Robin Cousins

Also by Martha Lowder Kimball:

ZERO TOLLERANCE with Toller Cranston

Robin Cousins

Martha Lowder Kimball

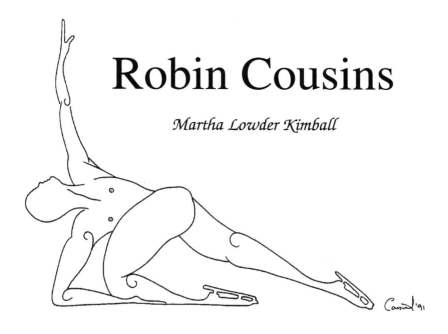

GATEWAY PRESS, INC.
Baltimore, MD   1998

Please direct all correspondence and book orders to:
Martha Lowder Kimball
P.O. Box 191
Jamestown, New York 14702-0191

Kimball, Martha Lowder, 1946-
  Robin Cousins / Martha Lowder Kimball.
     p.   cm.
   1. Cousins, Robin.   2. Skaters—Great Britain—Biography
I. Title.
GV850.C68K56   1998
796.91'2'092—dc21
[B]   97-51617
ISBN 0-9662502-0-6   CIP

Printed in the United States of America

To my husband,

Richard A. Kimball, Jr.,

for thirty-two years of loving support,

and to Laura Elizabeth, Richard Paul, and David Allen

for cheerfully indulging

their mother's enthusiasms

Acknowledgments

To Robin Cousins, for trusting me with his life story

To Toller Cranston, who demanded that I believe in myself

To Bob Houston, for the jump-start

To Lois Yuen, for tireless fact-checking

To Alice Zetterstrom, for moral and pecuniary support

To Robin's family and friends who generously shared their time and insights

Contents

Illustrations

Every reasonable effort has been made to give appropriate credit for copyright material that appears in this book. The publisher apologizes for any inadvertent error or omission.

End papers
Sketches by Robin Cousins

Prologue, page *x v*
At age two, with Fred: Photo courtesy of Robin Cousins

page 1
With Nick and Martin: Photo courtesy of Robin Cousins

page 10
Robin (right of Humpty Dumpty) in his first show: Photo courtesy of Robin Cousins

page 58
With John Curry and Michael Fish at Robin's first senior championship: Photo courtesy of Robin Cousins

page 86
With Pam Davies: Photo courtesy of Robin Cousins

page 87
His twenty-first birthday with grandparents, parents, and brothers: Photo courtesy of Robin Cousins

page 95
Simone Grigorescu: Photo courtesy of Toller Cranston

page 101
Carlo Fassi: Photo by Martha Kimball

page 174
With Peggy Fleming, Toller Cranston: Photo by Nancie Battaglia, courtesy of Gloria Ciaccio

page 182
Broadway and Tenth Street: Photo by Martha Kimball

page 185, top
With (clockwise) Brian Klavano, Celine McDonald, Gloria Ciaccio, Vin Cippola: Photo by Celine McDonald

page 185, bottom
With Vin Cippola and Amanda Rayner: Photo by Celine McDonald

page 189
With Vanessa Williams: Photo courtesy of Robin Cousins

page 191
With Dorothy Hamill, John Curry, Dick Button, Denise Biellmann: Photo by Celine McDonald

page 196
With Katherine Healy in "Lean on Me": Photo by Lois Yuen

page 202, top
"Busy Being Blue": Photo by Lois Yuen

page 202, bottom
With Brian Boitano: Photo courtesy of Robin Cousins

page 220
The Electric Ice Company: Sally Anderson, Simone Grigorescu, Allen Schramm, Keith Green, Tami Pennington, Elina Viola, Editha Dotson: Photo by Martha Kimball

page 280
Tristan Cousins: Photo courtesy of Robin Cousins

page 285
Fergie, Winston, and Thumper: Photo courtesy of Robin Cousins

page 286
With Nadia Comaneci: Photo courtesy of Robin Cousins

page 294
On the set of *The Cutting Edge*: Photo courtesy of MGM-Pathé

page 313
With the "freeze-dried people," *The Cutting Edge:* Photo courtesy of Robin Cousins

page 314
With Paul Glaser and Dean O'Brien: Photo courtesy of Robin Cousins

page 323
With Barbra Streisand: Photo courtesy of Robin Cousins

page 346
Number One Bedford Square: Photo by Martha Kimball

page 347
With Fred, Jo, Janet Mills, and Lee Mimms at the *Cats* premier: Photo courtesy of Robin Cousins

page 353   left
With Rachelle Ottley in *Cinderella*: Photo courtesy of Lois Yuen

page 366, left

The Duke of York's Theatre: Photo by Martha Kimball

page 366, right

Frank N Furter: Photo courtesy of Rocky Horror Ltd.

page 376

With Cindy Stuart in "Mr. Monotony": Photo by Lois Yuen

page 383

On the Sussex coast: Photo by Martha Kimball

page 386

Muffin-Pickle: Photo by Martha Kimball

I've never lived in black and white. I dream in color. I live in color. People say, "Come off the ether. Get with the real world." I've always been optimistic— optimistic and realistic at the same time. There are those people who say that realism is pessimism. I don't believe that.

Robin Cousins

Prologue

$\mathcal{A}$s a pond skater in suburban Albany, New York, I was captivated by my mother's long, black woolen skating skirt, lined in red satin, and her cache of programs from New York ice revues. Later I skated vicariously through televised events. Figure skating embodied for me the aesthetics of ballet, immeasurably enhanced by speed, glide, and freedom.

One day I heard about Robin Cousins, the British successor to John Curry. It seemed improbable that two such athletes should coincide on the same small plot of English earth. Robin had John's majesty and flow, coupled with prodigious jumps and a playfulness all his own. While he skated, I skated, too. Truly great interpretive movement, which springs from a skater's or dancer's soul, allows the sensitive observer to become a participant.

In 1980, Robin won the Olympic gold medal. Meanwhile, my new hometown had built a semienclosed rink. I had already begun adult lessons when Katie Baxter came to teach at the Jamestown Skating Club. I created her first summer school brochure, then launched a skating column for the local newspaper. That was followed by features in skating publications.

During the summer of 1983, the Electric Ice Company held open rehearsals at the nearby State University of New York at Fredonia. Although Robin had left for London by the time I returned from vacation, I watched the theatrical dance show on ice continue to develop.

Several years later, I met Robin through Katie at a Toronto bursary show. I believe that I informed him on the spot that I wanted to write his biography. His response was polite, so I persisted—after raising three children.

Those who know Robin best say that nothing he does surprises them. Actor, choreographer, commentator, creative consultant, dancer, designer, director, musicologist, painter, producer, singer, and skater: as he enters his fifth decade, he is an alphabet of diversity, a modern-day Renaissance man.

With his cheerful perversity, Robin likes to turn things upside down. Much like himself as an eight-year-old, confounding his father's expectations by using the soccer goal as a prop for handstands, he turns conventional wisdom onto its head. He abhors the label "gifted" with its elitist implications, preferring to adopt a pragmatic view. Whatever he is, whatever he has, came from his parents through their natures and their nurture.

He insists that his story begin with theirs. Their struggles formed his backbone. Their philosophy informed his character. Their delight gave meaning to his achievements. Ever a man given to imagery, he saw his family as a tree. His parents, the roots, gathered nutrients for the branches. They still do.

1. The Roots of the Tree

$\mathcal{F}$rederick Cousins and Edna "Jo" Higgs, born three days apart in December 1923, met on a dance floor in Northern Ireland during World War II. Both loved to dance, a passion they would one day bequeath, exponentially increased, to their youngest son.

Theirs was a classic wartime love story, set among the lush, emerald hills and granite escarpments of Ulster; in the searing heat of equatorial Africa; on soccer and cricket fields; on holiday beaches; in tuberculosis wards. Grand themes played out against the textured backdrop: romance, tragedy, grit, determination, and, in the end, abiding love. It was of that love that Robin Cousins was born.

Fred was a Londoner from the rough side of the

tracks, with talent enough to play professional soccer. "Football" was never a game for sissies, and the men from Millwall, a top English club, took that point to its extreme. Forty or fifty boys at a time demonstrated their skills, each hoping to be among the chosen. In 1938, at age fourteen, Fred tried out at the Den, the Millwall soccer ground. He was one of the lucky ones. He was accepted as an associate schoolboy.

A year later, Hitler invaded Poland. The great dial of history turned, sending Fred in a new direction. As soon as he was old enough, he joined the navy. He was a slender, handsome air mechanic electrician with the glint in the eye and the rugged features that he later passed on, like a blueprint, to his son Robin: the jutting cleft chin, the assertive nose, the spare cheeks, all topped by abundant dark brown hair that fell in waves.

Edna, a Bristol girl, spent family vacations by the sea. Ernest Higgs, an avid swimmer, had taught the sport to his athletic daughter when she was only three years old. He had the habit of doing "trudges," swimming for miles at a time—no mean feat in the frigid English Channel. His equally stoic daughter joined him in his trudges. Bit by bit, she increased her distance. A swimmer had to be eleven to be officially certified at a mile. Edna swam hers at age ten. She secretly vowed to swim the Channel, but her training ended when she joined the Women's Royal Naval Service.

At Wrens camp, there were two Ednas. Edna Higgs whistled a lot, so her friends called her Whistling Jo. She liked the new name so well that she kept it. If anyone calls her Edna, she pretends not to hear.

Jo was soft of voice but sturdy of character, a no-nonsense young woman of principle. In May 1943, she was sent as a supply assistant to the Eglinton Naval Air Station in the Londonderry district of Ulster, Northern Ireland. Fred arrived the following October at nineteen years and ten months—Robin's age when he left for America to train for the Olympics. How different were their wars.

Londonderry, perched on a bend in the river Foyle that divides Northern Ireland from the Republic, has been strife-torn since time immemorial. Vikings destroyed the first Celtic settlements. In 1689, Catholic forces fighting to restore King James II to the English throne laid siege to the Protestants within the walls. In time, William and Mary's forces triumphed, marginalizing the Catholics. The siege mentality remained entrenched—on the city's coat of arms and in ugly sectarian violence. World War II was just one more affront.

Residual traces of a grim history stand in sharp contrast to the tranquil, verdant Irish coastline. A small, paved county road leads along Lough Foyle to the hamlet of Eglinton: just the place for two young people with the same ideas of adventure to fall in love.

Civilians, Wrens, and sailors went to the "Orange halls" to relax and hear live music. The Eglinton hall, the Orange Box, had a four-piece band and a small dance floor. Shortly after Fred arrived, he and Jo became friends. It wasn't long before she had taken his true measure.

"I was stood up on our first date because a football match came along. As always, the sport came first. So the next dance was 'I will see you inside,' which meant I had to pay my own entrance."

Jo knew that the quickest way to Fred's heart was to watch all his soccer and cricket games. On half-day passes, they sometimes went to Londonderry for steak and chips or followed the coast to Portrush and Portstewart. It was in one of those enchanting seaside villages that Fred proposed a postwar wedding.

Jo stayed in Eglinton throughout her years as a Wren. Fred had been there just over a year when he was sent to Ceylon for a six-week layover in transit to Mombasa. While he was in Ceylon, his life changed forever.

Of all the cities in England, the war was cruelest to

London. Although Hitler had ordered the capital off-limits to the Luftwaffe, on August 24, 1940, two planes strayed and unloaded their bombs. Churchill ordered reprisals that were answered by counterreprisals. By September, the city was under all-out attack.

Night after night, terror rained down on Londoners huddled in the Underground, their ears ringing with the blare of air raid sirens. Hitler turned to Russia in mid-1941, but by August 1943, he was secretly testing two pilotless "vengeance weapons" to retaliate against England for persistent Allied bomber assaults: the V-1, a jet-powered bomb, and the more destructive V-2, a liquid-fueled rocket. In all, 518 V-2s wreaked their devastation on London, killing 2,724 civilians and injuring 6,000.

On March 7, 1945, as World War II sputtered to its end, a rocket obliterated two blocks of flats in Deptford, Southeast London. It was among the last of the V-2s—no consolation to Fred. That was the one that killed his mother and younger brother.

Three days earlier, William and Annie Cousins and their son Donald had visited Jo and her family in Bristol.

"His parents came to meet my parents and stay at our house for the weekend. His father had an engagement ring and put it on my finger for Fred. It was all by proxy. We wanted to get engaged, and there was no other way we could do it."

The Cousinses said good-bye to the Higgses and went home to London, where Annie volunteered as a camouflage seamstress. William went off as usual to his job. When he returned from work on Wednesday, his flat, his wife, and his child had all been blown away.

"The sad part," to Jo's way of thinking, "is that Donald would have been fourteen a week or so later and had been evacuated up until that time. He had only come home so he could go to the Naval College for an interview—to follow his brothers, of course."[1]

One column inch in the London *Times* of March 9, 1945, reported the incident in the perfunctory style of the day:

"A number of flats were destroyed and others were made uninhabitable when a V bomb fell in southern England recently. Some people, including children, were killed and other people were taken to hospital."

In a glass case in Westminster Abbey, the Book of Remembrance lists their names: Donald William Cousins, Royal Naval Cadet Corps, and Annie Harriet Cousins, Women's Voluntary Services, of 175 Folkestone Gardens. On the fiftieth anniversary of V-E Day, Fred made a pilgrimage to the Abbey.

Although Fred's older brother, at sea at the time, was permitted to return home to England, Fred was denied compassionate leave. In the throes of grief, inner turmoil, and frustration, he was sent on to Mombasa, Kenya, a populous island city in East Africa.

As an athlete affiliated with a professional club, Fred played for his station's soccer team. One day, he was kicked in the chest. The blow cracked a rib, and he hemorrhaged on the field. In Mombasa, his state of mind was such that he didn't take proper care of himself. In the squalid heat of equatorial Africa, known as "white man's grave," he landed in the hospital with TB in both lungs.

Tuberculosis was a debilitating, often fatal illness, conjuring grim images of isolation, painful treatments, and wracking coughs. Survivors faced years of bed rest. Fred was flown to the Wentworth Hospital in Durban, South Africa, a sprawling, modern seaport, where the doctors were unable to improve his condition.

Fifty years later, Fred and Jo relaxed in the sunroom of their country bungalow near the village of Borough

---

[1] In England, a "college" is a secondary school.

Green, looking back at their first great test of character. A warm breeze wafted through the screens as a chorus of birds twittered among the roses and rhododendrons in Fred's garden. What a stark contrast: the devoted, grey-haired couple sipping coffee in their sunroom and the terror-filled days that they recounted. They rarely think about those times. There's no point in looking back. Yet a sign in front of the bungalow identifies it as "Eglinton." Some things are worth remembering.

"In Durban," Fred recalled, "we were just given fresh air and rest, because no one really knew of any treatment. I was told to lie flat on my back with one pillow, and I was not allowed to move at all. I was lifted up in the morning by a big colored man while the nurses made my bed and bed-panned me. I was like that, basically, until I came home. They told Jo she was mad to marry me. I was going to be an invalid the rest of my life."

Fred spoke with the twinkle in the eye of a man who had outwitted fate. Jo fully matched his stubborn pleasure.

"They asked me if I knew what I was doing. He was never going to be able to work. He wrote to me when I was in Ireland and said he had TB, so we would cancel our engagement. I never got the letter, actually."

A lesser man than Fred might have thrown in the towel, yet even if he had wanted to give up, he would have had to reckon with Jo. She was fiercely determined, highly organized, and sure of how things should be done. If someone told her, "You can't," she doubled her efforts. Nothing short of Fred's full recovery would do.

Jo's sons dubbed her "the rock." Robin admired that strength. At the same time, he took his father as his primary role model.

"I've never known him to be a defeatist. To have coped when life was at its worst, when he almost didn't have a life, and then to go on and produce what he's been able to produce! There were many incidents early on that could have allowed him to give up and lead a ho-hum life. Fortunately, he didn't. But, then again, he was engaged to my mother."

The engagement withstood the best efforts of the naysayers. Fred transferred from the hospital in Durban to a sanatorium in the English village of Godalming, where he received a treatment called the "phrenic crush." Neck nerves were compressed, stilling the diaphragm. That seemed to slow the disease's progression.

When the war ended, Fred and Jo left the navy. Since William lived with his older son, Fred no longer had a home to go to. He was released from the sanatorium to Jo's house in Bristol, a city in southwest England, across the mouth of the Severn River from Cardiff. The Higgses cared for him while he recuperated.

Before Fred's release, Jo met with his doctor. Aware of the impending marriage, the doctor informed her that it would be a short one.

"You're not going to have long, you know."

He gave Fred five years, at best, to live.

"So?" Jo retorted. She didn't appreciate the blunt negativity. She became more determined than ever that Fred would beat the odds.

The bride wore a long, white dress for her wedding at Saint Mary's, Bristol, on April 19, 1947. Her situation was unusual, to say the least. Among other complications, the groom was out of work—and without qualifications.

As soon as Fred found a job, another hemorrhage struck him down. He was hospitalized in Bristol.

Then he had an amazing bit of good luck: he became a guinea pig in a drug test. Streptomycin, the first antibiotic useful in treating tuberculosis, was a wonderful drug, according to Fred, "but it was turning people blind and deaf." Researchers began testing it with a supplement to counteract its side effects.[2]

"I'd gone into a sanatorium outside Bristol, a place called Limpley Stoke. We all knew about the new wonder drug they were going to try, but no one knew quite what was happening. We went into a ward, and we were put into three groups of patients. We were all going to get streptomycin, but each with an addition. What I had was called a PAS capsule: para-aminosalicylic acid. We had to have them every night at a given time along with the streptomycin injections. All I know is how I reacted, and I had none of the side effects."

Once he received the new therapy, Fred made steady progress—although it was measured in years rather than months. Seventeen long years after the first signs of TB, the day he had been waiting for arrived.

"You used to go into the clinic for your checkup, and they gave you what they called a screening. They stood you behind a screen and took an X-ray. I'd had a 'wet film' three months previous. Normally a wet film meant they'd seen something they didn't want to see, so to speak. I went in with fear and trepidation and sat down on the chair by the doctor. My file was about an inch thick, and he was putting all these X-rays up. It seemed like an eternity to me, but it couldn't have been long. He suddenly put his hand on my knee and said, 'Old chap, I think we've won.'

"I haven't looked back from that day to this."

Barry's Legacy

In the early years of Fred's fight against TB, Jo gave birth to a son, Barry Donald, named for Fred's dead brother. A

---

[2]Those ranged from swollen lymph nodes, blood disease, blind spots, kidney irritation, and digestive disorders to deafness, anaphylaxis, and neuromuscular paralysis. Apart from the side effects, streptomycin alone left much to be desired in terms of antibacterial effect. PAS acted as a booster and prevented the development of drug-resistant strains of the bacteria.

benevolent future seemed to await the new family. Then, without warning, dawned the darkest days of their lives. Barry became ill. Fred and Jo summoned a doctor, who called in a specialist, but there was little to be done. Barry had meningitis. He was twenty-one months old when he died.

"He was the bonniest little boy," Fred said sadly, "and we don't know, from that day to this, why or how."

Jo and Fred left their little house, with its ghosts and anguished memories, and moved in with Irene and Ernest Higgs, swearing they would bear no more children. Jo was heartbroken.

The doctor took Fred aside.

"The quicker you have another child, the better it will be."

That was easier said than done. Throughout her second pregnancy, Jo insisted, "If it's a boy, I won't love him."

Once Martin Trevor arrived in October of 1952, Jo's negative thoughts flew out the window. She was thrilled to have another son. In March 1954, Nicholas David followed. Then on August 17, 1957, Robin was welcomed to the fold.

All three boys were cherished equally. Because of the pain of losing Barry, Fred and Jo never took their sons for granted. That was the central truth of their family life. In many ways, it explained everything.

After Robin won his Olympic gold medal, a well-meaning stranger asked Jo, "How is your lovely son?"

"Which one do you mean?" she replied, pretending not to understand. "The clever one, the musical one, or the skater?"

That became her standard reply.

Jo and Fred have no idea why they named their youngest Robin John. Only "Barry Donald" had a family connection. When Robin bought his parents a house with his first professional earnings, they named it Baridon House, in memory of the son they had never forgotten.

2. The Bristol Years: 1957-73

$\mathcal{E}$lvis Presley hit the music charts. Althea Gibson won Wimbledon. Monegasques greeted Princess Caroline, the first heir of Prince Rainier III and Princess Grace. The year 1957 was big in the Cousins household, too. During the third week of August, a black Austin 8 waited near a clinic entrance with two excited boys in the back seat: Martin, nearly five years old, and Nick, not quite three and a half. Fred appeared at the front passenger side and opened the door for Jo, who cradled in a shawl what little there was of Robin John Cousins.

Nick has a pristine recollection of that moment. It was a happy event, bound up in the boys' memory with the excitement of the family's move to their first real house.

Just before Robin's birth, the Cousinses moved from a cramped aluminum prefab to a semidetached council house (a government-built duplex) on Dingle Close, a cul-de-sac in the Sea Mills section of Bristol. A semicircle of uniform, rather drab middle-class houses, hedged in and topped by red tile roofs, surrounded a central green with fenced tennis courts. Beyond a gap in the hedgerow, the modest façade of number eleven looked out towards the forbidden private enclosure. The boys would later burrow under the steel mesh for the illicit joy of volleying tennis balls.

The ground floor of the house contained a living room, dining room, kitchen, and hall with a stairway that led to the second-story bedrooms. Robin's was the first on the left, opposite the bathroom—the smallest of three. Martin and Nick shared the middle-sized quarters.

Dingle Close was a pleasant place for active boys to play. There was room on the grass at the end of the courts for tricycle-riding and cartwheels. Martin and Nick were rough-and-tumble boys, glad to join Fred in a soccer game. It was expected that the youngest brother soon would join in. That expectation was quickly dashed.

Jo saw no early indications of physical precocity.

"The only indications we were looking for didn't arrive, and that would be for a footballer."

Robin was highly energetic, but no more so than his brothers. He liked to tumble rather than kick a ball. When the family went to the beach, he rarely did anything so prosaic as play in the sand. He preferred to jump, spread-eagle, off the piers and seawalls.

Nick found that Robin was not advanced in terms of motor skills.

"In fact, if anything, the opposite. It would be grossly insulting and unfair to call him the runt. That wasn't the case—but none of us were early developers in terms of physical maturation."

Robin was a late bloomer, to his advantage. He maintained a young child's flexibility longer than he might have otherwise.

His greatest natural asset, apart from flexibility, was spatial awareness: his innate ability to know where his body was in space and time. He never lacked for strength, but that wasn't key. Stamina was not his strong suit. Agility, flexibility, spatial awareness, a certain economy of motion, combined with an innate aesthetic sense: those were the physical components of his gift.

"I used to try to make my body do weird things. I'd do a handstand and throw myself sideways to get back to my feet, or I'd try to balance on one hand."

There were no boundaries, no conventions.

Robin had little patience for toys his brothers had enjoyed, in particular their model railroad and miniature farm. Jo believes that, as a young child, he didn't enjoy his own company (although he disagrees). She often went to great lengths to set up the trains. Having disappeared to dust or sweep, she soon found him at her skirts again, trailing after his mother like a young duck.

Robin viewed Jo as the bulwark who ensured that the household hummed efficiently. She drew a line that wasn't always easy to toe.

"She is a matriarch in the nicest possible way. My father, like me, is an internalist. Everybody else comes first, as long as he can cope with what he has to."

Fred was the fun-maker, Jo the caretaker. Their youngest, a happy-go-lucky child, had his father's even disposition. His inherited propensity to look at the bright side helped him to sail through disappointments, while his optimism goaded him towards challenges.

Robin was no angel, but the Cousins boys were not disposed to mischief. Time and forgetfulness faded any large blots in their copybooks. Robin was not a physical child in the sense of pushing and shoving, but he was kinetic, exuberant, always in motion. In contrast, he had a shy, quiet personality.

He did confess to one habitual bedtime crime.

"I would leave the living room while Mum and Dad were watching television but purposely leave the door open three or four inches. I could then sneak back down, squat at the bottom of the stairs, and watch TV through the gap."

He was drawn to anything theatrical, as long as it involved music and energy.

"I vividly remember the variety shows that we used to have quite a lot of in this country: 'Thank Your Lucky Stars,' 'Billy Cotton's Band Show,' 'Sunday Night at the London Palladium.' We watched those all the time, and Sunday afternoons the odd MGM musical; Fonteyn and Nureyev; anything to do with glamour and entertainment; jazz dancers leaping across voids: Fred Astaire, Gene Kelly, and Donald O'Connor going a mile a minute."

Robin has few early childhood memories.

"Music and movement; being taken to ballet class; walking from church to my grandmother's house; climbing frames in primary school; riding on the back of Daddy's moped."

Fred's "putt-putt" was a convenience rather than a form of recreation. Because running a car was expensive for a lower-middle-class family, Robin often rode to school on the back of the moped. The average sprinter could have outrun it, but even such modest speed thrilled him. He loved to fly down the road, as he later would fly down the ice.

All three boys began their educations at Doris Nash's Sea Mills Infant School, a progressive institution that emphasized a gentle pedagogical touch and hands-on learning. Educators visited from America to observe Miss Nash's practices. Fred thoroughly approved of her philosophy.

"She was one of the instigators of the learn-by-doing method. You feed the hens so much corn each day, and then you go and do data and find out how many eggs you have." Thus would the children develop their curiosity and their powers of inductive reasoning.

Doris Nash, who encouraged each child to express his own talents, was among the first to recognize Robin's love for music and his gift for interpretation.

"She could see the artistry in him while we couldn't, to be perfectly honest," Jo admitted.

Fred noticed his son's early talent for performance. At age six, Robin's stage presence allowed him to command twenty or thirty other children. His class was videotaped improvising to songs by the Swingle Singers. On the vintage tape, young Robin dances still, engrossed in the music and perfectly on the beat.

"When they did 'This Is Your Life,' they had footage of me doing extemporaneous dancing. It was part of a program schools were doing with children's sport and the psychology of music and movement. There I was, doing me thing, waving around me bit o' dry reed."

He has no independent memory of the event, but he recalls sensing an internal cadence that organized his external world.

"I know that, from a very early age, musicality—formation and theming and rise and fall—was a part of my life. Everything was organized. I've been meticulous for as long as I can remember: neat, tidy, things in their places."

Lilwern Patterson taught the children dance. Robin showed so much promise that she broached the subject of ballet, but Fred and Jo were unreceptive.

Robin's first public performance was as an angel in Miss Nash's Christmas pageant. The children ran onstage and circled the Christ Child in his manger.

"I remember getting carried away after all the other angels had left the stage. Here I was, doing what I was doing around the baby Jesus in his crib, and someone had to come on and get me off."

At home, all the Cousins cousins (as they were) joined in Christmas pantomimes, with Robin as the chief organizer. Even then, he liked to be in charge of the show. Fred's older brother had three daughters, while Jo's two brothers had five daughters and two sons.

"It would be a huge family get-together—one night at my house, the next night at my uncle's house. The kids did recitals. My father and uncles got party games together. I used to organize panto scenes, silly stuff. I directed and choreographed them. We had a great time. I couldn't tell you any of them, other than the fact that we never *didn't* do them. The adults had their cocktails, and we did our little sing-along and variety act. They all clapped and cheered, and then we went off to the dining room and put something else together."

Robin liked to play Fred Astaire, leaping over the banister from the fourth step up. He swung his legs over the rail in an open cartwheel, landed in the hall, and often finished the move by slamming into a door. While playing at his grandmother's house, he propelled his cousin Kate into the air and smashed a glass lampshade to the floor.

Although Jo was strict about bedtime, once she allowed Robin to stay up late in order to watch a television documentary about the training of dancers at the Royal Ballet School. Fred was a man's man, one of a long line of similarly disposed Cousins males. He watched the program with his son but was unprepared for the subsequent interest in dance lessons. It was not the thing in those days, especially when your father was good at soccer.

Fred had no time for ballet. What he mainly objected to was the clothing. He couldn't fathom why a Russian Cossack had to perform in tights, not trousers. The world of leotards was alien to a man who played contact sports in shorts and muddy, bloodied jerseys.

Then Fred read that Millwall Football Club had hired

a ballerina to put the players through barre work twice a week. Headquartered in a rough part of London, the team enjoyed its richly-deserved reputation as a band of toughs. If the men from Millwall could dance, so could Robin.

That is not to minimize the amount of attitude adjustment that was required. It was a measure of Fred's character and his love for his son that he acknowledged talent where he saw it and let Robin grow in his chosen direction, towards the light that he alone perceived. Fred's loving acceptance was a given throughout Robin's life, helping him to cope with others who were less broad-minded.

So Robin, at seven, began ballet lessons. It wasn't the artistry that interested him but the gymnastic aspects of dance.

"It was running and jumping and handsprings and cartwheels. It was all for *that*. It wasn't the barre work and the theory of ballet. I found all that quite boring, and I still do. I'd rather watch Mark Morris than the New York City Ballet. Great stuff. It provokes debate and challenges the dancers. Another of my favorites is the Eliot Feld company. If a shoe flew off, nobody would go into a shock, horror, gasp. That can't happen at the Met."

Gymnastics clubs and modern dance classes didn't exist in Robin's world. Ballet was what was available. He enjoyed it and excelled, although he had little patience for the tedious discipline of the barre. He preferred to leap.

Robin was the only boy in the class at the Joan Watson School of Dancing. A humiliating burden?

"That made it even better. I was the leader in that case. I wasn't intimidated by its being all girls and me."

His family thought it was just for fun, but Miss Watson was taken with his promise and recommended he submit to the proficiency tests administered by visiting adjudicators from the Royal Ballet. He passed his first tests *Highly Commended,* the second-highest standard. When he passed the third with *Honours*, Miss Watson suggested an audition for the Royal Ballet School in London.

"I was not leaving home at nine years old. I didn't even want to leave home when I was *fifteen*. End of story."

When he eventually gave up dance lessons, Miss Watson was keenly disappointed. "You'll never make a career out of skating, Robin," she lectured. Years later, she had to eat her words.

Robin never got over his penchant for gymnastics. The first competition he ever won was a "cartwheels for style" event at his junior school's sports day.

There was a certain sports master at the Sea Mills Junior School who coached both Martin and Nick in soccer and cricket. When Robin came along, the coach thought he had another Cousins to grace his soccer team. Instead, he had a Cousins who stood in the middle of the field, kicked the ball when it came to him, then turned around and threw himself into a handstand. The man was beside himself, trying Robin at every position. When he put him in goal, where Fred had played for Millwall, he found him hanging upside down by his knees from the goalpost. Like a monkey, Robin shinnied up one of the sides and used the crossbar as a jungle gym.

"Cousins, what do you think you're doing? You're supposed to be defending the goal."

Robin scrambled into position—until the next time no one was looking.

"He was always like that," said Jo, "and I despaired for him."

Nevertheless, it made a welcome change from all the cricket, soccer, and rugby in her life. What she and Fred eventually realized was that Robin had no taste for team games. He liked individual sports—swimming, gymnastics, tennis, running—that allowed him to win or lose on his own merits. Although he loved pairs skating, he never competed with a partner. He was too fond of being his own master.

"I'm not a good loser. I don't do anything half measures. I can't play for fun. That doesn't mean that I can't
enjoy playing, but I play to win. There is something, once
instilled in you, about having to be the best—not necessarily to beat other people, but to *do* your best. I'm not saying
I'm unhappy when someone beats me. I'm unhappy when I
don't do what I know I *can* do."

One summer, Fred, Jo, and Robin attended a holiday
camp that held amateur competitions. Robin won the limbo
contest, received a prize for drawing Disney characters,
and placed near the top in the singing competition with a
plaintive rendition of "Where Is Love?" from *Oliver!* With
his gangly frame and teeth that needed growing into, he
made a rather winsome Oliver Twist.

Bournemouth

In August 1965, around his eighth birthday, Robin had his
first encounter with ice. He and Jo, on vacation with the
family in Dorset, wandered into the ice rink in the seaside
resort of Bournemouth. It was a sweltering day, unusual
for England. The Cousinses had been enjoying the beach,
one of their favorite pastimes, when the tide came in. The
crowded beach grew smaller and smaller, leaving a slim
crescent of sand for the hot, teeming hordes. Fred, Martin,
and Nick went to the putting green to play miniature golf,
while Jo and her youngest son headed towards the shops.
As they passed the ice rink, the promise of cool air tempted
them inside. Robin's eyes popped when he saw the lobby
cards.

"There's going to be an ice show tonight."

"Sorry, Robin, we can't go. Our caravan site is too far
away."

"Please?"

"How would it be if I let you try skating?"

Jo, chilly in her shorts and sandals, was ignorant of

the costly ways of the skating world. She approached a nearby stranger in skates.

"If you are going onto the ice in a few minutes, would you mind taking my son down to the barrier where he can hold on?"

The man was an instructor who soon had Jo at the office, paying seven shillings and sixpence for a twenty-minute lesson. That was most of the money she had in her purse, but she was too embarrassed to back down.

Robin remembers "going like the wind and not wanting to get off."

At the dance interval, he was told to leave the ice. The instructor, Gordon Holloway, skated to Jo by the boards.

"I wouldn't believe that your son had never been in an ice rink if you hadn't mentioned it. He has built-in balance."

"Perhaps it's because of his ballet lessons."

"Yes, that's probably it. Where are you from?"

"Bristol."

"That's a coincidence. They're building an ice rink in Bristol. You should go and see it."

That became a popular Saturday-morning routine. Often while Martin and Nick were at school, everyone else headed downtown to do errands. Robin and Fred got haircuts, then met Jo for coffee. There was one proviso.

"The only way I was going to get my hair cut was if we drove past where they were building the ice rink."

They climbed through the rubble to observe the brown brick building taking shape. The foundation went up. Then the cinema appeared. The Bingo hall and disco materialized. Finally, on top of it all, stood an ice rink.

In April 1966, the Silver Blades Ice Rink, on a small, sloping road named Frogmore Street, opened to the public for the first time. Preoccupied with dance lessons, Robin let the grand opening pass without notice. Later that spring, he enrolled in the Young Blades course and took group learn-to-skate lessons once a week for half an hour.

In June, he received his very first Certificate of Proficiency "which was grade three," said Jo with bemused exasperation, "not one or two, but three—with the comment from the coach that he wouldn't make a good skater because he was too impetuous. He would go, but he didn't know how to stop."

In his scrapbook, below the certificate, Robin wrote, "Not a very good start."

As naïve as they were about skating, Jo and Robin had interpreted third-class to mean third-rate—but that was just the course designation.

Later Robin wanted to take the advanced class.

"I did all this in rental skates, and I will *name names* here. There was a coach in Bristol who did the advanced class, which included basic ice dance moves. He refused to teach me, because I was the only one in the class who hadn't bought my own skates. My mother and he had an argument about the fact that nowhere on the enrollment sheet did it say that you had to have your own skates in order to sign up for the class, and there was no way we could afford for me to have them. That coach was Alex McGowan. He was the one who told my mother I would never be any good."

McGowan didn't stay long at the Bristol rink, though he eventually went on to international prominence as the coach of world champion Debi Thomas. Before he left Bristol, he taught Robin after all. Jo had gone straight to the manager to complain. By then, Robin felt like a poor relation. Sensitive to the needs of his psyche, his parents bought him a pair of fifthhand skates: girl's white boots that Fred painted black. Such were the humble beginnings of a champion.

Just before Christmas, an old school friend asked Jo if Robin could skate with her daughters in the holiday ice show. Normally one had to be enrolled in private lessons, but the cast was short of boys. Robin was pressed into service as a soldier. That was his defining moment, though little did his parents suspect. Jo gave her permission, never thinking he would be any good. He'd received only a third-class certificate and a number of disparaging remarks.

Suddenly ice skating lessons were at the top of Robin's Christmas list. He had heard the siren song of entertainment. He had felt the lure of center ice.

The Smile

Poet laureate Sir John Betjeman, with a touch of hyperbole, called Bristol "the most beautiful, interesting, and distinguished city in England." It is an inland port on the River Avon where it flows into the Severn and then to the sea. John Cabot set sail from Bristol. Coleridge, Wordsworth, and Lamb gathered among its Georgian homes. Defoe and Stevenson found their inspiration in downtown pubs and hostelries. Among the city's modern-day attractions are the harbor, the cathedral, the Clifton Suspension Bridge, the Theatre Royal, and the Hippodrome.

The Silver Blades Ice Rink, now under the banner of John Nike Leisuresport, is in the City Centre, a short walk up from the Hippodrome. Access is by sixty-six concrete steps—or an ornery escalator.

"When everybody was entering the building, the escalators were only going down. Then at night, when everybody was tired, we'd come out of the rink, and they wouldn't be going at all."

The new facility boasted organ music, lighting along the barriers, and revolving mirrored balls that hung from the ceiling, scattering prismatic shards across the ice. Surrounded by that chilly glamour, Robin won his first fateful smile from Pamela Davies.

Pam was a Birmingham girl, nearly nineteen, when she decided to move to Bristol to take her first job as a skating teacher. Blonde, slender, attractive, enthusiastic, and somewhat given to drama, she had definite ideas about learning to skate. Before setting out, she dissolved into tears at the thought of leaving hearth and home. Her father, telling her not to be a baby about it, asked her what she wanted from life.

"Dad, what I really would like," she told him with stunning clairvoyance, "is to make a champion."

Specifically, a male champion. The prospect of beating the odds in the female talent pool was less likely. Her ambition was to find a promising boy. She didn't have long to wait.

Fred and Jo told their sons how much could be spent on their Christmas presents. When they offered nine-year-old Robin fifty shillings' worth of private skating lessons, he did some quick calculations.

"I could have six lessons for eight shillings each or eight lessons for six shillings each."

"That's right. Which will it be?"

"I want to have lessons from *her,* because she smiled at me."

Pam, as senior instructor, charged the most. Robin chose fewer sessions with Pam by factoring in the intrinsic value of her smile. That was the start of an association that lasted six years and took Robin to the top of British skating.

"It was just that lucky break. She had already made up her mind that she was going to teach me because I was a boy. There were other boys in the class, but I was the one who looked like he had ambition. She could have had her pick of fifty thousand girls, but she took one boy, of which there were probably about three."

Pam knew talent when she saw it.

"Robin had that raw quality right at the beginning. He was very agile, very lithe. To me, he was quite an exciting little boy. He'd throw himself into the air, and he'd fall, but he'd never be worried."

Robin was not particularly full of grace. He was skinny, all arms and legs, like a young spider. Pam chided him for his flailing arms. He was her first project. What she found rewarding was that he absorbed lessons like a sponge. Every day he learned something new.

"I used to scream and shout at Robin. He would quite often cry, and I would feel very bad about that, but I would always cuddle and love him at the end of the lesson. I would always say, 'Robin, I so desperately want you to be good. You *will* be good. You will be world champion one day.'"

Pam suspected that Jo and Fred were not pleased when she scolded their son.

"I didn't tell him off unkindly. If you asked Robin did he not like me telling him off, I don't think he'd say exactly that. I'd sometimes ask him, 'Why are you crying?' and he'd say, 'It's because I can't please you.'"

Robin's early skating was so wild, ambitious, and fast that Pam feared he would injure himself. She padded his hips with foam rubber. He was such a hard worker that she sometimes had to order him off the ice. During one late-night session, he tried in vain to master the double Lutz. As matters deteriorated, Pam decreed, "Enough is enough." Robin insisted on trying just one more. It cracked open his head and sent him to the emergency room.

"That was my first foray into feeling what it was like to do half a back-flip. I spent many hours in Casualty with bruises, falls, and cuts. I crashed all the time. I remember sliding into the barrier and dislocating my thumb once. I could never just warm up a little bit or skate slowly or practice a little. I had to do everything big—and sometimes things got in the way."

Pam dated a doctor for a while. His first meeting with Robin was for minor foot surgery. One of Pam's talents was dating men who could help her, and Robin was part of the package.

The Figures Dilemma

When Robin began skating, there were two phases of International Skating Union (ISU) competition: the school figures, worth 60 per cent, and the free-skating program, 40 per cent. The weight of figures decreased in stages.[3] In 1988, they dropped to 20 per cent, where they remained until they were banished altogether.

Even at 30 per cent, the proportion in effect during most of Robin's international career, their influence was greater than the math suggests. The numerical scores assigned by the judges were carried forward and combined with subsequent results. Since the range of scores was much wider in figures than in free skating, it was arithmetically difficult to make up a deficit.

Robin disliked school figures. The repetition didn't suit his expressive nature. Pam saw his point.

"Figures are clinical, boring in a way, very technical. You have your cold patch of ice, and you have to go meticulously around these circles, match them all up—two circles, three circles, brackets, rockers, loops—and dedicate yourself totally to that piece of ice. There's no admiration. I'm glad figures have been taken out. Somebody had the nerve to say to me the other day, 'Do you think Robin would have been able to do a triple Axel?' I said, 'Of course, if not a quadruple, but please remember that Robin also had to dedicate his time to figures.'"

Robin did, in time, do triple Axels. According to Carlo Fassi, his pre-Olympic coach, teachers then didn't push the three-and-a-half-revolution jump. They considered it too dangerous. One day Robin did a triple Axel. Carlo happened to capture it on tape. After that, Robin routinely practiced the jump. (Only Vern Taylor had performed one in competition, and a shaky one at that.) By then, Robin had moved far away from Pam's encouraging embrace, yet figures

---

[3] To 50 per cent in 1967; 40 per cent in 1972; and 30 per cent in 1975.

still hung around his neck like a barnacle-encrusted anchor, impeding his dominance of the sport.

Not all Robin's figures problems were matters of mind-set or temperament. Some were questions of logistics. The ice in most rinks was stark white (although it could be tinted) and brightly lit to accommodate public sessions. When Robin started to skate figures, his tracings were nearly invisible. Judges suggested that he eat more or take on ballast.

According to Nick, "They used to have to weigh him down, put weights in his boots or weights in his bottom, so there would be a tracing. I remember going to a competition with my father, to Billingham, the British Juniors, and the judges trying to find the lines on the ice. Rob was always light—one might even say, rather unkindly, kind of weedy."

Robin remembers no such "weights in his bottom," but the humorous image illustrates how thoroughly the topic was explored *en famille*. Of course, what the judges couldn't see, they couldn't properly evaluate. Moreover, a reputation for poor figures preceded a skater long after it ceased to be justified.

The argument had two valid sides. Those who supported the retention of figures, including many North Americans, felt that figures taught discipline, control, balance, form, and mastery of the edge. Those who opposed their retention, including Europeans and people who televised the sport, countered that figures bored and confused the viewing public and—a more altruistic concern—that they created a disadvantage in countries where ice time was scarce. Figures were notoriously susceptible to judging by agenda, and there was virtually no oversight.

Over time, the anti-figures forces won out. Not all the effects of that decision were positive. Jump-heavy wizardry, often at the expense of artistic expression and discipline of form, is a direct outgrowth of the abolition of figures.

Katie Baxter, a coach and former competitive pairs skater, analyzed the issue:

"When figures were part of figure skating, skaters had to grow up with their figures. We couldn't take our eighth test by the time we were twelve. We grew up as people, maturing with our sport. Now the federations and the coaches and the parents pour thousands of dollars into kids who then reach puberty and can't perform. They could if they had gone through it a little slower. They'd be novice at fifteen, junior at sixteen, senior at seventeen. You couldn't do it any faster, really. The end of figures hacked five years off all that."

In 1990, in Halifax, Nova Scotia, skaters contested figures for the last time on the world stage—small consolation to Robin. He would have won three world titles under the present system.

As a ten-year-old, he was blissfully unaware of the big picture. His challenge, as he toiled in the bone-chilling cold of the Silver Blades Ice Rink, was simply to survive the boredom of it all.

Building Character

Pam ruled by maxim. One of her favorites was, "Whatever you do, do it well." She liked simple, polished programs. While Robin was eager to rush ahead, she demanded that he master each jump before learning the next one.

Another of her key rules was, "Whenever there's music on, skate to it," even if it was someone else's music.

She insisted that Robin practice moves both clockwise and counterclockwise, as her coach had trained her to do. Applied to someone with his innate spatial awareness, that technique was brilliant. Moreover, it reinforced the way he had learned to dance. In programs, of course, moves were standardized. Pam sometimes had to remind Robin which way to jump.

"My natural way to rotate, I discovered, was both ways. The only thing I can't do in the reverse direction, in a way that I would want people to see, is a flying camel. I did actually get to the point where I did a double Axel, then, from the landing edge, did a reverse double Salchow. I did it Olympic year, and the judges missed it. In fact, one judge thought I had just done a really bad double the normal way, so we decided it wasn't worth the risk."

Robin and Pam experimented with spins. He had his own version of the Hamill camel two years before Dorothy gave her name to a similar move.

Over and above technique, Pam's cardinal principle was "Always be nice to people." That was a lesson Robin learned well, since his family regularly reinforced it.

Jo wouldn't tolerate a show of temper. Once, she caught Robin kicking the ice. She told him, "If I see you kick that ice once more, you'll be off and out."

A woman approached her.

"Excuse me. If you have a son who is talented like that one is, you should give way to his tantrums."

"I beg your pardon? I have three sons, and they never get away with tantrums like that. If you have a little girl of three or four who gets on this ice, falls over, and hurts herself in the rut that my son has made, you won't be happy either."

That was how Jo saw it.

"I was really cross with him. They all do it, I know. I appreciate that you have to get rid of your frustrations, but, as far as I was concerned, he wasn't going to do it there."

Fred contributed to Robin's character by promoting self-reliance.

According to Nick, "Robin owes the most to my parents, the way they've brought him up—and Dad in particular. He's a phenomenal bloke. I remember him saying, 'I'll always wake you up, but I'll never get you out of bed. I'll always tell you when it's bedtime, but I'll never push you upstairs.'"

Without the inner motivation thus developed, Robin would have remained a skater with potential.

Fred tried skating only once—in rental boots—and got "two whacking great blisters." Jo took several lessons. Then she fell. She realized that, as the linchpin of the household, she could ill afford a broken leg.

Martin and Nick took no interest. They were far too involved with cricket and rugby to want to risk injury on ice. Similar in terms of their sporting tastes, the older boys played together while Robin "did what he did on his own in a corner somewhere," as Martin put it (without meaning to sound callous).

The first time Martin began to think that there might be something to the sport was at a 1967 exhibition. A typical teenage brother, he squeezed the skating between two soccer matches—mostly to show off Robin's skills to a German exchange student who was staying with the family. What Martin saw caught him by surprise.

"There you had Robin just coming up ten, but, even at that age, what impressed was the speed. Of course, no matter what sport you're talking about, that's what you miss on TV. You don't realize how fast they go. You don't realize how high they jump and how far they jump. There I was—slouching, probably, really not bothered. Suddenly this thing comes by, and I actually had to look up. That's what I always tell people who say how lovely skating is. I say, 'Yeah, but what you don't realize until you go is how big these individuals are jumping and how fit and strong they do have to be to cope with it.'"

Martin and Nick were captains of their cricket and rugby teams. Nick, a gifted musician, played the bassoon. One hectic day, Robin had an interrink competition while Nick and Martin were due to play cricket across the city. Fred and Jo watched Robin's figures, then rushed to the cricket fields. Fred cheered one son while Jo encouraged the other, since they played on different teams. Everyone converged on the rink for the five o'clock free skating. Then they changed clothes and went to Nick's Bristol Youth Orchestra concert.

Each boy pursued his own interests with keenness and devotion. Skating, however, was the most expensive. Finances grew more difficult as the number of lessons increased. Fred, as a civil servant who oversaw the motor vehicle office, didn't have the bank balance then for all the lessons that were deemed desirable. Robin took what few the family could afford and made good use of them.

Pam refused to push Fred and Jo to overextend themselves, but she did make sure that Robin didn't squander what he had. When she found him playing on the ice with his friends instead of sticking to business, she stopped him and said, "You're not doing your work. I used to be like that, and I know what it cost my family."

As Robin got older, he lobbied to attend ballets and other live shows at the Hippodrome. Jo said, "I will take you, but you will have to give up a lesson. You can't do both."

Once, Robin wanted to see *Swan Lake*.

"Fine," Jo told him. "On Thursday, you won't have your ice dance lesson. I'll cancel the ice time, and we'll go."

On Tuesday, having canceled the skating, Jo was next in line to buy ballet tickets. She called out, "Okay, Robin. We're going to the theatre."

"No, that's all right, Mum. I'll go skate."

Back Jo went to the rink to rebook the lesson.

Although Robin accepted disappointment well, Jo and Fred were heartbroken each time they denied him. The great consolation came years later when Robin starred in his own show at the Hippodrome.

Through small acts of deprivation, he acquired self-discipline. It hadn't always been his forte. When things didn't come easy, he began better to appreciate what he had. There came a time when Pam felt he needed additional figures lessons. During a family discussion, Martin piped up: "I can do a paper round, and then you can have the other lesson." He went straight to the news agent's shop and signed up for an early-morning route. Later Nick did the same.

Jo bristled when asked about family sacrifice in the name of skating.

"We don't say that. You see, it was our choice, wasn't it? At any time we could have said, 'Sorry, Robin, that's it. We don't have the money. We want a new house. We need a new car, so you will have to stop.' But, you know, you don't spend all that time encouraging him, standing at a barrier, then suddenly pull out. He had the backing of the other two boys all the way. The problem we had was trying to do the same for all three sons."

Jo saved money by teaching herself to make Robin's costumes. Until she acquired a sewing machine, she did the work by hand. Robin took an interest, as he did in all aspects of his skating. Jo knew what fabrics would work and what they could afford, while Robin had definite ideas about color and design. He didn't want anything flashy.

"In retrospect, we thought we'd done a great job. We had no choice at the time. It's like wanting to have Bloomingdale's but stuck with K-Mart. Looking back at it now, it makes me shudder. It was that era, the 1970s. Flared trousers: that was the look."

His favorite costume was the one he wore for the junior championship.

"It was a burgundy all-in-one sleeveless jumpsuit. Then we had gone out and found a cowboy patchwork shirt in colors that matched it, so it was rather hoedowny, and I thought that was cool. It worked for the moment. I also remember having my mother make a costume for me in kelly green (which was a big mistake) and chocolate brown. I looked like the Jolly Green Giant."

Pam hired Robin to do odd jobs on her apartment grounds. She took a lot of off-ice interest in him, even so far as to drag him along on her dates. She fit her social schedule around training times, which sometimes meant a threesome at dinner, followed by a late-night lesson.

They cruised the record shops to satisfy Robin's ravenous appetite for music. The stores had listening booths, soundproof cubicles in which Pam and Robin sampled the wares. They listened and listened but rarely bought. When the store owners caught on, they yanked away the welcome mat. Eventually, through one of Pam's many boyfriends, they found a contact at Radio Rentals who let them listen with no strings attached. Later, B B C Bristol offered the use of its music library. Robin chose his own pieces and edited them with a broken-down reel-to-reel tape recorder.

Pam insisted that Robin study ice dance, which contributed to his upright carriage, flexible knees, fluid edges, and princely bearing. At the dance interval, she took his hand and spun him off in a tango or paso doble. They eventually withdrew his silver dance test application, in part because she couldn't twizzle under his arms. He had meanwhile passed his figures and free skating, which took precedence.

Robin decided to quit ballet lessons, too. While he was both dancing and skating, he felt like a "pig in the middle." Pam told him to relax, while Joan Watson urged him to stiffen and straighten up. In the end, he relaxed his knees but maintained his balletic upper-body posture.

He hadn't abandoned his dream of becoming a dancer. He had simply transferred the movement to a different surface, in a format that better suited his love of speed and unfettered motion and his independent personality.

"Only through seeing skating live did I realize that it was a version of dancing that, to me, was more individual and completely different."

Robin liked to be admired. He had a talent for "pulling it off on the day." He didn't sparkle until he could play to an audience.

He had one nervous habit. As a small child in the yard on Dingle Close, he had severed the tip of the index finger of his left hand in a fold-up deck chair. Jo had wrapped his hand in a towel and rushed him to the hospital, but the reattached fingertip remained numb. When he was nervous, he chewed on it. He called it his competition finger.

He also had the habit of yawning. Much yawning presaged a good competition.

Once, neither finger-chewing, drawing on crowd support, nor yawning could save him from disaster. Jayne Torvill, a month and a half his junior, described the day.

"When I was very young, I used to do a lot of little competitions around England. I remember coming across Robin one or two times then. He was always bright and cheerful and friendly, and he was always doing well in his own competitions. I remember one time he had a bad experience. I was watching him in a competition, and he had forgotten his program. He went to the barrier. His coach told him to get away, because when you touch the barrier, you get penalized."

Pam shooed Robin away. "Just skate. Just skate."

The fact that they had spoken to each other meant that he was disqualified. The referee, a Bristolian, didn't want to be accused of favoritism. Robin was upset.

"So literal they are, so literal with the rulebooks. I've never seen a situation like that one anywhere else. I've been at internationals, Worlds, and Olympics when coaches have been *screaming* at skaters while they're performing, but a ten- or eleven-year-old at a local club-level competition was not allowed to have that happen. They disqualified me, and I probably would have won, too. I didn't skip a beat. I carried right on and picked up where she told me."

Then Pam taught her pupil a lesson.

"Everyone forgets his program once. In the future, if your mind goes blank, remember you're still a skater. Listen to your music. If you can ad-lib until that bit that jogs your memory, you'll be able to pick up and continue."

Rather than letting setbacks get him down, Robin used them as a spur to greater effort. He never again blanked out and sought refuge in a smile.

Robin, Toller, and John

When Pam skated in Birmingham as a child, the strip of ice where she practiced her figures was next to the patch of a promising local boy, John Curry. Though he was a year or two younger, they trained with the same coach.

By 1994, when he died of a heart attack at age forty-four, his body ravaged by AIDS, Curry had become one of the world's greatest skaters, an artist and influential innovator. Pam was accused of modeling Robin's skating on John's, a controlled, balletic style. She claimed (correctly) that it would have been impossible to do so. The two were completely different from each other. If there was any influence evident, it was only because she and John had learned from the same teacher.

As for Robin, he never copied John's style, consciously or unconsciously. He felt too great a compulsion to be himself. Since he was eight chronological years and four skating years behind John, he used John as a benchmark to measure his own progress towards Olympic standards.

It is curious how, throughout history, two people of genius have so often coincided in time and place, as though two seeds had germinated in the same fertile ground and had sprung up independent yet adjacent. The great difference between Robin and John was in natural temperament and, to extend the metaphor, in the amount of care and watering each received.

Randy Gardner, who (with Tai Babilonia) won the 1979 world pairs title, knew both Robin and John.

"I think they were similar in that they had strong, solid technique and backgrounds in dance, but once they hit the ice, they had different looks. Same level, two different categories."

Fred Cousins believed that his son was lucky. His two notable predecessors, John and the great Canadian, Toller Cranston, were individualistic.

"They were two examples of artistry on the ice, both completely different. I don't think you could copy either of them."

Yet you could draw inspiration from them and perhaps find some of the courage necessary to be equally individualistic. They paved the way for other skaters to challenge the establishment, though none have done so to a comparable extent. Robin wasn't engulfed in controversy as John and Toller were. He was more conventional.

Toller saw their times as "the era of Cousins, Cranston, and Curry. We were all equal and no less than the others in our own ways and had entirely different approaches to the sport during the same time frame."

Toller was the Olympic bronze medalist the year John won gold. Living a continent away, endowed with lucid vision and wry wit, he had a unique perspective on the two British members of the triumvirate.

"Robin will go down in the annals as one of the skating greats, and he is a great entertainer, but he cannot lay claim to being one of the major forces of innovation in skating. He was an interpreter, not an innovator. John Curry, on that count, is at the top of the mountain—and of course *I* [dramatic flourish] am up in the heavens."

That may be a bit pat, as Toller likes to say. Robin broke ground on a number of fronts. Ironically, it was his prolific diversity that camouflaged his impact as an innovator. He gently pushed the barriers at multiple points.

While asserting his own ascendancy as an innovator, Toller deferred to John and Robin as gold medalists.

"I suffer from the same fear that Catherine the Great of Russia suffered from. I became a kind of leading aristocrat in the skating world, yet, in fact, I didn't have the credentials. Catherine the Great became czarina of all Russia but didn't have a drop of Russian blood and was always worried that her pedigree was going to cost her her head—similarly Elizabeth I and Mary Queen of Scots."

Toller was never in danger of execution (though he may disagree), yet the shadow of illegitimacy hung over him, prompting him to create an elaborate persona that defied anyone to challenge his theatrical primacy.

John and Toller tended to experiment brilliantly within their preferred genres, while Robin's body of skating work was both more diverse and more popularly accessible, which sometimes led critics to undervalue it. That phenomenon exists in all walks of life, but especially in the arts. Certain forms of expression are judged to have more cachet, whether or not they are superior. In the least flattering light, it amounts to snob appeal.

Katherine Healy, a skater and prima ballerina, was John's devoted protégée and Robin's friend and admirer. She loved John dearly and valued his work while recognizing Robin's wider audience.

"His is more a jazz idiom. When I think of Robin, I think of *accessible*. He's not one of these esoteric people who are creating art that perhaps two intellectuals will understand. You can give him eight bars of music and say, 'We need to get these people from this place to that place.' He'll do it, and it won't be just workmanlike. It will be something artistic, something with value, but it will also accomplish what it has to accomplish in terms of efficiency. He's pragmatic in a very creative way."

Ballet has its contemporary pieces that few understand or pay to see. There is a talent in appealing across a broad spectrum; letting people in on the meaning of one's work. Robin popularized skating. He was a genius at packaging and marketing, without being crass.

John operated on a different plane, Katherine felt. He sometimes performed numbers with narrow appeal—to his detriment, perhaps. He and Robin pursued different goals.

"John wanted to create a dance company, and he wanted to dance on the ice. I don't mean to say anything strange, but sometimes he was *really* dancing on the ice. He was a skilled dancer. Robin really was a skater. He worked more through the establishment of skating, and yet he was artistic."

While Robin and John grew up in England, Toller spent his early childhood in a cold, remote Northern Ontario hamlet the Indians had named Swastika. (It was not, as Toller was quick to point out, the last Nazi stronghold.) In several important ways, Toller's early reactions and experiences were much like Robin's.

"I would dance to music in the living room and perform for my mother's guests *à la* Isadora Duncan, which was probably amusing and embarrassing for my mother."

Off young Toller went to ballet class, but it wasn't all he had envisioned. His reaction to barre exercises was strikingly similar to his later reaction to compulsory figures. He found them tedious, repetitive, and confining. His formal ballet career lasted all of half an hour.

"But the need and the desire were still innately within me."

Then he found an outdoor hockey rink.

"I began sort of dancing on the ice, and I still believe I 'invented' figure skating. I'd never seen it, but I was skating in a way that no other person was skating."

Late one winter afternoon, a local Ice Capades skater

practiced on Toller's rink "and did the sorts of things I had been trying to do ever since I'd been on the ice—like spinning, which I had never seen."

Toller learned that what he had been doing intuitively had a name: figure skating. At his insistence, his parents took him to an exhibition.

"All of a sudden, my life unfurled itself before my eyes. I saw what it was that dance didn't give me. You're looking at a bird that can fly and a bird with clipped wings. The bird that can fly is the skater. I don't feel that skating should become dance on ice. One can experiment, but it must never fly off the common denominator of what the wonderment of skating is: that flow and speed and glide and spontaneous movement.

"Sometimes overchoreographed dance steps on the ice become more dance than skating. Then you kind of think, 'Well, why are they even bothering to put on skates?' The thing with all art forms, music or poetry or painting, is that the simplest idea is often the most beautiful. A simple spiral, beautifully done, can be far more gorgeous to watch than the most complicated series of steps."

Those familiar with Toller's work recognize recurrent motifs in both his skating and his painting (for which he became equally renowned). He unabashedly confessed to a single-minded vision.

"I never changed it, because the vision was always the same. Of course, technically, one becomes more proficient, but I was just getting better at what was already there."

John, too, followed the imperatives of a single vision: the vision, as he revealed in his autobiography, of a frustrated dancer. His parents had denied his wish to study dance as a child, feeling it wasn't manly enough. He found a way to dance and call it sport, which was marginally more legitimate in their eyes. In so doing, he took ballet on ice to a place where it had never been before. What he missed was some of the sheer fun of skating.

John battled not only his parents' prejudices but those of his early coaches. They forcefully curbed his artistic flourishes and tried to make him less elegant, more virile. He fought to be himself, which toughened his single-minded resolve.

Katie Baxter knew John, Toller, and Robin. She admired each of them, while appreciating Robin's versatility.

"Robin could do it all. He could do the Curry style. He could do the Hamilton style. He could do any style—and it's hard to do. You have to be an incredible skater, but Robin just wanted to grow, and Robin was thrust into an atmosphere where he *could* grow and grow. Toller was going to stay with *Malagueña,* and John was going to skate to Tchaikovsky."

Toller pleaded guilty to the charge, while adding that *Pagliacci* might have been a more apt accusation.

Of course, that's an oversimplification. John, for example, branched out into modern dance, though still with classical underpinnings. Toller, in many ways, was avant-garde, with original lines and angles that evoked sculpture. Yet, as a general point of comparison, it is valid. Skating in the late 1970s and early 1980s became ever more entertaining and versatile, thanks in part to the pervasive influence of television. Robin caught that wave and rode it for all he was worth, while John clung to the rock of his own identity, lashed about in the surf of a changing sport.

As for Toller, he sailed towards his own manifest destiny, unfettered by the albatross of others' expectations.

Evelyn Kramer, who coached Robin as a pro, offered a trenchant assessment of the three great male free skaters of the epoch.

"John was a traditional, elegant skater who always kept you at a distance with his skating. You watched him skate, and you watched his greatness. You had to look at him, and that was one of the great things about his skating. He didn't reach out. You would only be excited by him if you understood him, or *sort of* understood him—he was difficult to understand. You'd have to know what you were looking at.

"When you watch Robin, he takes you in. I'm sure everybody in the audience is in love with him and thinks he's skating just for them.

"Toller is an exhibitionist. He's the middle person, but he's not the middle person in style, and he's not the middle person in technique. He's just 'I'm going to do anything I want'—and he had the guts to do it, whether it was technically correct or not technically correct or way out there. He's fun, and he's arrogant, and he has a sense of humor about himself that neither of the other two has.

"John pushed people away, Toller doesn't give a damn (or it *seems* he doesn't give a damn), and Robin wants to share himself with others."

Toller found that Robin and John could laugh at themselves as well. John, like Toller, was self-deprecating. The pity was that he was also often puerile and picayune. As for Robin, he and Toller shared similar senses of humor. They frequently laughed at the same situations.

In a recent third-party exchange, Toller expressed a fascination with the flamboyant, over-the-top Brighton Pavilion in the south of England.

"Yes," Robin laughed, "he probably wants to buy it."

"No," Toller drawled melodramatically, "I do not wish to buy it. Tell Robin I will only consent to live in it if he buys it for me—which is only fair in light of our history."

Robin and Toller enjoyed a close relationship, born of the fact that they weren't true rivals as John and Robin were. Toller assessed his role in the hierarchy.

"Even though I can be poles apart from somebody like Elvis Stojko, I feel avuncular towards him, and I can talk to him in a way that Elvis could not talk to Kurt

Browning. I can talk to Kurt in a way that Kurt would never discuss anything with Brian Orser, and I can be like family with Brian Orser in a way that he could not possibly be with Brian Boitano—and the list goes on. I have always been like an older brother to Robin Cousins, in a way that John Curry could never have been.

"Over the years, I have been friendly with all of them, I suspect because I am always perceived as being so far out on a limb that they don't see me as competition. I have beaten Robin more than half a dozen times in competitions, both amateur and professional, yet there was never an ounce of malice between us. I think Robin cares very much for me, and I care very much for him. We are comfortable with each other, although I don't know if we've ever really had a talk about the meaning of life. Maybe it's not even necessary. I feel that Robin is almost sort of family to me—a cousin! He's my English cousin. We've never, ever had an angry word between us, and we've never, ever disagreed about anything in skating. With Brian Boitano, I could definitely say, 'You're a great skater, and you're not stupid, but I totally disagree with you.' Robin and I have had an entirely consistent understanding of the medium of skating."

John and Toller, close in age, had a chilly relationship—as John did with many others. Although John was substantially older than Robin, one might have expected the two compatriots whose lives ran on parallel tracks to be kindred spirits. That wasn't the case.

"In time, we became friends of sorts through respect for each other's work. We never spent time together. The only time I ever saw John was at skating events, and John was quiet and guarded. The fact that we were on the same ice at a practice was sometimes as close as it got. John was never easily accessible. I also felt that he didn't have any time for the commerciality of the sport, and I had every intention of being as commercial and as popular as possible. That was what made it exciting for me: the showy aspect of skating, which didn't interest John. Certain aspects of dancing that interested him were the reasons I stopped dancing in the first place. We were quite juxtaposed for a while.

"When I almost beat him at the national championships prior to the Olympics, it was probably the first time I realized that someone I thought was very great was actually extremely vulnerable. He was one of the greatest exponents of the art of figure skating. He has left so much to the sport. I had a great respect for him as a performer and as an artist. It wasn't always necessarily my cup of tea. I felt he could have been so much better if he'd allowed himself to be a little more adaptable to the fun of what skating is all about."

Katherine Healy was particularly sensitive to the fragile nature of Robin and John's relationship.

"There was kind of a rivalry. I had the feeling that they were aware of each other and that, in some sense, they were probably both insecure about each other— needlessly. Nobody said, 'There should only be Robin' or 'There should only be John.' I also had the feeling that they respected each other. John might never have come right out and said so, but he always respected people who were very athletic, who had no fear on the ice. Mind you, John was a great skater, but he respected that athleticism enormously, and I always had the feeling that there was a secret respect for Robin."

John was what Katherine called "a little bit prickly on the outside," but inside he was "a very, very nice man— no matter what anybody says. He was one of the nicest people I knew in my whole life, and I was so sorry when he died. I'm only sad for him that he didn't try to be more commercial, because I think, in the end, he would have been happier; but he consciously made the choice not to do that. I think that, in a material sense, he would have been more comfortable, but he chose the hard way. If there was a hard way to choose, he always chose it."

That, in Toller's opinion, was the drawback of John's approach.

"John Curry is perhaps better dead than alive, for his own sake. I think of him as being quite a tortured person and uncomfortable with his talent. He never took the positive thrill from what he had been dealt. Robin Cousins, on the other hand, has had a magnificent career with countless magnificent moments and has brought pleasure to millions of people all over the world."

John was, perhaps more than anything, easily misunderstood. He had a nasty streak that he wasn't skillful at hiding, while his goodness remained under a bushel. He labored beneath the burden of frustration. In his intensity, he didn't waste energy on diplomacy. He said what he thought, which antagonized people. He exhibited the sometimes arrogant air of one with deeply-held convictions.

Robin was less complicated. Like his art, he was accessible: cheerful, giving, voluble, full of fun. Fortunate as a child to have been supported in his ambitions, he didn't harbor frustrations and let them fester. Rather, he set them aside and processed them later. The lack of brooding made him no less the artist.

JoJo Starbuck offered a poetic analysis of the troika.

"As Tenley Albright would say, John was kind to the ice. He skated with great reverence for the space he was in. Each edge was silent. His blades whispered. They didn't speak loudly, but his heart and his presence spoke loudly.

"When Toller skated, there was total abandon. He would gobble you up, gobble up the space, gobble up the ice. He threw himself at everything: at the music, at the ice, at the space, at the people. He did it with great passion and heart, too, but it was totally different and much more *out there*.

"Robin was audience-oriented—not that John and

Toller weren't. He was a master showman. He could become like water rippling, and then he could also be like an ocean crashing. He had a propensity to do both brilliantly."

John's art was introspective. Toller's was flamboyant, pretentious on the surface, yet delivered with charming irony and self-awareness. Robin's found expression in bounding, optimistic energy. What a rich legacy each left.

Propitious Omens

When Robin was eleven, he and his parents set out in a borrowed Bedford Caravanette for the 1969 British novice championships. Hotels were out of the question, so they set up camp under a ramp in the brand new Billingham Forum's frozen parking lot. Undressing in the cold was torture. Jo cooked the food she had packed for the entire four-day trip over a camp stove.

Hardship took a back seat when Robin became the novice champion—after barely two years of private lessons. As a result, the National Skating Association (NSA) invited him to qualify for a coaching scholarship. He skated before a panel of judges at Solihull and received a cash sponsorship equal to 50 per cent of the fees he paid his coach. Because he could afford so few lessons, the weekly windfall worked out to a paltry sum. Other expenses continued to mount precipitously: ice time, equipment, costumes, travel.

With 1970 came what Fred viewed as a turning point in Robin's career. When Robinson's Barley Water sponsored a national search for a future British Olympic champion, Martin wrote an essay nominating his brother. The contest was open to participants in all sports, with the winner to be chosen through interviews. After advancing through regional competition, Robin went to the Crystal Palace in London as one of a handful of finalists.

His demeanor at the interview was, he admits, rather

pompous and arrogant. He remembers saying, "I will win," not "I hope I can."

Judge Emlyn Hughes, Fred's soccer hero, remarked, "Your son has a clear idea of what he wants to do." That was why Robin won.

"I remember being very positive and thinking that was normal. I never thought my ambitions were abnormal. I'm rudely, and probably wrongly, accusatory of people who don't have any ambition whatsoever."

Apart from the £250 prize, the triumph carried the weight of a favorable omen.

The same year, Robin won the Queens Cup at the Queens Ice Skating Club, London. A writer for *Skate* magazine commented, "This thirteen-year-old skated with such gusto that he nearly did us all a favor by increasing the width of the ice surface at Queens, and for this feat of trying to demolish the barrier all he has to show is a badly bruised knee."

Like everything else that year, the remark was portentous.

The Reluctant Scholar

Martin, Nick, and Robin all attended the Sea Mills Infant and Junior schools. At age eleven, they parted company. From the list of senior institutions, Martin chose Bristol Grammar School for its academic reputation. Nick followed suit. Both won scholarships to the all-boys private school. Robin, who wasn't academically-inclined, chose Henbury Comprehensive for several good reasons. Grammar school, with its two to three hours of nightly homework and Saturday-morning classes, wouldn't have allowed time for skating. Furthermore, grammar schools took their team sports seriously, while comprehensive schools offered more individual sports, a point strongly in their favor to Robin's way of thinking.

The family chose Henbury in particular, according

to Jo, because it boasted the best reputation in academics, art, and music.

"We weren't thinking in terms of the Olympics, but we knew by then that skating was definitely a part of Robin's life, as maybe ballet would have been. So that was where he went—and was happy, I think, inasmuch as he would be happy with any school."

As Pam observed, "Robin ate, drank, and slept ice skating. It was all he could think about. I don't think he liked school so much."

Derek Walkerdine taught Robin humanities (history, geography, and religious studies) from shortly after Robin's eleventh birthday until he was nearly thirteen.

"My impressions of Robin are of a quiet, middle ability boy. He sat at the back of the class and just got on with his work. His attendance was excellent; there are no absences recorded in the first year and only three in the second year. The marks which I have recorded for him are very consistently average. I cannot recall him making a large oral contribution to the lesson, but my memory is that he responded if asked. I have to say that at this early stage in his secondary school career, he did not make a great impression. I was aware that he was already a skater of note, but he did not talk about it or make anything of it. Robin certainly never came into conflict with authority at school, and I would describe him as an attentive trier, hard-working rather than brilliant."

Mike Waters, Head of Nicholas House, of which Robin was a member from age thirteen, retained only sketchy memories of him, which any teacher will recognize as a sign that he was neither exceptionally good nor especially bad. He was one of those middle-of-the-road students who keep a low profile, hoping to escape from school unnoticed and unscathed.

Waters commented wryly, "Robin was, I think, rather a shy lad. I recall one occasion when I had to go to the local council offices, which were near the ice rink. Robin had obviously been training, and I spotted him coming up Park Street in Bristol as I headed down the hill. He crossed the road to avoid me!"

Robin's lackluster academic career did not reflect a limited learning capacity. He simply liked to learn on his own terms. His intelligence had quirks. His recall of verbal and visual detail was remarkable, while anything numerical—a date, age, or competition placement—was best viewed as an estimate. One can only imagine what sort of math student he must have been and how vague his time line of history.

"Math was a disaster. I don't do tables. I sit at them and eat. To this day, I'm quite happy to use my fingers to count, and I actually do long division with bits of paper—or a calculator, better still. We used to have to do the sums, and then we would be allowed to use the calculator to find out if we were right. Well, why not use it in the first place?"

Robin attached little importance to quantification unless he was counting musical beats.

He didn't appear overwhelmingly either left-brain or right-brain dominant. His creativity and spatial awareness suggested a right-brain point of view, while his articulateness and his ability to interrelate dozens of peripheral details depended on the organizational skills of his left brain. To compound the puzzle, he was born ambidextrous, with a mirror-image tendency. When he tied his skate laces, he raised the numb tip of his left index finger—while involuntarily raising the right finger, too.

"I could *not* play the piano," he joked.

Robin was equipped with the right assets, from his bones and muscles to the way his brain percolated, to do what he knew he was destined to do—and he knew it at age eleven. He would have been a challenge to any school that turned out round pegs for round holes, rather than making triangular, oval, and trapezoidal pegs to suit the full variety of hole types.

The English school taught to the left brain, and Robin's left brain wasn't paying attention.

He lit into the topic with relish.

"The problem with the English school system is that learning is not made interesting. Geography was books. Open the book. Read page five. Very bland and monochromatic. All those places I then got to visit were far more magical and mystical, even East Germany, than they had ever portrayed to me in school. I couldn't teach skating, even if I had a textbook, by teaching the textbook. You have to color in, find peripherals, find common denominators with something else. In England, somewhat still, it's all geared towards 'This has worked for the last ninety years, and it will continue to work for the next ninety if you let it.' School uniforms. Everyone looking the same. It's all very Orwellian to me. How can you create individuality in children when you demand that they all look the same?"

He was purposely obtuse in describing his uniforms.

"Blah. Grey. Grey, black, and more grey. All I remember is grey. Short trousers for junior school, long for senior. Dark green sweater for junior school, blazer for senior. White shirt and tie. That was whether you were at private school, public school, or nothing school."

Waters offered a more lucid description.

"The uniform at Henbury in the late sixties was very strictly enforced. The boys had to wear a white shirt, a House tie (there were six houses, each distinguished by a different color, red in the case of Nicholas, orange, light blue, yellow, dark green, and light green), grey trousers, a navy blue blazer with the school badge on it, and black shoes. The girls were expected to wear a grey skirt and a white blouse, a school blazer like the boys, black shoes, and either 'normal' stockings—no fancy colors—or white ankle socks. In the summer the girls were allowed to wear a blue-and-white vertically-striped dress."

Robin's coping mechanism was to tune out, doodle, and think about skating. He knew even then that it would open the whole world to his eager mind.

At Henbury, he swam, ran, and tumbled on the trampoline. As Fred and Jo had hoped, the school was generally supportive when it came to skating. With success came the need to miss classes to attend competitions. Eventually the headmaster, John Luget, told Fred and Jo not to bother writing notes each time their son was absent. If he wasn't in school, he was sure to be skating. Luget could see the sparkle in Robin's eye each time he won a trophy. He wisely understood that it wasn't something the youngster simply played at.

Robin couldn't say that school was an unhappy experience.

"But it wasn't anything to write home about. It was no big deal, and school really should be a big deal. The idea of a school reunion to anybody in England would be the most hysterically ridiculous, stupid thing that anybody ever mentioned, even in college and university, yet it's a big deal in the United States. American kids like to go to high school. There's something other than education involved. It's a way of life.

"In England, school is a completely different thing. I've seen it on both sides. There are those people who cope brilliantly in academic situations and those people who, if they didn't have all the other things that go with American high school life, couldn't cope, but they aren't catered to in the English school system, which is why so many people drop out.

"Kids in America have their friends at high school. There are extracurriculars—which exist in English schools, but they're not fun; not on *your* terms. It has probably all changed, but that's how I remember it."

In time, Henbury made concessions, but not without impassioned discussion. Robin was allowed to skate during the midday session, provided that Jo pick him up at the beginning of his games period and return him to school at its end.

The former Lower School head wrote ironically, "I recall clearly the interview with Robin's parents in my study and the difficulty of the decision—much opposed, of course, by the P.E. department."

"It's funny," Robin mused. "They never saw my skating as education."

Years later, he asked the Soviet pairs skater Irina Rodnina, his idol, "What is it about the Russians? Why are they such great skaters?" She replied that Russians viewed sport as part of the curriculum, not as a form of recreation than one pursued without goals and standards.

Waters distinctly recalled "arguing with the then Head Teacher, John Luget, about his decision to allow Robin time off school to train at the local ice-skating rink. I strongly opposed this, as I felt Robin's education was more important than ice skating, and that the time he spent out of school might prove detrimental to his eventual examination performance, and so to his opportunities later in life. I have seen a great many young men and women with aspirations in a field outside education, and on average very, very few succeed. John Luget, however, had been convinced by those responsible for Robin's training that here indeed was a young man of exceptional talent for whom exceptional arrangements should be made. Mr. Luget's view prevailed. He was a man of great vision, and I am pleased for Robin's sake that his decision, as things so often turned out, proved correct."

Jo worked as a secretary to subsidize her sons' activities and education. She left her office in the late morning to collect Robin at Henbury. He changed into his skating gear as they flew down the highway, then rushed up four flights, took his lesson, changed clothes again in the car, and arrived at school in time for the noon meal.

After his blessed escape from Henbury, he was redeposited in its clutches. No wonder he daydreamed.

Martin was one of several senior boys invited to have lunch at his grammar school's high table. His headmaster grilled him on the effect of training and competing on his brother's schooling. The fact that Robin could fit in most of his schoolwork impressed the headmaster, but Robin had little choice. The rink was available for lessons only at dawn, lunchtime, and late at night. Even so, after the Olympics, there was a congratulatory letter from Martin's long-retired headmaster.

Superboots

Martin christened his younger brother Little Titch. Later, as accomplishments warranted, Nick promoted him to the rank of Superboots. As his brothers, they were sometimes caught up in the drama, humor, pathos, and intrigue of skating life.

Each year the various rinks held interclub team competitions. When Bristol skated against Streatham one hot summer day, the team consisted of Robin, a female counterpart, an ice handball team, a speed skating team, and some barrel jumpers. Martin accompanied Robin on the bus to London. The bag containing his skates, clothes, and music went into the overhead compartment. Cassettes hadn't come into use, so there was a record of "The Colonel Bogey March."

By the time the record reached London, it had "turned into a flower bowl," as Martin recalled. To make it playable, Martin and a friend put it under the hottest water possible. The theory was, "If it played odd, too bad. At least, if it was flat, you could put a needle onto it." They took turns holding the disk under the tap, flattening it against the sink bottom.

"I can't remember how well or how badly it played, and I can't remember how well or how badly Robin skated, because that was one of those nights when I was smoking myself stupid. I was responsible for him. But you know the old story: all's well that ends well. We won the match."

In April 1972, at age fourteen, Robin became the youngest boy to win the junior men's championship. There was a jump in level between novice and junior (a gap filled today by the primary classification). Robin hadn't been expected to win, but something had happened to tilt things in his favor.

For the 1972-73 season, the ISU had added the short program to competitions it sanctioned. Figures were relegated to 40 per cent. The long program accounted for another 40. The short program, at 20 per cent, was a technical variant of the long free-skating program.[4] In 1972, Robin staked out a historic footnote. The British junior championship, early in the skating year, was the first national championship worldwide to incorporate the short program. Since Robin was first to skate, he was the first to perform it in competition.

According to ISU historian Benjamin Wright, "It is impossible to verify that such was the case."

Robin found that odd.

"You should be able to look it up. I think we were the only country on the planet that had a national championship in the middle of the spring."

The short program favored Robin's panache and his outstanding ability to jump and spin. Taken together, the short and long programs constituted the combined free skating, for which the ISU conferred a separate title and

---

[4] The percentages, like the short program format, were later adjusted. By the time Robin won the Olympics in 1980, although the short program remained at 20 per cent, figures were worth just 30 per cent, and the long program had been upgraded to 50. There were originally six, then seven, and now eight designated elements that had to be performed, one attempt each: specific jumps, spins, and footwork sequences. As with the long program, two marks were given: one for required elements and one for presentation.

medal. Robin amassed a king's ransom in free-skating gold medals: fifteen in a row between October 1977 and March 1980.

In Billingham, he pulled up from fourth to win the free skating and the title, qualifying for senior competition. Ice dance coach Peri Horne pointed out that he would soon be out of his league.

"After today, you're not the best junior but the worst senior."

"Thanks a lot," he thought, but her words spurred him on.

Saint-Gervais

Not long afterwards, Robin received an invitation from the NSA to compete in his first "international"—late-summer and fall competitions that lend experience to up-and-coming skaters. The trip to Saint-Gervais, France, for the Grand Prix was his first foreign expedition. The picturesque ski resort at the foot of Mont Blanc, on the Gallic side of the congruence of France, Switzerland, and Italy, was also the site of Robin's first encounter with American Charles Tickner. Charlie was a steady, unflappable skater, consistent, if not blindingly brilliant, in figures and freestyle. He won the men's event, while Robin finished seventh following a poor showing in figures, an all-too-familiar state of affairs.

Though Robin was too "overawed" to skate his best, Saint-Gervais was a watershed. As Robin, Charlie, Randy Gardner, Tai Babilonia, and Linda Fratianne made their international débuts together, they ushered in an era. They continued to hit benchmarks together and formed links of friendship. Each went on to international stardom.

"We've all gone through what we've gone through, but there was a certain resilience about us: Tai and Randy, Lisa-Marie Allen, Linda, Emi Watanabe. We all skated because we wanted to. We loved what we did. That was the only reason to do it. There was no money involved. There were no agents. It was a very different time.

"Scott Hamilton and Rosalynn Sumners cusped that era. Skating started to become a business after that. As much as I wish I had been able to have offered to me what is now offered to the present stars, even before they *are* stars, I don't know if I could have done it under those circumstances. The pressures are different. We've all been able to suffer through anything we've had to and still come out the other end. I think it shows in the skating now that people forget why they're there in the first place. That's sad. Now children say, 'I want to be an ice skater because they make lots of money.' Nobody said that in our day. If you wanted to be an ice skater, it was because you liked to skate, not because of the potential pot of gold at the end of the rainbow."

Rosalynn agreed.

"Amateur was definitely amateur, but I was right on the cusp. You were starting to have managers, but you couldn't be seen talking to them. It was all hush-hush. We would have to stand at the other side of the arena so it didn't look like we were connected. Back then, your only choices were Ice Capades and Disney, and there were only two professional competitions. Now there are fifteen competitions to choose from and many tours. I tease Kristi Yamaguchi and Paul Wylie now and then: 'I'd like to see you guys survive that many shows a year!' Now it's all plush-plush. They're big, huge stars. They're on the cover of *USA Today* and doing 'Dateline.' It's a business, which is kind of sad. Things had to change, follow a natural progression, but having seen both sides, having been in the *then* and the *now*, I'm glad that I did it in the *then.*"

Rosalynn was happy to be the national and world champion when the all-around title still included figures. Skating was "still a bit innocent and naïve." As Robin, Scott, and Rosalynn paved the way for the Kristis and the

Pauls, mutual respect grew between generations. When young skaters no longer know their history, they may take their good fortune for granted.

Skating as a business, Rosalynn suggested, "starts when these kids are thirteen years old. It's like tennis now. They can support a whole family. The family quit their jobs. It's scary. I wouldn't want that kind of pressure. We skated because we truly loved what we did, and do still. That's where the longevity comes from that Robin and Scott and I have. Even though we had to turn our skating a little bit into a business, we did it all those years without being motivated by how much money we could make at a competition or how many television specials we could be in. It was all purely, 'Sure, I'll go to Erie, Pennsylvania, and do a show.' We didn't even know we were paving the way."

American David Santee harks back to the same era.

"I was part of a great, great time in figure skating, when the sport started to boom. There were a lot of us that people could follow, who had great stories off the ice and great personalities on the ice. It was a special time, and it has had an impact on what's happening now. Now skating is on TV every week, which is great, but it's the same people all the time. Everything has its drawbacks, but I don't think I would trade times. With the group that we had, with the talent that was there, it was pretty special."

Robin was invited to perform an exhibition, an unexpected honor for the seventh-placer. He and Pam bought Paul McCartney's "Live and Let Die" and choreographed it on the spot.

"I wasn't my best. It was a little much for me, being thrown into all that. I was fourteen. I think I had my birthday while we were away."

Randy saw the talent shining through.

"Robin stood apart from the rest of the guys. He was more talented. He was more musical. He had something special about him, and I could see it back then. I could tell he was going to be a star."

One of Robin's chief talents was mimicry. He reproduced voices, personalities, and skating styles, operating in an *on* mode around his fellow skaters, who thought of him as funny and outgoing. Those who knew him best in private life were more aware of his shyness and reserve. That duality persists.

Garnet Ostermaier, the sometime runner-up to German champion Dagmar Lurz, was born in California to German parents. Destined to be Robin's lifelong friend, she first met him at Saint-Gervais.

"He was skinny, tall, and gangly-looking. He hadn't reached his full potential, but you could see that there was a big talent there."

Saint-Gervais showed Robin his future. It set him and his cohorts on the long, bumpy road to Lake Placid.

One of the Men

Robin had begun missing school each Wednesday to study with Gladys Hogg at Queens. By December 1972, he was ready for his first senior championship, contested, as usual, in Richmond's Arosa rink (since razed). Seeing television lights, Martin was struck for the first time by the enormity of the affair. It suddenly hit him, "That's my little brother out there." He was hooked.

Haig Oundjian didn't defend his title. Robin, skating with an injured hand, finished third behind John Curry, who regained the number-one spot he had earned in 1970.

Robin felt compelled to confess, "Yes, I was third in my first senior championship, but there were only three in it."

Although Robin was third in figures, his second-place free-skating programs received warm receptions from the crowd and optimistic predictions from the press. The NSA expressed its own confidence by naming him to compete at the European championship at Cologne, West Germany. The age of innocence was drawing to a close.

Martin was twenty, Nick eighteen. Both had left for universities by then. If the three boys were treated equally, that didn't mean they were all the same.

Martin, the "clever" son, was the least extroverted.

"Martin was the one who had the wild and crazy days when he was at university. He was the one who went through the long-haired Yippie and Monty Python phase. Woodstock, Jimi Hendrix, he was into all that, and he was the one with the motorbike."

Today Martin is an insurance broker. He and his wife, June, have two sons, Robin and Tristan.

Nick, the "musical one," was colorful in his own way, gregarious, happy-go-lucky, and protective of his younger brother.

"Nick was the one who would go to town for his music lesson and leave his bassoon—it's *not* a small instrument—on the bus. He has even driven to town from the house and come home on the bus. But my favorite story about my brother is of the time he was proudly putting up a towel rack and screamed for his wife to come and help him look for a vinyl screw—and it was between his teeth. Then, to finish it off, he threw the towel gallantly onto the rack, and the whole thing fell on the floor. That's my brother. 'I don't know how I'll do it, mother, but you know I will. I will.'"

These days Nick heads the physical education department, teaches history, and serves as house master to a flock of young boys at the esteemed boarding school Dulwich College. He is among the ten top-ranked English soccer referees. Nick, Helen, and their four children, Thomas, James, Claire, and Oliver, dwell amongst what appears to be blissful chaos.

"Yes," Robin agreed, "which is only chaos to everybody else around him. He has it perfectly organized in his head, but he's not written anything down. Nobody knows where anything is. How he runs the school and keeps those boys in order and has a family—!"

Nick is a masculine man, athletically gifted and proud of it. Loughborough University, his alma mater, is a premier English bastion of physical education.

"My circle of friends were very much centered on the rugby club. Now, rugby buggers are notoriously narrow-banded individuals, and although I've never been embarrassed, ashamed, or put off by the fact that my skills are in rugby and cricket and Robin is an ice skater, you're aware sometimes that people will look down their noses at skating in general or your brother in particular, and those people would tend to be in the sorts of groups in which I was moving—and so they'd say some unkind remarks. You can imagine the sort of thing: 'effeminate' remarks or 'dressed in sequins,' or whatever it might be."

When the Loughborough men saw skating on T V, they were quick to change the channel. Then Robin appeared in person.

"Here's Nick's brother, the pansy ice skater, the fluffy one, coming to where all these jocks were."

In the gym, Robin turned the tables. The P.E. majors, stunned by his superior trampoline prowess, suddenly saw the "pansy ice skater" as an athlete. From then on, Robin (or Rob, as Nick calls him) was just one of the men.

Nick admitted to a single lingering aversion.

"One thing I couldn't stand was when he costumed out in sequins. That has always been a downer for me."

Nick graduated from Loughborough with a joint honors degree in physical education and history. Martin earned a degree at Birmingham University. Robin went on to obtain what may have been the best education of all, through his skating travels and in the school of life.

3. The London Years: 1973-77

$\mathcal{F}$amily and friends borrowed a twelve-seater van for the week-long trip to Cologne, where Robin, the youngest competitor, finished fifteenth in his first European championship.

"Loved it. I was a star. Well, *Pam* was a star. Pam was the hit of the championships. She was so gorgeous and glamorous. Amongst all those fuddy-duddy skating coaches, she was a hit. She was coaching this 'hot new talent.' The stars at that time were Ondrej Nepela and Sergei Chetverukhin. She had them both champing at the bit. She held court in the lobby. Everybody was talking about the child who had so much potential. I don't usually take in a lot of what people say, but I do remember enjoying the celebrity it was going to entail. I actually skated very well. I had a good time, and I wasn't *last*—even in figures."

When the NSA had chosen Robin for Europeans, the comment at school had been, "Is it really necessary? Do you have to have time off to skate?"

Jo was taken aback.

"He was just fifteen then, and of course it was quite a big thing—but not for a certain schoolmistress."

Robin offered pedants a cautionary tale.

"There were one or two teachers whose names I cannot remember—probably it's a good job—who wished I'd stop playing at 'that thing that you do when you leave' and get down to some work. If this person had made her geography lessons half as interesting as the places that I was visiting, or had *included* the places I was visiting—but that was never an option. To have been to Germany and France at that age was far more interesting to me than to be reading yet another story about how the pyramids were built."

In his disenchantment with school, he found an unexpected ally. The NSA strongly urged that he skate in London full-time, now that he was a member of the British team. Pam had taken Robin as far as she could, although it broke her heart to let him go. To her credit, both Gladys Hogg and later Carlo Fassi were full of praise for the foundation she had laid.

Going to London meant quitting school. A year later, that wouldn't have been in the cards. The school-leaving age was about to be raised to sixteen. Jo and Fred went to see Headmaster Luget.

"Give me a week, and I will think about it," he told them. Then, having spoken to Robin's teachers, he agreed that leaving school would be for the best. Only half of Robin's heart was at school. The rest was in the ice rink.

"If skating is to be his life, as Robin insists that it is, then that's fine," Luget concluded.

It wasn't as fine with Nick. He returned from

Loughborough to an agonizing family discussion of the pros and cons of Robin leaving school to live by himself in a London bed-sitter. The situation was laid out, and Nick was asked for his opinion.

"My mum was in tears. To my chagrin, I remember banging the table and saying, 'You're not thinking of him leaving school? He has no qualifications. This is absurdity.' It was me playing the archconservative. 'This won't last. What if it all goes wrong?' At the end of the day, of course, off he went. The rest is history."

Like Nick, both Jo and Fred valued an academic education. Fred remembered his own youthful dilemma.

"I was going to be a footballer. No way was I going to *work*. In 1946, I came out of the navy with no qualifications. Hadn't done my schooling. I had to start at the bottom rung. That's why I say, no matter how good you are at any sport, you must have some education."

Stepping off the academic ladder was a permanent decision. Night school was the only alternative. Luget reminded Jo and Fred of that option. It was enough to allay their worst fears, so Robin left school at Easter.

He was alone in London, living in what amounted to a converted bathroom in an old five-story house at Notting Hill Gate. It contained a tiny gas stove, a sink, a bed, a stand-up closet, and a wind-up record player, with a flowered comforter and skating posters for decoration. Robin disciplined himself to a rigid schedule, managed his meager finances, and fixed his own meals.

Each Monday morning, with a heavy heart, he caught the 7:17 train for London. Once he hit the ice, he was fine. Still, each Friday evening he returned to Bristol. Fred and Jo thought it wouldn't be long before he stayed in town for the weekend, but that didn't happen. From time to time, Jo stumbled on party invitations.

"You didn't want to go?"

"No. I came home, didn't I?"

Queens was on the ground floor of a brown brick and grey stone building of flats in Queensway, Kensington. The ice surface was an abnormally long and narrow oval: 220' x 65'.[5] The distinctive smell of man-made ice permeated everything in the building. The locker rooms, a friend remembers, were "squalid and primitive." There was a café where the skaters lounged between sessions. Music played in the background, while dance intervals punctuated public sessions. In the morning, small children and grandmothers populated the rink. In the afternoon, when school let out, chaos was unleashed like the unmentionable horrors of Pandora's box.

Robin found a part-time job stocking shelves, wrapping packages, and occasionally running the till at Whiteley's Department Store, a huge, somewhat run-down emporium down the street from the rink. There, in an architecturally pretentious corner building with massive columns and a small domed cupola, he earned about £5 a week to help meet expenses.

"Clocked in, clocked out, took the money, and ran— not very far, unfortunately."

Fred told a reporter, "Having to be careful with cash is a good thing. It builds character."

Robin was on a £30-per-week budget, austere even at 1973 prices. Weekly rent was £8.50. Skating costs came to £10, half for coaching and half for ice time. Train fare at £4 per weekend left £7.50 for food and incidentals.

Each dawn, Robin rose at 5:00. Free-skating practice ran from 6:00 until 8:00. Often the only time the ice was clear enough for a five-minute run-through was at the inhospitable hour of 6:45. Gladys was wont to say, "If you can do it at this hour, you can do it at any hour." It was all part of the character-building process.

---

[5] A regulation Olympic surface is 200' by 100'. The Queens Ice Bowl of today, at 165' by 65', accommodates ten-pin bowling.

Between 8:30 and 9:00, the singles skaters did compulsory figures at one end of the rink, while the dancers filled the remaining ice with the broad, curved tracings of compulsory dances. From 10:00 until 12:00, the public took over, more or less limiting the efficiency of practice depending on the day. After resurfacing, there was an additional figures patch. Ninety per cent of the British team trained under those conditions, threading their way through public sessions together. It was Grand Central Station at rush hour, with a lot more speed.

At 1:45 P.M., Robin hurried to Whiteley's, where he worked until 5:00. Then he went home to the bed-sitter, cooked a simple dinner, and turned in at 8:00 in order to be up again as the cock crowed. Fred and Jo never heard a complaint.

"What was there to complain about? There was no alternative."

It was at that dreary point that Robin's life intersected the rather more interesting existence of Trish Bernays, a modern married woman in her early thirties. Tall and flamboyant, with a long blonde ponytail, Trish was too ill with hepatitis to hold a full-time job. Figure skating had always intrigued her, so she tried it. Her skating time increased with her strength. She took an interest in Robin, and they became good friends.

As a student in Bristol, he had formed few close friendships, partly because of his demanding schedule and partly because the more typical teenagers found his lifestyle unusual. In London, the situation was worse. While he was at the rink, most boys his age were in school. He was stranded without family, peers, and Pam.

As for Trish, her recuperation bored her. When she stumbled upon a boy who touched her heart, she and her husband, Mike, virtually adopted him. Robin made a number of adult friends, never having been one to pigeonhole people by age.

Trish found, "Robin was much more interested in other lives than skating. He didn't have such a narrow field. It wasn't my habit to hang around with fifteen-year-old kids. Kids were kids to me, but Robin was like a twenty-year-old. He had such a presence, such a strength of character."

Most fifteen-year-olds focused on themselves and their immediate social and creature needs. Fifteen-year-olds who were serious about skating often took that narrow view to its extreme. Robin was articulate. He enjoyed art, music, and the theatre. The cruel irony was that he lived amidst a smorgasbord of cultural delights yet had no money with which to taste them.

Nick observed a paradox. Trish enjoyed Robin for his mature and eclectic interests, while it was also Trish who provoked and reinforced them.

"She introduced him to an adult lifestyle. He knew nothing different. I mean, that was the point. He missed out on the intermediate teenage years. They just didn't happen for him. One minute he was a little boy at home—and he was a *little* boy—and the next minute he was living in a bed-sit in London, being looked after by two very well-to-do people (and very nice nevertheless), but their interests were not those of a fifteen-year-old, so he gravitated upward. He missed out on all the middle bit, the normal fifteen years old, because there was nobody he knew who was age fifteen. It could have been a total disaster. I don't think I was too much out of order suggesting that he shouldn't be up in London in a bed-sit when he was so unworldly-wise at that time."

Robin, Trish, Mike, and their friends drank cream teas, enjoyed the park, went to the movies, or shopped. Trish and Mike often picked up Robin's tab. They invited him to their flat for sandwiches and TV, and he liked being part of their family.

Meanwhile, he made himself useful. He cut up snake

skins for the patchwork purses and belts that Italian women bought by the armload from Mike's stall on Portobello Road. Sometimes he threaded glass-bead necklaces. It was fun because it wasn't what normal people did. It was more exotic, romantic, and colorful than anything he had known in Bristol.

The 1970s were in full bloom. Watergate overflowed its banks. Billie Jean King battled Chris Evert at Wimbledon, while Bjorn Borg burst upon the quarterfinals. Princess Caroline went home to Monaco after two years at an English convent school. Oil was in short supply; hot tubs were not. Robin reveled in the no man's land between Bristol and Bohemia.

"Trish was hip—there are no two ways about it—and her friend Julia was a model, so that was even cooler. They were always up to mischief, and they would do it on purpose if Gladys was watching. They knew it would make her nervous. Julia was extremely well-endowed, which was her forte on television. She was one of the stars of what we affectionately call 'jiggle TV.'"

Robin wasn't Trish and Julia's sole conquest. Gail Keddie, a future British champion from an affluent, straight-laced Scottish family, found them entertaining as well. As innocent as the hijinks were—turning Julia's windshield wipers outward to spray pedestrians—they had the mouth-watering taste of forbidden fruit.

Trish found Robin "pushier" than the other boys at the rink. He had a ferocious determination to succeed, and with that went self-discipline. He sat in her flat until mid-evening, then said, "Tell me the end of the movie, Trish. I must go."

He never invited Trish or Mike into the bed-sitter.

"There wasn't room for two people. It's a cliché, but you could *not* swing the cat around."

Trish and Julia offered Robin an alternative to the "bitchiness" of the rink.

"Some of the other skaters used to laugh at him because he had such pretty movements. It was difficult for him. I think having Julia and me around helped. I don't know much about choreography, but I do know what looks attractive. I'd say, 'No, no, Robin, that doesn't look sexy enough' or 'That looks gauche and awkward.' A French boy probably could look sexy. An English boy can't. They have very little sex appeal at that age. At fifteen, he was an awkward, gawky young man, full of ideas but too embarrassed to carry them out. Tall and gangly but tremendously charming. All in all, I helped him through a time when he was quite lonely, away from his parents. I think it was an era he'd rather forget."

The Redoubtable Miss Hogg

Robin had presence on the ice, though he was reluctant to let it show. When he skated, people watched. He was fluid like a ballet dancer, able to interpret music. His sense of style was alien to his coach.

The late Gladys Hogg MBE was an elderly woman even then. A roller dancer and international fencer in her youth, she had won professional ice skating titles in both dance and pairs and had taught at Queens since its 1930 opening.

Gladys's tastes had formed when artistry in male skaters was unacceptable. Her great love was ice dance, and she coached many champions. Robin shared her attentions with Janet Thompson and Warren Maxwell.

To complicate matters, Gladys was afraid to fly. She traveled to competitions by train or boat, arriving days behind her skaters. If she sent a substitute coach, invariably it was one who specialized in ice dance.

With heavy irony and mischief in his eye, Robin spoke of "the great Gladys Hogg." He didn't mean his remarks unkindly—but, in truth, she scared him to death. She stood on the ice in heavy boots or old-fashioned skates, firmly planted on legs encased in sensible tweed trousers, her torso and arms bundled in a bulky overcoat. Everything about her was no-nonsense, from her manner to her short-cropped grey hair to the glasses through which she peered severely. Her voice was frightening to imaginative boys like Robin.

"She was average in height only. She had a face that had been through and seen, she would have thought, anything there was to see in skating. She was one of the great coaches, but she taught the way she taught. There was no room for embellishment on her theories, which were absolutely textbook and could not be faulted. She was an old schoolmarm. You said 'Good morning, Miss Hogg' as you walked in the door. If not, you didn't get a lesson. Obviously respect and politeness were in order, but they were demanded in such a way that I was terrified of the woman.

"She wasn't endearing whatsoever, but she didn't want to be. It was, 'This is how I taught so-and-so, and that's how I'll teach you.' Anybody who was somebody she'd either started or had taught at some point, so who was I to argue? All I needed to do was to learn the hard facts of how to take off a triple properly and how to do figures. I don't know how to describe her. She was Sister George!"

Robin had learned Pam's lesson well and never forgot his programs. With Gladys, however, he developed a new trick: changing them on purpose. She despaired. Spontaneity was not in her vocabulary. She and her pupil had nothing in common except a slab of cold, hard ice.

Robin confided wistfully, "That's not how I want to do it, Trish. That's not what I'm about. She doesn't understand. She doesn't listen to the radio or go to the movies, so she certainly never would have heard that style of musical."

Even then, Robin absorbed influences from other media and used them to enrich and diversify his creations. Like a dry sponge, he drank up everything: good, bad, and indifferent. That was beyond the ken of Gladys Hogg, under whose nonetheless capable tutelage John Curry had felt equally frustrated.

Her disinterest in individuality notwithstanding, Gladys overhauled Robin's figures and prepared them for championship standard, a feat that one cannot overstate. Her wealth of experience, combined with Pam's solid stylistic foundation, stood him in good stead in the years to come. More important, every trial he underwent in London, every hardship he met and overcame, set him up mentally and emotionally for the rest of his life. He later wondered, had he not had to struggle, if he would have achieved his goals.

"There wouldn't be the color about what I do. I know what I had to go through, and what I went through by choice, to get to the top. I don't mean to *win*, but just to get there."

During his first summer of full-time study with Gladys, Robin passed his inter-gold figures, which allowed him to continue to compete at the senior level. The gold test was another story—one that explains a certain antipathy on his part towards the English judging establishment.

As Christopher Dean conceded, "Everybody is a character. Sure, there are some judges who are colorful and have their own opinions. What they say goes. It's like anything that subjective. It lends itself to eccentricity."

British tests followed a strict sequence: preliminary, bronze, inter-silver, silver, inter-gold, and finally gold. In Robin's day, you either passed all sixteen figures on all three judges' cards, or you failed. The NSA administered the figures and freestyle tests in tandem. In front of seven world-caliber judges, four of them observers, Robin executed creditable gold figures.

The who's who of the British hierarchy made "a rather intimidating group." Pauline Borrajo, Sally Stapleford, Pam Davis, and Mollie Phillips were among them. Two of the three official judges found Robin's figures excellent. Even Miss Hogg was satisfied and told him to change into his freestyle boots. What the third judge thought remains a mystery. "Not today, dearie" was all she told Robin.

"Apparently one judge, who shall remain nameless, was kept waiting in the lobby. The cafeteria was closed, and she was told, 'No, you can't be in here.' She was in a foul mood and just decided that was it. She turned around, and that was her response: 'Not today, dearie.' Then she walked out. Gladys collared her in the lobby, and I remember a furor going on. I was gobsmacked."

Other judges told Robin, "Don't think anything of it. You were fine."

All he could do was stammer, "But, but—"

Such was his fury at the hierarchy that he never retook the test. He wouldn't give the judges the satisfaction.

1973-74: Firsts

That autumn, Robin flew to Calgary for the first Skate Canada international, gaining experience and recognition if not a high placement. At nationals, he was runner-up to Curry for the first time. Then he went to Zagreb, Yugoslavia, for the 1974 Europeans, memorable in at least one respect for a naïve sixteen-year-old.

"The official hotel was the local hangout for all the hookers. They weren't even subtle: scarlet knee-high plastic boots with miniskirts. Gladys's room was stuck right between two of them. She was *not* a happy bunny. It was funny to see all the male skating officials running around with their tongues hanging out. Karena Richardson and I laughed our heads off. Gladys was beside herself."

Zagreb was the occasion for several more firsts: Robin's first triple jumps in international competition and his first significant injury. The latter aborted yet another first: his maiden world championship.

Great Britain didn't have a team doctor. As Robin saw

it, "We would rather send substitute referees or judges who *may* get picked to judge an event rather than send a physician who could look after the team properly."

In truth, only the Soviets and East and West Germans then traveled with doctors. Dr. Wolf-Dieter Montag of the Federal Republic of Germany was an orthopedic surgeon, a physical therapist, and the first Western physician involved in skating to be educated in sports medicine. He pioneered the philosophy that regarded injured athletes as healthy patients. Montag became a family member to the skaters he patched up. Germans, Canadians, Americans, and Russians still show him their scars and ask, "Do you remember this one?" Irina Vorobieva once sought him out while her coach and an official kept the Soviet doctor at bay. Luckily Robin knew Montag. Pam had met him the previous year.

In Zagreb, Robin was on the verge of withdrawing.

"No, no, no," Dr. Montag told him. "You should not stop."

"I can't skate."

"Okay, I'll tape you. Then you try again."

Robin finished sixth in the long program, eleventh overall. When he returned to England, X-rays indicated a bad sprain. At the Munich Worlds the next month, although Montag pronounced Robin fit to compete, Miss Hogg decided that he couldn't skate convincingly enough to make a positive first impression. That was just as well. New X-rays later revealed a bone chip.

Emi Watanabe, in a little Eskimo outfit, found Robin in tears in the lobby of the competitors' hotel.

"What's wrong?"

"I've just had to withdraw from my first world championship."

Fred and Jo arrived to witness their son's devastation. There would be other Worlds, but the wait seemed unbearable.

1974-75: Glimpsing the Future

The new season began with Skate Canada in Kitchener, where Robin placed third in the free skating, sixth overall. Toller Cranston, nearing his competitive peak, noticed the young Briton.

"Robin Cousins, like so many people I've seen over the years, has a special, quintessential, unique star quality that anyone who also possesses it can spot a mile away. The marks he got at that competition, and possibly for the rest of his life, could not accurately depict the quality of his skating and who he was, because he is one of a kind. He has a God-given talent and uniqueness that transcend skating: the child-of-destiny syndrome.

"He has a fineness and a refinement. He also has an ability that not all great skaters have: he can step on the ice and undergo a metamorphosis, both physically and spiritually. He becomes an instrument that inspires awe, like Janet Lynn. Janet was not Marilyn Monroe, but when she hit the ice, she had an ethereal beauty. Neither is Robin Mel Gibson off the ice, yet he becomes noble. He has an aristocratic countenance that sets him apart from everyone else."

At the British championship, one child of destiny gained ground on another as Robin edged closer to John.

At Europeans in Copenhagen, Robin caught the flu and finished eleventh (eighth for combined free skating). Not all the drama was on the ice. Nine members of the Cousins entourage set out in a minibus for the Harwich ferry, only to learn that the Sir Winston Churchill, the boat that was to take them to Denmark, had broken down. They went to Bremerhaven and drove through Germany, but when they reached the Hamburg docks, the minibus balked and had to be towed onto the ferry. The first stop in Denmark was a garage.

Those pilgrimages rank among Fred and Jo's fondest memories. Each year they went to either Europeans or

Worlds, whichever was accessible by car. Amateur skaters, by definition, made no money in those days. Their training costs were an enormous drain on family resources. The Cousinses camped or stayed in bed and breakfasts, bringing along all their food. One journalist who accepted a lunch invitation was shocked when his hosts pulled out Cup-a-Soup and crackers.

The best part of those trips, to Jo's way of thinking, was the côterie of fans who went along.

"When the Bristol supporters went, they weren't so much ice skating supporters; they were Robin Cousins supporters. The only way they could go was the cheapest way, and they did (and their children came, too). I don't know of another Briton who had his own supporters at fifteen or seventeen years of age. By then he had left Bristol and was living in London, but they still came, and they still followed him."

That was a bonus John didn't enjoy to the same extent; nor was he fortunate enough to possess a visible, united family like Robin's. In Copenhagen, the Bristol supporters both pleased and embarrassed John by signing a good luck card—his first, according to Fred.

The 1975 Worlds afforded Robin another glimpse into his future. At the Broadmoor World Arena in Colorado Springs, since torn down to make way for an expansion of the resort, he had his first taste of top-class American facilities.

The Broadmoor Hotel and its accoutrements, all in salmon-pink stucco with a Mediterranean motif, perched on the edge of a man-made lake with a large waterfowl population. The Rocky Mountains formed the backdrop. Originally an equestrian ring, the main rink had high, arched ceilings and wooden seats numbered in brass. Skating history suffused its every beam.

Gladys had put Robin in the hands of Ron Baker, her former ice-dance partner. The youngest of twenty-two competitors, Robin finished twelfth overall—not bad for a first Worlds. His triple Salchow/double toe loop was the most difficult combination of the event. Gladys's tutelage was paying off, no matter the unhappiness it entailed.

In early April, Robin competed in Skate Safari at Johannesburg. In his second meeting with Charlie Tickner, he won the long program but finished second overall in a three-two split.

Encountering apartheid unsettled him.

"When you go into an ice rink early in the morning, you find people cleaning and doing menial jobs. You get used to saying good morning and 'Hi, how are you?' One day we were walking in the street, and I saw two of the people who worked in the rink walking towards us. White South Africans crossed the road in order not to pass them— and it was one thing for us to acknowledge them, but we 'really shouldn't be doing that in public.' I found that all very odd. I would never refuse to greet people because either they didn't speak my language or they weren't the right color.

"It reminded me of sitting on a train during the East German tour, listening to Warren Maxwell having a discussion about history books: our history books compared to German history books; what they were saying about us, and what we were saying about them. You understood their point of view when you knew what they were being taught—and they had no reason to believe it was a lie, any more than we had reason to believe that what we had been taught in school was a lie."

When Robin visited Jo's friend on a ranch in Johannesburg, the question of her black servants arose. She explained that their educational level was so low that if she spoke to them in full sentences, they wouldn't understand. Only "You sweep!" was comprehensible. Robin didn't buy that. He wondered, "Why aren't they being educated so they *do* understand?"

South Africa had already been excluded from the Olympics. The ISU soon imposed anti-apartheid sanctions of its own. South African skaters were banned from hosting and participating in ISU competitions: a symbolic act that forced individual athletes to pay the price for society's sins. Not until 1992 were South Africans welcome again at Worlds.

Lenel van den Berg met Robin at Skate Safari and later starred with him in Holiday on Ice. Although Lenel won seven South African men's titles, he could never compete at Worlds or Olympics.

The tour that followed Skate Safari included four days in Durban, where Fred had languished with TB. Ironically, it was in South Africa that Robin experienced the first signs of his own chronic health problem—one that cast a long shadow of doubt over his future skating life.

1975-76: Second-rate Knees

Every time Robin bent his right knee, he heard snapping noises like dead twigs. The knee developed a tendency to lock. It was cartilage trouble, an athlete's worst nightmare.

Doctors blamed the constant pounding of landing jumps on the right blade. Only Fred knew the depths of his son's despair. Robin liked to keep his troubles to himself.

Although sports medicine was virtually unknown in England at the time, Fred knew, from his soccer days, that healing sports injuries required specialized knowledge. He took Robin to Les Bardsley, the physiotherapist for the Bristol City Football Club, a practitioner well-known in athletic circles. Surmising that the symptoms pointed towards surgery, Les sat Robin down and prepared him for the worst.

"Right, you're seventeen? Let's face it. You could come out of this operation with a stiff knee. Come on, if you come out of this operation with a stiff knee, what are you going to do?"

"Well, I could still teach," Robin replied after some thought.

"That's it. So all is not lost."

Les had made Robin admit that, if everything went wrong, he'd still have a future, albeit different from the one he had planned; he could still use what knowledge he possessed. That was a great psychological boost. Les arranged for Mr. Clough, a specialist who had operated on a well-known cricketer, to perform the surgery.[6]

The practice of the day was to remove the cartilage as completely as possible.[7] Clough eyed Robin and took aim.

"You probably won't ever be able to skate at the same level again, so get that out of your head."

As expected, Robin was perverse.

"That's the exact reason I said I *would*."

Arthroscopic surgery, in its early experimental phase, was not an option. The invasive procedure to remove the torn meniscus involved lengthy recuperation.

Fred moved the car out of the garage and rigged up a knee-strengthening mechanism with a sandbag on one end and a gallon of water on the other. For a teenager with a sore, atrophied leg, the pulley device could have been a ton of bricks. Robin worked it for two hours a day, spent another two hours walking, jogging, and running, then swam—a measure of how desperately he wanted to skate. For eleven weeks, he had nothing else to do but watch television, draw, and make up programs in his head. When he returned to the rink, Les went along to advise him. With only half a year until the 1976 Olympics, Robin was restless to train. He admitted to being a difficult patient.

Hoping to do little more than survive the British

---

[6]Like many British physicians, Clough's title was Mr. rather than Dr.

[7]Today shattered fragments can sometimes be sutured. Experimental techniques involve the harvesting and propagation of human cartilage. The development of artificial cartilage is not as promising, since no suitable material has been found. The joints reject foreign matter.

championship, he won the third figure and both free-skating programs. John skated so poorly in all three phases that Robin called his performances a disaster.

"It was as if he were wearing someone else's skates. It was one of those nightmares that nobody wishes on anyone—three days of nightmares, not just five minutes."

Such were the vagaries of scoring that the mathematics barely favored John, who then swept Europeans, Worlds, and Olympics. John's near miss was a lucky break, a wake-up call that sent him rushing with conviction towards the Olympic podium.

John had been skating in Denver, Colorado, under Carlo Fassi, the coach who led Peggy Fleming to Olympic gold in Grenoble in 1968.[8] In 1976, Fassi would achieve the same results with both John and Dorothy Hamill. Before inviting John to Denver, Carlo had made a pitch to Toller Cranston.

"I, either being a creature of integrity or a fool—but I suspect the former—could not possibly imagine violating the loyalty and love that I had for Ellen Burka. I thought that if winning meant destroying that friendship at *le moment critique*, I would prefer not to win, so I did not go to Denver. John Curry did, and the rest is history."

England, unlike Canada, offered few rinks and little ice time. Robin later traveled John's route.

"Carlo had a way of being able to make you feel and understand exactly what you needed to do without saying too much. If you didn't get it then, then he said too much. I'm sure that's what he did with John."

Innsbruck

Robin placed sixth at Europeans in Geneva with a fourth in free skating and a standing ovation: a good warmup for the

[8] Fassi was an Italian men's and pairs champion, two-time European champion, and 1953 world bronze medalist. He died in March 1997 at the world championships in Lausanne, Switzerland.

1976 winter Olympics at Innsbruck, Austria.

"I don't think anybody who has experienced an Olympics can describe properly what it feels like to be an Olympian. The size of it! Then sitting down at lunch one day and realizing I was sitting next to Franz Klammer" the champion ski racer.

Robin was amused—although he might have been appalled—by the practice facilities. There was the "bubble rink," a portable enclosure with an air-supported plastic dome entered through a decompression chamber. Landing a flying sit spin, Terry Kubicka put his toe pick through a pipe, and "the Trevi Fountain shot up." At 6:00 A.M., the figure skaters ran through their long programs at the center of the outdoor speed skating track, while the speed skaters raced around them in great blurry ovals. Robin never saw John on those predawn practices, but Gladys made sure that *her* students were there every morning.

"It was freezing cold. You'd be fighting the wind in one direction and flying down the ice in the other. You couldn't jump. It was horrible. I remember it vividly.

"I feel fortunate having been a winter Olympian. We got to experience exactly what the Olympics are all about. I don't know how I would have felt if it had been 1980 or 1984 and I had been a summer athlete who had trained all my life for someone to tell me that, for political reasons, I wasn't going to be able to prove I was the best in the world.[9] No one can take away the Olympic gold medal, but it doesn't quite mean the same if you haven't been able to beat the people you should be competing against.

"I think we're lucky that the skating fraternity is small and the winter Olympic Games have always been a poor relation. We were never used for political reasons. At

---

[9]On December 27, 1979, the Soviet Union invaded Afghanistan. President Carter asked the IOC to move the Moscow Summer Games. When that didn't happen, the USOC voted to boycott. The Soviet Union retaliated in kind against the 1984 Los Angeles event.

that point, the winter Olympics didn't have as much money invested in them and weren't as commercialized as the Summer Games. Certainly for me, Innsbruck and Lake Placid were what the Olympic spirit was all about."

Robin was relaxed when his turn came to compete. The pressure fell on John as he won Great Britain's first Olympic gold medal in men's figure skating and ended his country's twelve-year gold-medal drought. Robin learned a great deal by watching how John handled both the good and the bad.

It was in Innsbruck that Robin first felt the sting of high-level international skating politics. Despite five triple jumps, superior spins, and the only triple combination, he placed eighth in the long program, tenth overall. He hadn't "paid his dues." A German journalist complained with wit that he had "skated to the symphonic variations on the theme of 'Three Blind Mice' in front of Nine Blind Judges."

Toller, on the verge of winning the bronze medal, quivered backstage, waiting for his own rendezvous with destiny.

"I remember Ellen Burka telling me that Robin Cousins had been totally fantastic and completely under-marked, and what a joke that was—which didn't help my ego."

The Olympic season ground to a halt at Worlds in Gothenburg, Sweden, where Robin gained one place over Innsbruck despite a long program mishap. A slack skate lace turned his last three triples into doubles. The skating year ended, not with a bang but with a whimper.

1976-77: A Time for Decisions

In July, Robin won another Grand Prix. Christopher Dean turned eighteen.

"We shared a room at Saint-Gervais, he and his

brother Nick and me, three of us into this tiny room somewhere up the mountain in France. Jayne and I had just
started in international competition. Our first competition
together was Oberstdorf. We came second. The couple that
beat us, who were Russian, weren't going on to France. As
we arrived, I remember Robin saying, 'That's great. You're
going to win.'"

"How do you know that?" Jayne and Chris wondered.

"Oh, trust me," Robin told them. He was right.

Chris barely finished his program before collapsing
with food poisoning. Nick was the team's de facto chaperon.

"The British organization was sort of nil. We must
have had a team leader, but I can't remember who it was,
and whoever it was wasn't doing very well. Christopher
probably shouldn't have skated. We looked after him and
took him off to the hospital."

Jayne had planned to go along but was called to accept their medals. She stood on the podium in her street
clothes, alone and mortified.

Scott Hamilton, like Jayne and Chris, was a prospective member of the Olympic Class of '84. He was on the cusp
of eighteen, a year younger than Jayne and Robin.

"Robin came to Saint-Gervais, which is generally a
junior development competition. He decided he needed to
blow all the young skaters away. He came in and gave us a
nice waxing. I went from Oberstdorf to Saint-Gervais and
had the real fortune of knowing that, in my second international competition, I was going to compete against the
guy ranked ninth in the world.

"With Robin, it was fun. His brother Nick was a
friendly, great guy. They're a wholesome, down-to-earth
family. I remember admiring Robin's abilities, being in
awe of him, because I was at that age where I was just
starting at the senior level. Being in a competition with
Robin, knowing he would someday be on the highest step

of the podium, was kind of thrilling."

Scott had a frizzy permanent, a vanity of the 1970s. Upon meeting Robin, he announced with embarrassment, "I don't usually look this way." Although Scott is no longer a candidate for a permanent, he might enjoy knowing that he has a namesake in a certain guest suite in England: a hairy stuffed gorilla.

After the victory at Saint-Gervais came a second-place finish at Skate Canada in Ottawa. The Austrian judge awarded Robin his first perfect 6.0 for artistic impression.

Several months later, Robin performed some im-promptu choreography a bit too near his bedroom door, breaking the little toe on his landing foot. He couldn't lace up a skate until a week before nationals. Three busloads of Bristol fans encouraged him to victory with a banner dis-playing a red, inflamed toe.

There was vocal support for the long program to *El Dorado* by the Electric Light Orchestra and Debussy's *Clair de Lune*, although Robin scrapped four of its five triples. Mollie Phillips, known for enthusiastic judging, awarded Robin's second 6.0. Dennis Bird rhapsodized in the London *Times*, "He skates better with a broken toe than everybody else does with ten perfect ones."

Robin regularly performed injured or ill. He deli-vered sparkling programs while hampered by respiratory infections and stomach flu. He skated competitive routines with his back in spasm. That was not his preferred *modus operandi*, but often his only alternative.

"I always had colds or flu or *something*. To this day, something always gets in the way a week or two before the event. Maybe it's a psychological mechanism. Rarely does everything go according to plan. Even with the best of in-tentions, something will happen."

At Europeans in Helsinki, Robin turned in substan-tially improved figures. He was second to East Germany's Jan Hoffmann in both free-skating sections, with the highest presentation marks and a bronze medal overall. The result might have been better had he not doubled all but one of his triples. His flow, élan, and musicality to the beat of *Hava Nagila* thrilled the audience and upstaged both higher-ranked skaters.

Jan was an eminently capable but rather wooden free skater. Silver medalist Vladimir Kovalev of the Soviet Union, a dramatic, humorous character with a black wardrobe and a roving eye, was what Toller called a "hammer-thrower," a skater short on finesse.

Gladys couldn't travel to Helsinki. Competing at a championship without one's coach was nearly unthinkable. An English writer complained that if no remedy were found, it would serve Great Britain right never to have another international champion.

In Finland, Carlo Fassi took Robin aside to make a welcome proposal.

One of the nice things for Robin was that others were saying, "I want to go to Carlo," and there Carlo was, asking, "Will you come to me?" He didn't do that often.

Since Gladys couldn't fly to Tokyo, Robin arranged for the Fassis to advise him at Worlds. The NSA showed no real interest in the situation.

"The association always disassociated themselves so much from the skaters that there was never any thought that I could phone them for advice. You saw the judges at a championship or at a test. You spoke to them only when they spoke to you. There was nothing friendly about the way they projected themselves, although there were one or two exceptions—out of fifteen or twenty. I'm still terrified of them."

It had occurred to Robin that third in Europe, ninth in the world, might be the end of his road.

"The other skaters were doing more training in a day than I had in an entire week. I thought, 'Do I want to stay and do what I'm doing now and be bronze medalist for three more years, or do I get out and go?' I would have quit skating if I hadn't gotten to Carlo."

Disaster in Tokyo

Early one Sunday in Bristol, Robin was warming up when his left knee emitted a sickeningly familiar *crunch*. When it locked in bent position, he was carried off the ice. That afternoon, Mr. Clough repositioned the cartilage. With Robin insisting on continuing to train for Tokyo, Les experimented with supports. He and Clough conceded that they could postpone surgery without risking permanent damage.

While waiting for the swelling to go down, Robin remained in Bristol, training at his home rink until he and Les could develop taping procedures. The NSA erroneously reasoned that if Robin wasn't training with Gladys in London, he wasn't training at all. Rather than phoning to check, the association sent Fred and Jo a letter suggesting that Robin planned to withdraw as soon as he arrived in Tokyo, subsequently vacationing at their expense. If he withdrew within the first two days, they demanded he pay for the costly trip himself. (Worlds were one of the few competitions that came with an NSA subsidy, although skaters still underwrote coaches' expenses.)

Fred and Jo were incensed. Then things got worse. The officials telephoned.

"We hear Robin's not on the ice, and he has no intention of skating."

"How dare you tell me what my son does or doesn't intend to do?" Jo demanded to know. Then she slammed down the receiver.

Robin arrived in Tokyo with Martin, who had taken out a loan to finance the trip.

Garnet watched Robin teach himself moves on the "wrong" foot, aided by his inborn mirror-image quirk and by Pam's early insistence on bidirectional rotation.

"He just decided that he was going to learn how to do the jump sit spin in the other direction, the way a left-handed person would. It amazed me that he was able to switch it around and land on the other knee. He did it beautifully. Some of the better skaters can do an Axel in the opposite direction, but it's awkward. You never would have known with Robin."

Dr. Montag was by then the ISU medical advisor. At first he found Robin a skeptical patient. The biggest hurdle was convincing him that there was no medical reason why he shouldn't compete as long as his knee had support. Once Robin made up his mind to trust Montag, he said, "As long as you are here, I am convinced nothing can happen."

But then, "nothing" is relative. Several times during practice sessions, the cartilage became dislodged. A painfully vigorous shake of the leg slid it back into place.

The ice had been laid over the swimming pool in the Yoyogi Olympic sports complex. Irregularly supported by a wooden platform, it cracked. Moreover, the first layer had been made before the paint on the platform dried, leaving dizzying stripes instead of a uniform light-blue cast. That sheet of ice had been removed and the platform repainted grey—which turned to Stygian murk under ice. TV officials hit the roof. BBC commentator Alan Weeks tripped on a Zamboni divot and broke his ankle. With a gaping cavity below, skate blades speeding across the ice made a hollow roar, punctuated by the heavy thud of jumps. Those were the least of Robin's worries.

Dr. Montag obtained special permission for him to skate on the last training session before each phase of competition. Prior to practice, Montag drained the fluid one last time and applied fresh taping. Then Robin stayed in his skates until he finished his event.

He had a lucky break in the compulsory figures draw. He had to start only one on his weak leg.

During the short program warmup, his knee gave

out. Dr. Montag strapped it so tightly that it barely bent. Figuring that the worst had already happened, Robin went for broke. He couldn't pick with his left foot to do a toe loop, so he performed a triple loop/double loop—something he had never done in competition—and a back flying sit spin. In acute pain, he skated without error and placed fourth, pulling up from tenth to sixth overall.

Montag, standing by the boards, was awed by the quality of Robin's movement and the silence of his blades. Sally Stapleford awarded first-place marks.

During the long program, Robin's luck ran out. When his cartilage slipped during routine footwork, he scrambled to his feet and kicked to realign it. Then he executed a camel spin on his left foot, hoping the backward momentum of the free leg would snap the cartilage into place. When he stepped out of the spin to skate away, his injured leg wouldn't hold him. For years, he was haunted by the memory of crawling ignominiously off the ice. Imagine his surprise when a video recently proved that he had hobbled away with slightly more dignity.

While the British team leader ran to the referee to announce Robin's withdrawal, Martin hurried to the dressing rooms, where he witnessed a touching scene.

"The thing that impressed me most was the concern that was being shown by all the other skaters, Russians and East Germans included. You hear stories in all sports about the rivalries, and the press has tried to stir them up at times, but the one that I can remember who was really concerned was Kovalev. Imagine, he was a Russian and Robin was a Brit. These guys were waiting to go out and do their one-off performances of the year. They were interrupting whatever preparations they were making and coming over to see if he was okay."

Robin didn't regret the trip to Tokyo.

"Another minute and a half and I'd have been fine. Well, I wouldn't have been *fine*, but—!"

That episode was the beginning of a long-term relationship with the Japanese who had bonded with him in his misery. Nick joked, "You're big in Japan," but Robin saw the evidence.

"I still find myself showing up in teen magazines, and I have more Japanese fans than I have probably anywhere else. They write the most beautiful letters and send gifts and origamis. Japan is the only place I've been where I had to have a bodyguard. At Pro Skate, they rocked the bus. It was scary. Screaming, adoring fans. I loved it."

There was one practical benefit that arose from Tokyo's ashes. Robin took to the Fassis. He decided to move to America.

Pennies from Heaven and Pounds from the SAF

Six days later, Robin was in Saint Mary's Hospital, Bristol. The removal of his left meniscus went better than the earlier surgery, due to the added experience of both doctors and patient. The nurses soon restricted his rampant ambulation.

Just over a month later, Robin was honored as Bristol's Sportsman of the Year at a luncheon that coincided with his return to the ice. A journalist reported that Robin had "virtually no pocket money, and in fact has only recently been able to earn himself a little personal cash by selling some of the delightful drawings he executes in his spare time."

Acts of kindness by relative strangers punctuate many successful athletes' stories. Robin received generous private donations from James Miller, a Scottish builder, and his wife, Iris Lloyd-Webb Miller, one of Gladys Hogg's former pupils. There were also small but steady gifts from the Bristol Skating Club. When the local grocer put out a seven-pound pickle jar, shoppers responded with more than £100. Nonetheless, Fred and Jo predicted that it would take a whopping £5,000 a year at 1977 prices to pay for their son's American training—and they couldn't even manage his airfare.

Robin was not one to be deterred. He didn't know how he would get to America, but he would do it—much like Nick's cheerful assurance that he could nail up a sturdy towel bar. The Cousins men refused to be dissuaded, even when reality reared its ugly head.

"It was a question of Mum and Dad sitting me down and saying, 'Is it the training, or do you just want to go to America? Is this serious?' There was no money to spare. If that's what I was going to do, we had to try to find it some-where."

Next to nothing in the way of financial help came from the NSA. The Sports Council spread its wealth among many associations. The little NSA was far down on the list. Private support like the Millers' was rare, while corporate sponsorship was all but nonexistent.

The outlook changed when the Sports Aid Founda-tion, an independent entity set up by the Minister for Sport and the Sports Council to provide financial assistance to amateur international competitors, came forward with the help Robin needed for his final push towards the Olympics.

The SAF had begun awarding grants in 1976. Be-tween May 1977 and March 1979, Robin was to receive seven installments totaling £1,833: six at £250 and one at £333—nowhere near the full cost of training, but enough to enable Fred and Jo to keep their heads above water.

Early in 1979, the SAF introduced the Supplementary (now Elite) Grants that offered further assistance to those who demonstrated the highest ability and potential for Olympic medals. Robin was among the first eleven re-cipients.

The most exciting development was the SAF's launch of the Sir John Cohen Memorial Award, named for the Tesco supermarket founder who had organized a lottery for the benefit of amateur sportsmen. The grant was to be disbursed in four installments of £1,560 (for a total of £6,240) through January 1980. Over the years, Robin repaid the largesse by attending fundraising functions and serving as Governor of SAF-South West.

The second recipient of the Cohen award was the great middle-distance runner Sebastian Coe. Both athletes went on to Olympic gold.

4. The Denver Years: 1977-1980

$\mathcal{R}$obin's invitation to train in Colorado was traumatic for Jo.

"We had to make up our minds, 'A, do we want him to do this?' and then 'B, can we afford it?' So having decided yes, we would and yes, we could, that's when the tears came."

In the summer of 1977, Queen Elizabeth II fêted her Silver Jubilee while Tracy Austin ate Wimbledon strawberries and cream. Across the ocean, life was less formal. A man named Jimmy inhabited the White House, Luke Skywalker blazed across movie screens, and feminists burned their bras. Prince Charles, visiting the Colonies, was photographed in a Native American headdress.

88

After spending most of his life at sea level, Robin
moved to the Mile-High City, a glass and steel cosmopolis
flanked by the Rockies. Denver left him breathless in
every way.

Summer school would be a two-way tryout. Robin
explained to his coach that his parents' chief concerns
were his physical well-being and his happiness, not his
progress in skating—hardly a typical viewpoint. Carlo went
to great lengths to assure them that he would not leave
their son to his own devices in the American equivalent of
a bed-sitter.

At the airport, Jo told Robin, "If you have a problem
on or off the ice, and you either want to come home or you
want to talk about it, you just ring us as if you were next
door."

In her practical mind, transatlantic calls were for
emergencies. Robin had been gone only days when the
phone rang.

"What's wrong?" Jo asked anxiously as soon as she
heard his voice.

"Nothing. I just thought I'd phone."

All was well, and continued to be, but he had established a pattern of playing fast and loose with the family
phone bill—a no-win situation.

"If you call, it's, 'What's wrong?'

"'Nothing's wrong.'

"'Why are you phoning, then?'

"'I'm phoning to say everything's all right.'

"If you don't phone, she phones.

"'What's wrong?'

"'Nothing's wrong. Everything's all right.'

"'Then why haven't you phoned?'"

It was a typical state of affairs between a mother and
her youngest son, newly launched into the world.

"We had postcards from wherever he was and, as I
remember, the odd letter, but in the main he rang. It was

nice. You could always tell by Robin's voice whether he was happy. You still can."

Robin bailed out of his first hosts' strict religious environment. The Risbergs, his second family, matched him to a T—except that their daughter, a junior lady, lacked Robin's dedication. If she didn't get up for early-morning patch, he didn't have a ride to the rink.

The third match was made in heaven. Robin moved to the home of B.L. and Bob Wylie, their daughters, Dawn and Clare, and their son, Paul (who would be the 1992 men's Olympic silver medalist). B.L. and Bob were devoted to each other, to their children, and to the sport. They treated Robin like one of their own, and he thrived in the homelike environment.

"It was a family that was run very much the way my family was. There was open affection all around."

That included the boarders.

Skaters as children, B.L. and Bob had continued the tradition when they married. When Bob found work as a geophysicist in Dallas, they joined the local club. Later their children went along. Paul's first skating experience was prenatal. B.L. was expecting him when she performed in the club show in 1964. Like Bob, B.L. took U.S. Figure Skating Association tests and even judged at one time.

"I don't anymore. It just got to be too much when I had all those kids."

The Wylies were surrogate parents to a parade of boarders. Theirs was a family Carlo relied on to care for young skaters far from home. Although the skating world is known for its itinerant nature, the Wylies' boarders tended to be long-term. B.L. didn't know of another family that housed as many boarders for as long as they did. The skaters became their extended family. When Robin arrived, he joined Cindy Perpich and Chris Sherrill.

The house in Bow Mar South was a large, Bavarian-style brick split-level: four upstairs bedrooms; kitchen, living room, dining room, and study on the main level; and family room, bedroom, and laundry room below. The Wylies had recently arrived from Texas. Robin lived in the study, with a moving box for a closet, until he was promoted upstairs.

Except in Robin's case, skating followed a full school day. B.L. ran the Skatique at the Colorado Ice Arena (CIA), returning with the youngsters at 8:30 P.M. Since the Wylies were "a real meal-oriented, together-oriented family," even at that hour they ate a sit-down dinner. Then came homework and bedtime.

The Wylies honored the tradition of the family photograph. Robin went along on one such occasion.

"I hadn't presumed I would be part of their family portrait. They're all in suits, ties, and beautiful clothes, and there I am in a sweater."

Like the other boarders, he did his own laundry and cleaned his room. (B.L. was delighted when her children followed suit.) When he packed for a trip, which was often, he neatly laid out everything in advance.

It fell to Dawn, the patient, quiet daughter, to teach Robin to drive. He slid behind the wheel of the Wylies' Buick station wagon and passed his driving test on the "wrong" side of the road. Dawn went away to college soon afterwards.

"Clare was more my speed," Robin laughed. "She went off to Ice Capades and was into the showbiz and the glamour of skating. She was never the big competitor. Paul was more studious and was obviously much younger then and was learning. Dawn was a skater, but certainly not into the showbiz and glamour. She was more interested in poetry and reading. It was interesting, Dawn being the eldest: Dawn was more like Nick, and Clare was more like Martin. They were tremendous, and I was very comfortable there."

Of the two other full-time boarders, Chris was the

artist. He followed his own lights, even more than Robin, whose more vivid impressions were of Cindy.

"Cindy and I got along great, then we didn't get along at all. We were far too much alike. We were all sort of sixteen-, seventeen-, eighteen-year-olds. It was just that strange age. A lot of the teenage angst and growing up that I normally would have gone through at thirteen, fourteen, or fifteen, I went through when I was sixteen, seventeen, and eighteen. I actually went through it with that family maybe more than with my own family."

Skaters, like serious gymnasts and dancers, often exhibited arrested development. They lived in a narrowly circumscribed environment, focusing on their goals.

"They are expected to be so mature on the ice, and they are," B.L. noted. "They live that role well."

Socially, however, they missed out, passing up certain teenage activities until they were older. Although they experimented sexually, they were less likely than their nonskating contemporaries to form mature bonds. It was hard enough to claw their way up the competitive ladder, dealing with setbacks, competitors' mind games, training discipline, and growing bodies, without simultaneously coming to terms with their sexual and social identities. It is interesting that Robin consistently underestimates his age at various milestones. He was nineteen when he went to Denver, though he remembers being younger.

"We tend not to continue to mature like the rest of the world does. A seventeen-year-old figure skater, I think, still has the mentality of a thirteen- or fourteen-year-old. There is a form of retardation that happens, not only in skating, but in any area where you become so insular that the rest of the world continues at a different pace. You are coddled. Your coach looks after you, and your parents. The mental growth happens later, when you have the time for it."

B.L. didn't see the similarity to Cindy that Robin perceived.

"Robin was more serious, because he was in a different situation. His parents had sacrificed everything in the world for him to be there. Not that Cindy wasn't serious, but Robin leaned a little more towards the artistic side. He could spend hours by himself. Cindy always was going and doing and having people over. Robin, though he was certainly social, didn't go that much. The things that amazed me about him were, A, how happy he could be alone and, B, how little money he spent. This kid lived on next to nothing, and without complaint—without seeming to suffer."

Garnet also trained in Denver by then. She found Robin at that stage—six feet tall and one hundred and forty pounds—shy and introverted.

"I think he felt a little awkward because he was very tall. He was that height when he was fifteen years old—and really skinny. You would look at him and say that he could never be a good skater, just because he was so thin, but when he'd get on the ice, he'd always surprise you. It was one of those bodies that matured and became stronger as he got older, but he went through a gangly, awkward-looking stage. I think that was a hard time for him, especially the first two years. He went through things most kids go through when they're home with their families. The saving grace for him was that the Wylies were like a second family. They loved him, and he loved them. That didn't happen for many kids who went to Denver during that period. There were a lot of dormitory situations, but few kids found families to live with who really jelled with how they thought and felt."

Was Robin homesick in Denver? Probably, although he hid it skillfully.

"We had a good time," B.L. recalled. "I always felt he fit into the family very well, but Robin has a way of keeping things to himself, and I'm sure there was probably quite a bit of homesickness."

If so, it was nothing like the wrenching affliction that had colored his London days. The time in Denver passed happily, filled with the satisfaction of progressing towards goals.

B.L. interpreted Robin's quiet side differently from others who knew him.

"I think, rather than shy, I call it more of an artistic temperament. He had a lot of his own moments. There are times when you have thoughts for yourself, and you don't want to be disturbed. This is kind of where I saw him— definitely his own person."

As Simone Grigorescu so aptly put it, "Robin had a side that was very private. It was a part of him that had a *Do Not Enter* sign. A lot of us during those years were hard-driven and emotional people, so we all had parts of our consciousness locked up in a little lock box. We hid the key and didn't let anybody look inside."

That is still the case. As friendly and entertaining as Robin is, he shares his inner self neither often nor deeply.

As at other times in his life, art was Robin's companion.

As a young child, he drew whenever he wasn't in motion. When he started school, he began to draw in earnest—mostly doodles and cartoons. Fred urged him to be more original.

"He was a great copier. I tried hard to get him to sit in the garden and sketch, but no, he wouldn't be interested. But give him a postcard, and he could reproduce that when he was very young and be perfect—and he could reduce it, make it smaller."

In time, the drawings became more fanciful. The little cartoons—whimsical, detailed, and brightly colored— reflected Robin's optimism. By Denver, he had entered an art deco phase. Line dominated color: curvilinear forms, geometric motifs, bold outlines.

Simone saw the art as mood-driven.

"I think he has always used drawing as an emotional release rather than through the wish to be an artist. It was almost a necessity."

The Wylies kept an acrylic painting from those days: a woman with a fur.

Jo and Fred couldn't travel to America during the pre-Olympic years, but B.L. enjoyed Nick's visits.

"He was great fun. We always loved having him. Nick taught Robin how to do a back-flip in our back yard. We had two dogs, and we said that Robin *had* to land the back-flip. Otherwise he landed in you-know-what."

The back-flip was by then illegal in amateur competition, which didn't dampen Robin's interest. He asked Nick, who had taught gymnastics, to show him the move on grass. First Nick taught him a flick-flack, a back handspring. Then he spotted him in a no-hands back somersault.

"He was marvelous. Anybody could have taught him. I just showed him what to do, and then he did it."

Enter Carlo, who had come to "tea" and happened upon the illicit activity, to Nick's chagrin.

"He was very, very cross with me—he wanted to send me home—and very cross with Rob, because he didn't see that this had any part in what he was doing. I was banned from teaching him thereafter, and he was banned from doing the back-flip."

Robin did it anyway, but he wasn't caught again.

Simone

Robin found a staunch ally in Simone Grigorescu, the 1973 Romanian junior champion. Under the Communist régime, she had lived in a "small, airtight environment," able to skate only five months out of twelve. The Romanian sports in official favor were gymnastics, kayaking, handball, and volleyball.

"We were always lagging a little bit behind. The Russians did send some coaches one summer, but I think they put an end to that because we improved too quickly. They saw potential competition."

Not long after Simone won her title, her family left home one day with no prior notice and defected to Yugoslavia, then to West Germany. They ended up in New York City, where they read a newspaper item about the Dunfields, coaches at Sky Rink. Sonya and Peter took the shy, quiet youngster under their wing as she returned to the bottom of the skating ladder and worked her way up through the American test structure.

The upheaval was overwhelming, especially since Simone at first spoke no English. Intensely intelligent, with a sad, doe-eyed beauty and a lyrical touch on the ice, in 1978 she found sponsorship and went to train with Carlo Fassi. Karena Richardson, the once and future British ladies' champion, became the Grigorescus' boarder.

Robin visited often in his role as Karena's big brother and advisor. Sometimes he sat under a tree in the back yard and beaded costumes—an outlet for his rampant creativity. He used metal backs with prongs that poked through to the right side of the fabric and bent over onto the beads through brute force. He liked to maintain quality control over all aspects of his on-ice performance.

Simone, at a charmingly naïve seventeen, grew attached to the elegant ice stylist several years her senior and so obviously bound for glory.

"There was always an air of confidence about him. He was a people person. One of the things you noticed about Robin from the start was that, even at a young age, he had a great deal of charisma. All the younger kids were more or less in awe and tried to emulate him. We had a wonderful skating environment for those couple of years that we trained together at Colorado Ice Arena. The whole rink was absolutely full of world-class competitors from all over the world. We had a strong and healthy competitive environment, but we all liked each other. We helped each other out. It was one of those experiences I haven't encountered in amateur skating anywhere else. It was quite inspirational."

Robin knew what his talents were and where they would take him if he worked hard enough. While he navigated by an internal road map to success, he had a way of sweeping others along in a rush of enthusiasm. That's one of the reasons Simone was "infatuated with being around him," despite his occasional self-absorption.

"You try to get some of that energy and apply it to your own lifestyle or your own craft. With people who are very self-motivated and self-directed, at times you tend to feel that the selfishness is a drawback, but you realize afterwards that it's necessary for those who want to succeed. He liked people being taken by him and in awe of him, and I guess I was one of those. I think maybe that's one of the reasons he liked me. I was more or less willing to do anything for him. I was willing to always be on his side and ignore his less charming qualities."

The British press made more of it than that, reporting hints of distant wedding bells. Robin was focused, body and soul, on becoming the best skater in the world. Distractions were laughable, but he couldn't afford to laugh. Simone played along. As taken as she was with his regal on-ice persona, his off-ice vulnerability equally charmed her.

Robin and Simone went out together, but it wasn't all that the British press implied.

"British newspapers—well, American newspapers like the *National Enquirer* and the *Star* and such—love to associate people in a romantic way. At the time, we were all high-strung competitors. We were driven. Naturally we were always together—not just Robin and I, but the whole group. I was the one the papers saw as closer to Robin than anyone else. Skating has always been a sport of images, the same way old Hollywood used to look upon its stars. It's not enough to have a lot of talent and charisma. You also have to back that up with a healthy home environment. Well, not now anymore. Now trash is in, but back then it was important, especially in skating, to have a complete image."

Somehow it wasn't enough that Robin possessed talent, charisma, a squeaky-clean image, a loving nuclear family, and—almost—an Olympic gold medal. To satisfy the press, he needed a girlfriend and marriage plans.

Paul

Robin shared with the Wylies a deep love for music. He had a talent for ferreting out obscure recordings, especially when he traveled. He spent much time cutting programs for fellow skaters, including Paul.

"He went through a tape recorder," B.L. joked.

"There weren't any little wheels left by the time he was finished."

Paul followed in Robin's footsteps.

"They both loved to put on a piece of music and just skate to it. I'm sure Robin had influences in that direction, although Paul as a little guy, as a three- and four-year-old, had a lot of music in him."

Paul, twelve and a half when Robin arrived, already had the makings of a gifted artist. Robin knew that.

"I was able to help mold what Paul was about to do, and he was able to watch what I was up to. I worked with him on the ice. I got to do his programs and his music. The one thing Paul had right from the beginning was that charisma and the ability to make a program look brilliant even if he'd fallen five times. I tried to present that to him. That was the *affect*. I've always said to him, and to other people I work with, 'Your program has to be interesting, even if there are no jumps in it.' That was one thing Paul had to offer that others didn't."

Paul was fortunate to have Robin as a prototype, and John Curry before him. The Wylies were in Denver during John's last summer there. By watching John, Paul had learned to appreciate stretch and extension. Then Robin arrived, modeling the same qualities. When Paul won the Junior Worlds in December 1980, Carlo told the press, "Robin had a tremendous influence on him. A little piece of this title belongs to Robin."

Paul later confessed, "I was like a mockingbird, picking up pieces of everybody." In time those pieces, combined with his own compelling interior dictates, evolved into a unique, extraordinary style.

Scott Hamilton, another Denver alumnus, got to know Paul through Stars on Ice.

"I think Robin's direction artistically had a lot to do with Paul's development. Robin's strong, dynamic personality is contagious. If you look at a lot of the people who have enjoyed success in skating, you'll see that they're at times a little bit over the top, bigger than life. They can bring people in. It's charisma, a way about them that makes you kind of lean in a bit. Robin is like that. I think that Robin's presence and rapport with the audience influenced Paul's artistic vision quite a bit. If you look at what Paul's doing now, it's classic, dramatic, artistic skating. Skating has not been presented like that for a long time. People have all gone the other way—jumping, more of the athletics. Paul has really stayed home with the program and carved his own niche in the sport."

Celine McDonald, one of Robin's New York friends, remembers a visit from Paul.

"He must have been maybe sixteen or so. He was kind of a chubby-faced kid, and he so idolized Robin."

Paradoxically, Paul credits John with the greater influence, despite Carlo's assertion that John spent little time working with Paul. John was fifteen years older—physically and temperamentally remote—whereas Robin and Paul were "brothers" and friends with all the complex emotions inherent in rough-and-tumble daily life.

The Wylies watched Robin progress through most of an Olympiad, from mid-1977 through early 1980. That exposure served as a dry run for their own subsequent trials, as B.L. revealed.

"It certainly gave us a lot better feel for the international skating community and absolutely taught us what international skating was about. When Paul reached that point, there were no surprises. We'd been there and done that. I think the fact that Robin had to struggle for so long may have been an influence on Paul. Robin had such a time with the figures and with getting things to the point where he could go off and command the respect he should have been getting all along. Paul watched Robin go through his struggle. When it came time for Paul to go through it, he wasn't the first person in the world that he'd ever seen do it. It was much more, 'Oh yeah, this is okay. We've been here before.'"

Robin was touring with Champions on Ice during Paul's Olympic moment. On the night of the men's final, the cast huddled in the basement of an old theatre, watching what they could between shows, while Liz Manley held up the television antenna to improve reception. To Robin, Paul's performance was transcendent.

"That's one of those moments when it doesn't matter what color the medal is. He could have been twenty-first. With that performance, he will be remembered in the history books. That was one of those magical moments, like Jayne and Chris with *Bolero*. It really had nothing to do with the judges."

Polishing the Diamond

The training schedule at the CIA was more hospitable and infinitely more flexible than the schedule had been at Queens. It was never exactly the same from one day to the next, so the routine didn't become boring—a key feature, to Robin's way of thinking.

There was one main rink and a smaller figures rink. A syndicate of local businessmen operated the complex. Carlo Fassi was one of three limited partners who owned 25 per cent of the enterprise. The remaining 75 per cent belonged to investors. Although there were two managers, Carlo oversaw the figure skating.

The blue-green metal building with a slightly peaked roof—chilly, cavernous, and industrial—served its purpose. It was exciting only on the inside.

During his early days in Denver, Robin tried to make up for the have-not years. If somebody didn't use his scheduled patch, Robin grabbed it. It took him a long time to recognize psychologically that more than enough hours were available. It was like growing up in modest circumstances, then continuing to be careful with money.

"You *always* are careful. It's not that I don't like to spend it, but I know what it's like not to have any, and I don't think you can ever take it for granted."

Robin approached his sport and his coaches the same way.

Christa Fassi, trim, petite, and impeccably groomed, was a fifteen-year-old German skater on the day she met Carlo at a competition. After they had dated for a year and a half, Christa left her Austrian coach and went to Milan to train with Carlo. They married—over her parents' mild objections—when she was barely eighteen. He was thirty.

Carlo explained with a twinkle, "The parents' objection was mainly because she was German and I am Italian. The Germans thought all Italians go around with a mandolin."

Christa became an Italian citizen. She won the 1961 national ladies' title, then advanced to Europeans. The ISU canceled Worlds when the entire American team, along with their coaches and families, died in a plane crash en route to Prague. Three months later, the newlyweds moved to America to help rebuild the U.S. program.

Carlo, a short, sturdy teddy bear, loved his wife and adored their three children, Riccardo, Monika, and Lorenzo. Robin liked spending time with them. No matter where he was, he sought out a homelike environment.

Christa was the softer side of the team. Carlo credited her for much of Robin's success. She played a significant role in the musical and choreographic aspects of his training and served as a buffer.

Carlo, a workaholic, was the boss and the technician, according to Robin.

"We had our own opinions that he listened to. Then he told us why he was right."

Carlo had a gift for making things click for each individual skater. When training went badly, however, he bellowed in exasperation, "Christa, here. Work with him." He was smart enough to know when to assert control, when to leave Robin alone, and when to call in reinforcements.

Robin was easy to work with, from Carlo's perspective, though he didn't accept criticism well.

"He trained hard. With the kids you have now, they are so full of complexes. I think he was very, very simple and very, very nice."

While recognizing Robin's physical gifts, Carlo credited Gladys Hogg for knowing how to direct them.

"Gladys was probably one of the great coaches, if not the greatest one, because those two kids [John and Robin] developed with me, but they would never have been that good if she hadn't made them that good to start with."

Robin saw his coach as a master gemsmith.

"Carlo didn't go and find the diamonds. He knew how to cut 'em and polish 'em to make them pretty for other people. He and his wife were the master polishers of cut diamonds. Even with a bad diamond, he could still polish it to look pretty good. Some people thought that was a gift, and some people thought it was a con, but the whole point, when you go out to do your long program, is to make what you do look as good as possible: to look fabulous, feel great, and perform the tricks to the best of your ability."

Robin developed a great fondness for his coach.

"He thought he spoke perfect English. With Carlo, instead of stand straight, it was always 'stand it in.' 'Stand it in. Straight it. Pointed the fingers.' That's toes, Carlo. 'What I say? I be in America seventeen years and I speaked the perfect English.' People imitated him all the time. It was just the way he said things that was endearing and funny. There was English, Italian, French, German, American, and Carlo. He was a language all unto himself, and he wouldn't have been the same without that."

One Christmas at the Fassi house, young Lorenzo was pounding on a keyboard. Carlo called out in irritation, "Lorenzo, stopped it. You have the music uppity down."

Robin could change the Italian glint in Carlo's eye into a flash of Italian temper. One sure way was to make spontaneous modifications in his program.

"He used to get crazy with me, because I changed things. He'd say, 'No, no, no, no, no. We change *nothing*.' Then Christa would say, 'Carlo, leave him alone.'"

Garnet witnessed the occasional clash between the sometimes stubborn pupil and his stubborn teacher.

"Carlo used to get so mad at him, because if Robin was off the beat of the music even a split second, he couldn't do a jump. If he had fallen or tripped and was a little bit off the beat for his triple loop, he wouldn't do it. Carlo would be screaming his head off.

"'Why didn't you do it?'

"'I was off the music. I can't do it unless I'm on the music.'

"'I don't care if you're off the music. Do the triple loop. That's what's important.'"

Technically, Carlo was right. If Robin didn't do the triple loop in competition, that would be a much bigger issue than straying from the beat.

Garnet remembers "big, upsetting sessions where Robin would say, 'Look, I just can't do it if I'm not exactly on this beat. Do you hear that *mmmm* in the music?' There would be a hundred million notes. If he pointed it out to you, though, you'd say, 'Ah, I hear that.' It would be one instrument way in the background that he would hear and connect with, and that was his take-off edge. I know it sounds corny, but he really did become one with music when he skated to it. I remember laughing with him about that years later. Now I realize that was the way he timed his jumps. He told me, 'I heard the sound of my edges and the sound of the music, and I made them together. That's how the jump worked.' If he had music, he could do anything.

"Robin was always listening to music. He had the newest, weirdest thing from Timbuktu, the most avant-garde stuff, and he tried to educate everybody else. He brought cassettes to jazz class on Thursdays and said, 'Try this.'"

Music was a stimulus to Robin. It called forth a physical response and gave order and beauty to the constant movement that was in his kinetic nature.

In childhood, music had surrounded him. Fred and Jo listened to Big Bands. Martin liked pop. Nick preferred jazz and the classics. Like his brothers, Robin sang in the school and church choirs. When the time came to learn more about music in order to skate to it properly, he was predisposed and only too eager. With Nick's help, and with his own ear for pitch and tempo, he was able to find and splice pieces that flowed together.

Pam Davies recognized the central role that music played in drawing out and highlighting Robin's physical strengths.

"You have to have an awful lot of qualities to be a skater. You have to be physically good; you have to look the part; you have to have good, strong muscles; you have to be able to appreciate music; you have to be able to feel that music right from your heart and from your soul; and you really have to be able to live what you're doing. You can't just go on and skate empty. You'll see a lot of good technical skaters, and you'll say to somebody by the side of you, 'What are they missing?' They're missing the soul. Then you'll see Robin. He skates with some extra God's gift inside him. He has an excitement that he gives to the audience. It's a pity that you can't teach that."

When Robin left Pam and Gladys to work with the master polisher, he had a formidable box of tools. Some were God-given; some he earned through training. Some had physical properties, while others were aesthetic. Yet the most powerful tools were character and will. Without them, the rest would have gone to waste.

Of the physical tools, perhaps the greatest, as Nick suggested, was spatial awareness. One of its complements, the ability to revolve in both directions, contributed to the quality and diversity of Robin's spins. Nick marveled.

"He was so superior to everybody else: because he could spin virtually faultlessly on the spot, and because of the hand and arm movements he was able to engender within the spin. He had an innate ability to move right to left or left to right and know precisely where he was. I'd say to him, 'Spin as fast as you can.' Then I'd say, 'I want you to stop facing the clock.' He'd do it. You see this guy spinning at a phenomenal speed. Then he can choose to come out at any time, any distance."

Robin's flexibility and aesthetic sense came into play in sit, cross-foot, and camel spins. With his body line in harmony with the laws of physics, he spun quickly and sustained multiple rotations.

That rotational ability, combined with explosive strength, also yielded high, powerful jumps. Correct air position in turn facilitated quickness, efficiency, and the long glide of a controlled landing. Economy of motion contributed the illusion of ease. Those, embellished with grace, majesty, and *ballon* (midair suspension), produced jumping magic. Robin's use of hang time was especially effective in delayed open Axels, tuck Axels, and Russian splits-to-Axel combinations.

As Nick said, "It's almost impossible for him to look inelegant. You could see thirty top-class skaters on an ice rink, and you'd still pick him out, even if he was just skating around. He has that priceless gift of elegance and beauty, which he's always had, combined with natural flair in the skill of jumping."

Some of Robin's signature moves came about by accident. That was the case with the Cousins slide spiral, a languid swoop culminating in a spray of ice.

"The slide, really, was a mistake. I was trying to move out of somebody's way in a hurry."

Christa saw it and told Robin, "That was really neat. Do it again."

He performed it out of a right back-outside spiral, with his knee slightly bent and his weight on the center of his blade. He compared the movement to the swipe of a windshield wiper. The secret was to slide gently through the arc.

Even compulsory figures took on some polish under Carlo's practiced eye and through his shrewd psychology.

The problem, as Carlo saw it, was that Robin was too happy-go-lucky and didn't always concentrate.

Toller found Robin's figures much better than expected.

"But there was one funny thing about them that sometimes surprises people. He was tall and statuesque, yet I found his figures to be diminutive."

Robin's explanation was simple: Gladys taught small figures. Until he arrived in Denver, he didn't know they could be larger. With Carlo, they expanded.

"I wasn't as bad as people said I was. I was never a fifth- or seventh-place figure skater. Maybe I was always terrified of judges, but that was the way I had been brought up in England. I blame the system for putting the fear of God into children taking compulsory figure tests."

In retrospect, he realized that he had never understood what figures were about until Carlo showed him their creative value.

"I actually came to enjoy the process of creating beautiful patterns on the ice and finding the lyrical feel of paragraph change loops. Gladys never made the connection between figures and free skating."

Once Robin established that connection, the final barriers to the top of the podium began to fall.

On the Road with the Fassi Force

There were many who felt that Fassi's power went beyond good public relations. Toller called him a kingmaker.

"The Carlo Fassis of this age are Jurassic Park

creatures. You can no longer politic behind the scenes in the way that he did. You cannot arrange things and make deals, all of which were very much the fashion of the day."

It is true that Carlo promoted his students shamelessly. He was proud of what he had accomplished with them, and he had every right to be. He had no qualms about pointing out their strengths to international judges.

The Fassi factory embraced, among others, Emi Watanabe (Japan); Claudia Kristofics-Binder (Austria); Kristina Wegelius (Finland); Jean-Christophe Simond (France); Hae-Sook Shin (South Korea); Reiko Kobayashi (Japan); and Susan Driano, an American who represented Italy.

Scott Hamilton had trained in Denver since 1976. He hadn't seen Robin since his "waxing" in Saint-Gervais. Then suddenly Robin appeared at the CIA.

"It's a great environment when you're skating with somebody who is so well-respected and has so much talent. It brings out better things in your skating. It was nice, too (because I was just developing as a senior), that I wasn't the number-one guy in the rink. There were a lot of good, high-ranked international skaters there. Just to be in that environment with Robin, to see him work, to get to know him pretty well on a personal level was neat. I think it did a lot for my development. I was down the street from Charlie Tickner and skating every day with Robin Cousins."

When the group traveled to competitions, they were an international family, the "Fassi Force." That pleased Jo.

"We think Robin was lucky when he went to America. Carlo had champions there. Here's this young Brit, and the other fellows and girls could have taken exception, to a point. You know what it's like to have a usurper come in, but they were so friendly."

The Fassi Force went out together to movies and other amusements. On occasion, they sneaked six-packs of beer behind the rink. There was a place where they could sit undetected and "hang out, talk, and mess around," as

Scott phrased it, like young people everywhere.

Charlie trained in a rival camp. He and Robin often passed each other driving in opposite directions. Their coaches didn't particularly hit it off. The rival students weren't supposed to either. Yet they did, as much as possible under the strained circumstances of competition. Robin regretted the strain.

"You only tend to see each other at events, and I think there were a few of us who probably would have been much better pals had we been allowed to *be* pals."

On the ISU "world tour," a traveling series of exhibitions following Worlds, the "kids" (as they were invariably called regardless of age) escaped the isolation of their own rinks, renewed acquaintances, and indulged high spirits, something Randy Gardner fondly recalled.

"We used to tease Linda Fratianne. She was the butt of a lot of jokes."

Once, the skaters were in a bus on a runway, waiting to board a box-shaped commuter plane. Robin told Linda, "We're going to stay in the bus, and the bus is going to drive right onto the back of the plane." Linda believed him. She believed more or less anything the boys told her.

"I was the one they picked on. Nothing mean. Just a lot of teasing, because I was shy and gullible."

Emi Watanabe was gullible, too.

"They set themselves up for it. What can I say?" Randy laughed. "It was fun for us. Robin could pull it off. He'd be the front man. I'd sit in the back and giggle."

Linda was quick to insist, "My memory of Robin is that even though he teased me a lot, he was always very kind to me and very kind to everybody else. I became a big fan of his, early on."

On one tour, Robin landed in the middle of a prank played by Warren Maxwell on Canadian Ron Shaver. For a year and a half, Warren had been terrorizing Ron with the threat of a pie in the face. After a while, Ron forgot and let down his guard. One night in Bristol, at the end of Ron's performance, Robin called him over to meet a friend. There was Warren with a shaving cream pie that dripped from Ron's face throughout his encore. At the end of the evening, the announcer summoned Warren and Ron and presented them with two pies that they in turn "presented" to Robin when he appeared for the finale.

Robin was not usually a mischief-maker.

"Don't do mischief—things kids did on tour, like setting off fire alarms or putting fire extinguishers in the lifts. I never found any amusement in stuff like that. I wasn't a ringleader."

Robin's preferred genre was the bawdy joke, which he was capable of turning into a tale worthy of Boccaccio.

"They're not original, I have to say. I'm usually good at remembering them, and I do tend to turn a joke into an epic. I embellish a lot."

According to Scott, "He has a pretty outrageous sense of humor. He is a physical person. He likes to joke around and laugh. If you want to hear a good, filthy joke, either he'll tell it to you or he's heard it before. It was always fun with Robin. It has been many years, but what jumps out is that he was always laughing and joking about something."

Occasionally there were bouts of gallows humor. On a trip to Vienna, a Canadian official invited some skaters to dinner, among them Robin, Cindy Perpich, and Garnet's younger sister, Brigitte. After they left the restaurant and returned to their lodgings at a university dormitory, the official died of a heart attack. Brigitte spoke both German and English, so she communicated with the Viennese authorities and the paramedics. The biggest snag, according to Robin, was that the university was closed.

"We were the only people staying there. I think the paramedics actually arrived, couldn't get in, and went away again. Poor Brigitte was running between the English-speaking people and the Austrians on the phone—

a pay phone at that. For a thirteen-year-old to be in charge of something like that was quite *trau*matic, and it was very *dra*matic."

Brigitte felt responsible for the unfortunate man's fate and became hysterical. Robin walked her into a quiet part of the dormitory and attempted to lighten her mood. He looked around and remarked, without weighing his words, "Gosh, this place is really *dead*."

According to Garnet, Brigitte "completely lost it. She flailed her arms and screamed 'How could you *say* that?' It was like *Gone With the Wind*. Robin had to slap her. For years, she was so mad at him. She really held a grudge."

A Slit in the Iron Curtain

Travel afforded the chance to know Eastern Bloc athletes when that was both a rare privilege and a daring challenge. In those days, there were ladies who sat in chairs on each hotel floor to watch who came and went. At the arena there were burly men in overcoats. Defection was an ever-present threat to the Soviet government, which vigorously impeded exposure to Western ideas. Yet Robin noticed that there was always a way for East and West to meet over a glass of vodka.

"We were a great group. There was nobody but *us*. We had coaches who really didn't talk to each other. We didn't have agents then, and we had a lot of time when we could find each other."

During the Moscow world tour stop, acquaintances in the kitchen helped Irina Moiseeva and Andrei Minenkov sneak into the skaters' hotel. They were hanging out with Robin and his friends when their chaperon knocked on the door. The rest of the group whisked Min and Mo into a closet.

"It's just us. Sorry we're being noisy," they chirped.

Linda Fratianne stood in the corner giggling. To the Western athletes, those incidents were humorous. For the

Soviets, they were no laughing matter.

"We had fun when we were around each other," Robin recalled. "They brought gifts and vodka—Moiseeva's mother was a master vodka maker—and Russian records and books. Beautiful things. 'I bring for you.' They always came bearing gifts and were so polite and nice—when they were allowed to be. I did get off on the fact that these were people who appreciated what I did. We enjoyed mutual respect. I loved their quality. When we were in Russia, four or five of us went to the Bolshoi. Everybody stood up when we walked in. There was a great pride about the work and a great respect. The books and records I have are prized possessions."

They include the entire collected works of Tolstoy in Russian.

Paul Wylie's Junior Worlds long program music was another Russian gift to Robin: a Khatchaturian ballet, *The Onion Man*. Martin had the synopsis translated into English. Robin later skated to a different cut.

Once, a chaperon approached Robin's dinner table and ordered the Soviets to move.

"No,'" one of the Russian men retorted in English. "We have dinner with our friends."

Elite athletes eventually gained the power to risk disobedience, especially when they were out of their own countries.

Not all of Robin's Eastern Bloc adventures were pleasant.

"I also remember Emi Watanabe and Toller and me being taken off a train and held at gunpoint in East Germany. When you showed up at an East German hotel, you handed them your passports when they checked you in. They put slips of paper in the passports, but we threw them away. We weren't told they meant anything. We reached the border. I remember Frau Müller getting up and saying something. Officials pushed her to the floor. They took

Toller, Emi, and me off the train at gunpoint, and the train took off without us. Cutting a long story short, they phoned back to the hotel, went through the wastepaper baskets, and found the slips of paper that had been in our passports. They put us on the next train, and we ended up getting there before the others—but that wasn't the funniest part. The funniest part was Toller trying to stop Emi from crying by making jokes with the East German border guards."

Robin developed a colorful view of the dynasty coached by Jutta Müller, among them his chief rival, Jan Hoffmann.

"He was not a bad free skater. He just didn't do it very nicely. He had the stuff. He did all the triples, but nothing in East Germany was very inspirational at that point. Gabi Seyfert had inspiration in her style, but it was still quite Germanic. Christine Errath had some heart behind her, and then Anett Pötzsch was pert. It went to Katarina Witt to break out and give the skating some kind of emotion, but all Katarina was, was an emotional version of Anett, who was a pert version of Christine. The technique was identical. The choreography was pretty much the same. The only thing the one had to offer was something the other one didn't. Then Frau Müller built on that, she built on that, she built on that, until you ended up with Katarina Witt.

"That was what made Frau Müller what she was: her ability to turn out performers. Katarina, to me, was the first person who took the Frau Müller style and gave it some emotional content. She had something to say with it, but if you took the flesh away from the structure, she and Anett and Christine and Gabi were identical, and Sonja Morgenstern before them. Frau Müller was good. She was the East German Gladys Hogg!"

1977-78:   Perverse   Arithmetic

Robin, at twenty, was one of nine Fassi skaters at Skate Canada 1977 in Moncton. His work on figures paid off so handsomely that he wanted to ship home the ice around his paragraph bracket. Losing the figures decision by a scant four-five split, he won his maiden international gold medal and beat Charlie for the first time. Then he successfully defended his British title and flew to Strasbourg, France, for Europeans.

A poor first figure doomed his chances. He couldn't close the gap between fifth place and first, even with two winning free skates. His short program rated a 6.0 from the Austrian judge. His long program, technically adequate, was an artistic triumph that drew another 6.0—this time from the French judge. Two judges placed Robin first overall. The seven others chose Jan on the strength of his figures. Vladimir had no first placements but won silver with a majority of seconds. Robin made do with another bronze medal, a free-skating title, and a slight hangover.

He never ate a meal before an event. In Strasbourg, he became ill drinking the beer offered as "inspiration" for the doping test. Paul Wylie once said of the urinalysis, "It's not my idea of a victory ceremony." Robin found it odd that an alcoholic substance was routinely used as a primer for a drug test.

Meanwhile, Christa phoned Carlo in Denver and told him that Robin had skated an excellent long program.

"My wife always kind of shielded me from the problems," Carlo admitted.

Then he turned on the television and saw the last minutes of Robin's program. In his estimation, it was subpar. At the airport, he berated Robin.

"Baloney. You skated lousy. You could have skated much better."

The words stung. Carlo cited that incident as the time Robin nearly left Denver.

Before the 1978 Worlds at Ottawa, Robin caught a virulent strain of flu, losing eleven pounds that he ill could spare. The Canadians housing Fred and Jo improved his outlook with roast beef, Yorkshire pudding, and trifle.

The Ottawans, passionate about skating, glided along the Rideau Canal in a scene from Currier & Ives. Simone Grigorescu joined them. She laced her skates in the heart of downtown and headed south to the Civic Centre, where the men's event was about to start. As the day warmed, the canal melted.

"It was like skating through quicksand. I had quite a workout, going through all those miles of slush. I was afraid that I was going to miss the event."

Robin learned that a young friend, Vicki Wylde, who had recently been hit by a car in London, had managed to make the transatlantic journey to root him on. While she was in the hospital, he had bombarded her with get well messages. Like Simone, she wasn't about to miss his big moment.

"That settles it," he declared. "I've just got to win for her."

Robin was fourth after the figures, ahead of strong technician David Santee. Vladimir led the pack, followed by Jan and Charlie.

David was first in the last short program group. A short-circuit in the Civic Centre sound system briefly interrupted his music. Robin skated next. An explosion sounded over the loudspeaker; then his music began alternately to cut out and blare. Announcer Wilf Langevin, who worked in the electronics industry, grew agitated. The problem was intermittent, which made it difficult to correct. Technicians never pinned down the cause, although the Altec mixer was the chief suspect.

When Robin finished his program, he went to the referee to lodge a complaint on behalf of the next skaters.

According to Langevin, "The technical people were

not instructed to stop the music during Robin's program or indeed during any other skater's program. In retrospect, the referee was the only person who could have stopped the competition and asked for corrective action to be taken."

Although Robin was second to Jan in the short program (with one first placement short of a majority), the disruption may have cost him crucial tenths of points. He remained fourth overall.

David could afford to be philosophical.

"I was fifth at the time, and Robin was battling it out for the lead, so it was a more sensational problem that he had."

Vladimir skated next without incident, though poorly enough to drop one place.

Although Robin won the long program, when all the marks, from figures to long program, had been added together, four judges had given Jan the highest total; three had placed Robin first; two had given the nod to Charlie. No skater had the required majority of five.

The result hung on a majority of second placements (counting firsts and seconds together). Because Charlie—with a career-best performance—had the most second-highest totals, he was the victor, followed by Jan. Robin, the free-skating champion, dropped to third by one judge and won his first world medal in one of the closest decisions in skating history.

David had watched the event from the calm eye of the vortex.

"Jan and Robin were fighting it out, and Charlie waltzed in there and won. Hoffmann's side had Robin in third, the Cousins side had Hoffmann in third, and everybody had Charlie in second. That's how he won. Charlie was in the right place at the right time. That's one of the things about our sport: sometimes you catch a break, and sometimes you don't."

There is evidence of soul-searching in high quarters. The ISU officially denied any cause and effect, but after Robin graduated to professional skating in 1980, there was a rule change that would have favored him retroactively. A revised ISU scoring system, based on factored places, went into effect in 1981.[10]

1978-79: From Bronze to Silver

Robin began adding to his triple jump repertoire. To the loop, toe loop, and Salchow, he added the flip, Lutz, Axel, and Axel in combination. Although he practiced the new jumps, he was leery of risking them in competition.

"I had triple flip and triple Lutz in my long program for about five minutes. On a good day, it was great: two of everything, including flip and Lutz. On a bad day, not even close. Scott could *make* jumps happen. Not me. Triple Axels were easier. On the days I felt like doing them, I did them. On the days I didn't feel like doing them, I didn't even try. That would be the same for triple flip and triple Lutz."

The triple Axel was unnecessary and constituted an undue risk, especially for someone who believed, "It's not what you do. It's how you do it." In Robin's judgment, five triples with two repeats in a clean program beat five different triples with the risk of a fall. (Today, only combinations may contain repeated jumps.)

Robin's underlying problem was that he had practically no cartilage, the connective tissue that cushions the knee joint, preventing bone-against-bone impact. Stopping the velocity and torque of a triple jump on a fraction of an inch of steel blade was unwise for someone who had

---

[10] Rather than calculate results by adding together raw marks, the ISU assigned each judge's decision an *ordinal* mark, based on the relative order in which he had placed the various skaters. The highest total earned the ordinal one; the second highest, two; and so forth. The order of finish was then converted to factored places based on the weight of the event. That remedied the unfair advantage that had disproportionately aided strong figures technicians.

undergone two major cartilage surgeries and could ill afford knee joint rotation due to the weakened state of his cruciate ligaments.

"I don't talk about the injuries that much. People forget, which is good, but I can't afford to forget."

All the jumping caused a left shin stress fracture that required six weeks of off-ice rest.

Robin reclaimed his British title, then returned to Denver to train for Europeans—away from home at Christmas for the first time. At Zagreb in January, he won another free-skating title. As in Ottawa, the arithmetic was Byzantine. Robin settled for bronze while the skating public scratched its collective head.[11]

At the 1979 world championships in Vienna, David particularly noticed Robin on the practice sessions.

"He would get on the ice and within five minutes go into one of these Axels that was about four hundred feet long. He took over the whole practice. I think that it was freestyle practice sessions that took Charlie Tickner out of the competition. Charlie was intimidated by Robin coming out and doing his huge jumps, especially the Axels and the double Axels, and by the response of the people watching the sessions. I was awed just being there. I can imagine what Charlie must have felt. He had to watch, knowing that he was trying to defend his title. It was something to see, and I've never seen anything like it since."

After the first two figures, Charlie was third, Robin fourth, and David fifth. David performed what some perceived as a relatively poor third figure, then went to the referee with a piece of rubber from a Zamboni tire.

"I caught this little piece of rubber on the top of one

---

[11] Robin had the highest totals on the cards of three judges. Hoffmann had three, Kovalev two. None had a majority of five. On the basis of the majority of the highest and second-highest raw sums, Hoffmann and Kovalev tied. The tie-breaker, the sum of placements, put Hoffmann ahead of Kovalev and left Robin in third—even though he had a lower, therefore better, sum of placements than Kovalev.

of my loops, which caused it to kind of skid a bit. I didn't want that skid mark there, because the rest was very good. I went to the referee, Ben Wright. My intent was not to reskate the figure. My intent was to say, 'Can you tell the judges that the reason there's a little skid is because I went over this piece of rubber?'"

"You're entitled to a reskate," Wright told him.

David informed his coach, Mary Scotvold.

"What for?" she wanted to know. "You have to be nuts."

"I'd kind of like to do it, because I know I can probably do it a bit better."

It was the left back paragraph loop "which nobody in his right mind would want to do twice in a row."

No one in the press room could recall a reskate since the championships had moved indoors. David placed second for the reskated figure and edged into fourth overall, dropping Robin one place.

Fassi had a heated argument with Wright.

"I felt David Santee did a lousy figure and then said that, during the figure, he hit a piece of rubber from the Zamboni. I did not believe it. I think he had the rubber in his pocket."

David stuck to his story that the original figure was good.

"Then why," Carlo asked with his mischievous glint, "did he do it again if it was good?"

The truth is long lost in a pile of Zamboni shavings.

Nerves were frayed, tensions palpable—not among the athletes, however. They were gentlemen who respected one another. Fred was amazed at how much goodwill there seemed to be among them, and how little rancor.

Robin's third figure was nothing to write home about. He ended the segment in fourth place, then fell during the short program—his first significant fall in five years. All the front-runners went down except Kovalev and Scott Cramer, who dropped in the long.

Jo was particularly tense.

"My friend Peg was always so positive about Robin. I get in a state—not about winning. I don't care where he comes, as long as he doesn't hurt himself. Peg was nervous for him, too. She kept saying, 'I have every confidence in him.' I looked at her and said, 'Shut up, Peg.' She thought I was angry with her. Then when Robin skated, I grabbed her hand and clutched it so hard that I drew blood."

People soon learned not to hold Jo's hand.

Robin won the long program and another free-skating title, climbing philosophically to the second tier of the podium.

"I have geared my entire career to winning gold at the Olympics next year, and I think it may not be such a bad thing to be in second position at this stage," he told the press.

Vienna was notable for a key episode in the Cousins family saga. It was there that Martin met June Baldock, a noncompetitive skater who was staying at the same hotel with a group from the Richmond club. They married on July 21.

The high point of the 1979 world tour was performing before Queen Elizabeth and Prince Philip at the Wembley Arena NSA Centenary Gala. Fred and Jo intercepted Robin at his hotel to tell him that his grandfather, Ernest Higgs, had died. His grandmother had never seen him skate. That evening she did.

The boys adored Irene Higgs. They called her Nanny or Nan.

"Although," according to Robin, "we affectionately nicknamed her Granny Grimble, or, even more affectionately, the Old Boot. I have to say that Nick was the only one with enough charm to get away with calling her the Old Boot."

As Nick told the story, "My grandmother, Nan to us,

was a wonderfully maternal figure. Now, her husband, my Pop, was not a warm man, and I think he'd given my mum and my Nan probably a fairly tough time. He was a man's man, an engine driver, but he was still our grandfather. Rob was deeply affected, much more so than any of us ever thought he would be. He produced a little requiem he had choreographed himself, an extraordinarily emotive piece with high strings, in memory of his grandfather: a sort of eulogy, very poignant and beautiful."

Robin has forgotten the name of the music.

"But I do remember that I cried through the whole thing."

Nan was thrilled when Robin met the Queen, but she was proudest during the encore that he dedicated to his grandfather. Then he crossed the ice and gave her a rose.

1979-80: The Final Ascent of Olympus

Although the Sports Aid Foundation had relieved the financial burden, one pressure that escalated as the Olympics approached was the burden of growing fame. Throughout the fall of 1979, competitions, exhibitions, and demands from the media consumed a large part of Robin's time and energy. The Fassis received, on average, ten requests daily: from rink openings to judging the world disco championships. Although they winnowed the worthy from the absurd, engagements piled up.

What annoyed Carlo the most were the constant demands to compare Robin to John.

"It was very difficult. They were so similar in many cases, so different in others. It was stupid to ask, but the press kept going, kept going, kept going."

One day Carlo told a reporter, "Robin is more the athlete, the physical champion, and John was more the mental champion. Everything John did, more than with his body, he did it with his brain."

Two weeks later, he received a postcard: "Thank you

for the article. Your untalented pupil, John Curry."

In October, Robin won the Rotary Watches Ice International (later called St. Ivel). He took figures for the first time—flourish of trumpets, roll of drums—after a night awake with food poisoning. He had eaten two dollops of whipped topping, his own and Karena's. He paid for his gluttony, vomiting spoiled cream until time to skate figures. Surviving on glucose water, he won the short program that same evening. The next day, with an omelet and dry toast added to the menu, he previewed his Olympic long program to enthusiastic reviews and first-place marks. Why had it taken food poisoning to produce a figures win? Robin was too sick to be nervous.

A week and a half later, he returned to Tokyo, the scene of his biggest disaster, to compete in the NHK Trophy free-skating competition. Despite his squeamishness at returning to that blackest of ice, he easily won before a supportive crowd.

Shortly before nationals, Robin was at home in Bristol when a representative of the NSA phoned to inform him of a commitment made on his behalf. Seduced by the lure of revenues from the telecast of the ice dance championship in Nottingham, the association had promised an exhibition by Robin as the guarantee.

"I can't," he said. "I have the Ennia Challenge Cup in The Hague."

"You owe it to us to do the exhibition."

Robin covered the receiver.

"Mother, if you don't take the phone, I'm going to slam it down on this guy. He's drunk, and he's telling me I *have* to be there."

In the end, Robin complied—unhappily. Between the short program and the long, he flew from the Netherlands to England to skate the exhibition. Leaving the Nottingham arena at 1:00 A.M. amidst a dangerously enthusiastic mob, he was pushed up against the family car. A foot landed sharply on his ankle, which blew up like a balloon. He iced the swelling, got a few hours' sleep, and left at 6:00 A.M. to return to The Hague. That afternoon, he skated an undistinguished long program. The NSA had made it a Pyrrhic victory.

Back in Bristol, Robin learned that even a world silver medalist practiced between midnight and 3:00 A.M. By the time he arrived in Richmond, tired and drawn, he had an ankle infection caused by an ill-fitting boot. He won his fourth British title in front of a crowd that overflowed into the street with the most embarrassing long program of his life.

"Abysmal," he called it. He went home and slept for sixteen hours. Carlo canceled an Australian rink opening so Robin could return to Denver to prepare for the triple challenge that lay ahead.

British Airways flew Robin to the 1980 European championships in Gothenburg, Sweden, on the cramped but luxurious Concorde SST. His figures propelled him into third place, behind Vladimir and Jan. There he remained when his short program combination wilted into doubles. Carlo called Robin a chicken, a commonplace epithet with which he goaded his students.

A British journalist asked, "May I quote you?"

"Yes, quote me."

Carlo was piqued that Robin might have discarded the European title—and with it a psychological advantage at the Olympics. By the time he reached his hotel, his phone was ringing off the hook.

"This is BBC London. Is it true that you called Robin Cousins a chicken?"

"Yes."

"This is BBC Bristol. Is it true that you called Robin Cousins a chicken?"

"Yes, it is true."

The next call was Fred and Jo's, politely expressing

their disappointment in Carlo's choice of words.

"Sorry," he told them. "Those things come out in the heat of the competition."

The provocateur had found his target. Robin awoke the next morning raring to go. He earned three 6.0s on his way to the title. Headlines clucked <u>The Chicken That Laid the Golden Egg</u>.

Then it was back to Denver for the final tune-up.

Robin made a fetish of finding fresh music. He didn't like to use the same piece twice. Nonetheless, he was skating to an "old" short program, *The Railway Children* (albeit a new combination of cuts). Carlo had repeatedly said, "We need something like *that*." Finally they decided that *that* was what would do the trick.

For the long program, classical music was the safe and customary choice. Robin was able to interpret it with great feeling. Still, he didn't like to play it safe. He had decided to express his vibrant personality with something more upbeat.

The five-minute program began with a slow pop passage, "Belle de Jour" by San Tropez, then segued into a disco section, "Dragons at Midnight" by Mike Theodore: three separate snippets spliced together, one sped up and two slowed down. The third section came from Richard Rodney Bennett's film score *Murder on the Orient Express*: lush, lyrical music with classical overtones. The explosive finish, from Johnny Harris's instrumental version of the Rolling Stones' "Paint it Black," highlighted Robin's athleticism and gave his ebullience free reign.

Garnet had watched the program develop.

"The disco thing was big then. He had a dancing section, and I remember Carlo not being sure about that, thinking it might be too much for the skating world. It was a lot more conservative then."

Carlo was correct where the staid British judges were concerned. After the Rotary international, Robin promised to make changes—a promise that he kept only superficially. Yet when Carlo trumpeted the "new" program at the next competition, those same judges nodded in satisfaction, saying they liked it much better.

Just before their boarder left for Lake Placid, the Wylies moved, trading houses with another Denver family.

As B.L. told it, "We had a daughter in college, a daughter skating and in private school, and a son skating and in private school. We could not afford the food we were putting on our table. That's why we moved. We did go to another five-bedroom house, but it was smaller and less expensive. (I couldn't afford anything. Here I went to all these magnificent overseas competitions, and at every gala I was in the same little blue blazer.) I did all the packing myself. It was a nightmare. I had to be out of our house by three o'clock in the afternoon, because *their* moving van was pulling up to the front door."

As for Robin, "It was probably the best thing that ever happened to him, actually. We moved within the week or two before he left. The poor kid had to pack up his room, and I think probably it took his mind off what he was doing a bit, but the concentration was so heavy that he kept driving to our other house. It shows you how focused he was."

A German television crew arrived unannounced at the Skatique and told B.L. that they were headed for her house to film an "up close and personal" segment. When the family got home, the Germans were everywhere, plugging great heaps of equipment into the house power. Bob went outside and stared at the electric meter. The numbers were changing at "eighty thousand miles an hour."

"That's the kind of thing that went on," B.L. laughed, "and that was what we had to protect Robin from. I remember him just being blown away by that aggressive television crew. He was so good to them that we had to be careful they didn't take advantage of him."

Each new crew wanted shots of the Wylies eating. There was equally heavy demand for footage of Robin back-flipping in the snowy yard. Neighborhood children swarmed like bees to the hive.

The Wylies were mindful of their responsibilities to Robin and the strain he was under—although he concealed it. They wanted to make sure that he ate well, rested, stayed healthy, and went to the Olympics in the best frame of mind possible, according to B.L.

"We were hopping. We were working full-time at this Olympic thing. I had the responsibility of it on my head. It was so important for us to send Robin away feeling confident and not confuse his life at all. I think that's the thing I remember the most: the real responsibility of not letting anything happen to him—in spite of the fact that we moved."

The week before the Olympics, Robin spent four days in bed with the flu. He was used to going into a downslide before the big sprint.

"I can turn off and go into a lethargic low gear. Sometimes it would mean getting a cold or whatever. It was my body saying to me, 'Calm before the storm.'"

He lay in bed without panicking, without worrying that he ought to be on the ice. By the time the machine was purring in high gear, the momentous day had arrived to leave for Lake Placid.

Lake Placid

A winter sports enthusiast goes to Lake Placid, New York, as the priest and prioress to Canterbury. West of the North-way linking Albany to southern Quebec, a remote, birch-lined, two-lane road winds towards the outskirts of town, then swoops past the luge and bobsled runs and the ski jump. A left turn at the only traffic light on Main Street leads to the heart of the village, the Olympic Center. Its 1932 and 1980 rinks evoke the times when Lake Placid was the center of the world.

The people of Lake Placid billed their Games as "An Olympics in Perspective." The venues were first-rate, the athletes spirited, the ambiance warm, yet there were struggles. Lake Placid was a speck on the map, a one-road town. In early February, that road was jammed with cold, irritable athletes and spectators waiting for phantom buses.

In late January, the biggest worry had been the lack of snow. Wallowing in mud and slush, the organizers had a nightmare: they were about to host the first Indian Summer Olympics. Once the snow fell, worries turned to cramming 13,000 members of the "Olympic family" and a projected 50,000 daily visitors into a hamlet with a normal winter population of 2,997.

Ticket-holders had to leave their cars up to sixteen miles away and ride shuttle buses. *Bus* became a three-letter curse. At first, the shuttle system broke down because of a labor dispute. Then it began breaking down spontaneously, for no apparent reason other than perversity. The governor of New York and the Olympic Organizing Committee hired Greyhound to rescue the floundering network.

The opening ceremonies were disappointing for the British athletes. Officials held them on buses in the arctic cold until it was time to parade into the stadium, then herded them back onboard. Because the usual ten-minute ride to the village took two hours, Robin missed his practice session in the new 1980 Olympic Arena. Meanwhile, Fred, Jo, and Nick joined a three-mile trek to the village. Eight hikers required treatment for frostbite.

Carlo and Christa had rented a house on Mirror Lake, a few minutes' walk from the arena, to share with the Cousinses: a good place for Robin to hide out and unwind. His confining cubicle in the athletes' village was the last place he wanted to be. The house was seriously overpopulated. In the morning, one had to climb over rows of slumbering bodies in sleeping bags.

Six months after the bombing death of Lord Mountbatten, allegedly at the hands of the Provisional I.R.A., the British team was under heavy protection. The Olympic security force was not pleased when Robin was on the loose. Luckily, no one knew that the house belonged to Irish-Americans, a fact that became obvious to Carlo when a son returned from Ireland. Far from threatening Robin's security, the hosts hung bed sheets down the front of the house as good luck banners for their adopted Englishman.

Christopher Dean beheld the Olympic spectacle with amazement: a hundred-strong press corps from the U.K. alone, focused on Robin as its principal medal hope. Chris and Jayne were still green enough to be awed by the international scene, though they viewed the publicity circus with a certain detachment.

"It was fascinating to watch. I suppose, in a way, maybe Jayne and I got something from that for when our turn came around."

If Robin was the star, there were few perquisites. The NSA hadn't arranged tickets for parents, whose practice credentials were invalid at competitions. Fred and Jo watched Robin compete only through the kindness of the BBC's Alan Weeks.

Jo went on a tranquilizer regimen. It didn't help her state of mind that back in England the birth of her first grandchild was imminent. Members of the British press floated the rumor of a family rift. Nick was in Lake Placid, while Martin was nowhere to be found! Events soon silenced the rumors, although one reporter in particular was bitterly disappointed at the dearth of scandal.

As Robin left the ice after his second figure, he was handed a note: "Phone your brother in London." He stood in front of the bleachers, looking up at his parents.

"Quick, phone home. I think I'm an uncle."

That became headline news. Martin and June named their baby Robin Clifford. His uncle, glad to have something to think about besides his third figure, ended up an encouraging fourth, then pulled up to second after a brilliant short program. A flurry of 5.9s accompanied the Canadian judge's 6.0 for artistic impression.

Following an early-morning practice the next day, Robin had time to himself. He and Nick headed up Main Street, a road jammed with shops selling food, gear, and Olympic memorabilia. There was just one problem.

"The thing I wanted to do most of all was get out in the crowd and wander. I couldn't walk past anybody who didn't turn around and shout 'Good luck tomorrow.' I was definitely trying not to think about it."

Charlie's prospects had dimmed when he faltered in the short program. Robin felt like his honorary stand-in. If it was going to be the Brit or the East German, it had to be the Brit—in part because the Brit trained in the Colonies.

Robin drew to skate first in the final long program group. He stood at center ice, alone with his reflections.

"God, I hope I don't screw up in front of all these people. That would be really embarrassing."

As he moved with precision and languid fluidity through a technical minefield, a two-footed triple loop administered a twinge of disappointment.

Rather than wait in restless agony for five more skaters, Robin strolled to the practice rink to watch Linda Fratianne run through her program.

She skated to the boards.

"How did Charlie do?"

"I don't know. He's not finished yet."

Robin turned on his heels and headed back towards the main rink just as Nick intercepted him.

"Where have you been? We were looking for you. It's all over."

Nick had come from the BBC Radio box, where the

unofficial consensus had Robin on top. They went to find Fred and Jo and await the official results.

At 11:15 P.M. on February 21, 1980, Robin, Nick, Fred, and Jo stared at a television monitor hooked up to a computer. In a nanosecond, that chunk of electronic wizardry digested the marks of the last competitor and flashed a revised list of names onto the screen—names in Russian, French, English, German, and Czech. At the top was "Cousins, Robin" preceded by the numeral one. Fourteen and a half years' worth of dreams had just come true. Among the tens of thousands of eight-year-olds who had grown up with the same ambition, what were the odds of being the one at the top? Relief and joy combined in equal measure. The quest had ended. The Holy Grail was in hand.

The outcome had by no means been assured until that moment that Nick recalls so vividly.

"It had been the most extraordinary fortnight of my life—and, I know, of Robin's life, too. He'd been built up, as the British tend to do when they think they *might* have somebody who *might* win something. We just go bananas. The press corps, the papers, and every minute of every day, the interviews. Every move was scrutinized, and the pressure was unbelievable.

"The result was tight. I don't think Robin knew what was going on because of the way skating is judged. We were in the press box when the computer screens came up with the standings. There was a moment, before anybody else did, when *we* knew he'd won. My mum said, 'You've won! You've won!' He let out the most extraordinary sound. I couldn't possibly describe it, and I wouldn't want to—sort of a guttural animal grunt. All that huge pent-up emotion, terror, fright, all the negative aspects which had welled up in there (that he'd never brought out to the surface) exploded in an unbelievable, rather frightening sound, which then gave way to a sea of tears and emotion and that wonderful ecstasy."

Workers rolled a carpet onto the ice and assembled a podium. As the awards party stood by with medals and flowers, three men waited to hear their names and take their places.

"Robin Cousins."

Robin skated out and numbly ascended the podium. As he reached for the highest step, he tripped.

"Normally it's one, two, three, but they had half a step in between, and I did that wonderful trip up onto the podium. My legs had done the job they needed to do for the night. I was miles away."

During the playing of "God Save the Queen," Robin's eyes met his parents' across the Union Jack.

After the ceremony, after the victory lap, after the press conference, after the doping test, after the hugs, kisses, handshakes, bouquets, and many congratulations, Robin, his family, and his coaches went to the athletes' village for a champagne celebration. The Pinkerton's guard refused to let them in. There they stood in the glacial cold at one thirty in the morning, arguing with a determined pit bull. Brandishing the shiny new medal didn't help one iota. Fred found that amusing.

"There was the head of the Olympic Committee, there was the Minister for Sport, and of course us, but she was adamant. It took about twenty minutes, half an hour, before they could get through to someone who could supersede this lady."

Sic transit gloria.

In England, friends, neighbors, and strangers had stayed up half the night to see the event's conclusion. Bristol school children had watched and waited. The start of classes the next day would be ragged.

Jo's reaction was, "We were wishing and hoping he would win, but when I hear that four million people sat up watching until 4:00 A.M., I say thank goodness he *did* win."

Of the four million, Pam Davies had been the most nervous of all, repeating like a mantra, "Can anyone see my heart moving?" Then, Pam had always been like that.

"Just standing there making no physical effort at all, my heart would be beating by the end of the program just as if I was skating it."

Garnet was in the hospital that night.

"I had a bleeding ulcer, which is probably why I cried so hard when he won. I wanted to be there—not just for me, but to see Robin, my friend, do this great thing. You watch him do his run-throughs every single day, and then, a week later, he's at the Olympics."

She cried when he won. Then she cried again when she saw the gold medal around his neck.

B.L. had watched with her family in Denver.

"It was awful. Paul was so nervous that he nearly died. We bought a new television for the Olympics and a videotape recorder. My husband set it up, and we were just a wreck. It was like having your own child go off. Somebody gave us a call. I think we knew he had won before we saw it on television. Then Robin called. It was about three o'clock our time, as I recall, and he'd been partying all night. They had gone from one thing to another."

The London *Observer* spotted Robin "back-flipping in Cell Block J in the Olympic Village in the early hours of the morning after his victory—entertaining the poor man who was on night-guard duty." It was indeed Cell Block J. After the Games, the Olympic Village became a minimum-security federal prison. For some golden athletes, hounded by the media, it was a prison before the Games ended.

The next morning, it was June and Robin Clifford whose picture filled the front page of the *Daily Express*. Under the headline Robin Cousins is Good as Gold, a wag noted that he had yawned and gone back to sleep.

"I was just on cloud nine," Martin said. "I had a brother who was Olympic champion, and then I was a dad."

"It doesn't come any better than that" was Robin's opinion.

"You just said what I was thinking," Martin told his brother.

"We rode a roller coaster. Robin had his roller coaster going abroad, and I had my own little roller coaster going over here. We had this wonderful day when little Robin was born. Three nights later, I then had a night when my brother won the Olympics. June used to work in the Canadian High Commission, and a friend of ours from there came down and brought some steaks and beer. I had a wonderful, stupid phone call—at least I thought it was stupid—from the BBC."

"Will you be watching your brother tonight?"

"No, I think I'm going to go to sleep!"

"Where will you be watching?"

"In the flat. I have a friend coming over."

"Would you mind if we came along and watched it with you?"

BBC Radio audio-recorded Martin's reactions. He slept for one hour that night, the very hour the segment aired. He still hasn't heard it—probably just as well. What he uttered when Robin two-footed the triple loop wasn't fit for the public airwaves.

The next morning, Martin went to work.

"I didn't do anything, but I went in."

At 5:00 P.M., the *Daily Mail* was due at the hospital to photograph him with June and the baby. Meanwhile, he received a call from the BBC, summoning him to the London studios for a live satellite video linkup with Robin in Lake Placid and Pam in Bristol. Stuck in traffic, he missed the linkup. No problem, said the BBC. Can you come back at six o'clock when the taped linkup airs? Fine, said Martin. He rushed to the hospital for the photograph, telling June, "Watch the television tonight. *I'm* going to be on. Never mind Robin." Then he returned to the studio.

"I had to go back down to do a proper visit, which meant I had no time whatsoever to think about anything. I turned up in the hospital to visit my wife and baby with the TV makeup still on. There were lots of funny looks."

Back in Lake Placid, Robin and Nick set off for a second time to stroll around the village—in a substantially improved frame of mind, by Nick's account.

"We found and bought a wooden plaque he was going to put his medal on. I remember that the bloke couldn't get over it. Rob had obviously just won the gold medal, and there he was, walking into that little man's shop."

The aftermath of the Olympic victory was even more frantic than the buildup. Robin's countrymen, friends and strangers alike, inundated Lake Placid with messages. Even better than the telegrams from Michael Jackson and Queen Elizabeth was the message "We were all rooting for you," signed Paul and Linda McCartney.

Lyricist Carol Connors, moved by Robin's interpretation of "With You I'm Born Again," one of his two exhibition numbers, sent him the sheet music. He had it framed—his favorite Olympic memento.

A humorous incident at the gala, broadcast live to millions, illuminated Jan Hoffmann's personality. As he stood with downcast eyes, legs spread, arms outstretched, waiting for his music to start, the tape deck destroyed his program recording. Long minutes ticked by. Any other skater would have left the ice, but Jan stood his ground. Periodically he glanced up, but he never changed his position. When a backup tape was located, there he stood, a stoic through and through, waiting in his opening pose.

Robin entered the closing ceremonies hand in hand with ladies' silver medalist Linda Fratianne. Charlie had won a bronze medal. Of the Saint-Gervais group, only Tai and Randy left Lake Placid unannointed. Randy, with a numbed groin injury, had withdrawn during the warmup, ending their amateur career in heartbreak.

A Footnote to History

David Santee claimed a dubious Olympic record. After his fourth-place finish, he reported to doping control. He noticed Jan having a beer and thought, "Hey, great. I'll have one, too." He drank two on an empty stomach, chased with apple juice and water—with no measurable results. After forty-five minutes, officials sent him to the American press conference with a minder.

"Those two beers really had an impact on me. I definitely remember feeling a little bit fuzzy. Scott was already there. He looked at me and started to laugh, because he could tell I was not entirely with it."

Back in doping control, the monitor and a Marine gave David hot tea and made him run stairs. The breakthrough came when the Marine put David on his honor.

"I was so dehydrated from the competition that it took me about two hours and forty minutes to finally get the job done. They were pretty amused when I finished. It was 1:15 in the morning, and they all clapped."

The Americans and Russians communed on their last night together. (The Russians supplied the vodka.) The U.S. team was due to gather at 6:15 A.M. for a trip to the White House. David rolled up to his Lake Placid trailer at 5:45.

"I packed, got about ten minutes of sleep, and went to meet President Carter. I was *not* feeling all that great."

No Tea on Downing Street

Fred and Jo returned to Bristol to find their usually quiet home deluged with marriage proposals for Robin, bushels of letters, and phone calls. Business went up 50 per cent at the Silver Blades Ice Rink. Window dressers erected Welcome Home signs.

On the floor of the House of Commons, Liberal M P Clement Freud asked, "In view of President Carter's fine example in inviting the victorious American ice hockey team to dinner in the White House, will the Prime Minister emulate that by asking Robin Cousins to have tea at No. 10 Downing Street?" Mrs. Thatcher replied drolly, "I rather thought that he deserved more than that. Is the honorable gentleman fishing for an invitation?"

Isolated from the whirlwind, Robin returned to Denver. The world championships at Dortmund, Germany, loomed. There was pressure to match John Curry's vaunted sweep of the Europeans, Olympics, and Worlds.

Fred told the *Evening Post,* "People think Robin has only to put on his boots to win again, but Hoffmann will be even more determined this time." As usual, Fred was right.

There were crowds at the Denver airport, a party at the CIA, and mounds of mail that rivaled those in England. The Wylie phone rang nonstop while sightseers cruised past the house. B.L. was alert to events around her—and careful about the location of the gold medal.

Through it all, Robin stayed focused—and if he didn't, B.L. thought he faked it well.

"He did keep a lot of things inside. I'm sure that's how he survived through the whole thing."

Once More, with Feeling

Robin's Olympic win had an immediate payoff for Fred. On the way to Dortmund with a busload of Bristol supporters, he steered the cross-Channel ferry the last few miles between Dover and Zeebrugge. The celebrity of the group was Robin's seventy-eight-year-old grandmother who had never traveled farther than the Isle of Wight. The family had pooled its resources to finance her first skating trip.

Normally when Fred and Jo appeared at the practice rink, Robin acknowledged them without interrupting his work. It was enough for him to know where they were in the stands. In Dortmund, Irene Higgs had barely emerged through the canvas curtain when Robin spotted her, shouted "My Nan!" and skated straight in her direction.

By Jo's account, "She went down over those steps

like a ten-year-old." The press swarmed like locusts, and Nan was on television before Robin was.

The Germans treated Nan like the Queen Mother. For some reason, they called her Granny Castles. She didn't mind. She couldn't enter or leave the Westfalenhalle without someone snapping her picture. Robin received bouquets at the end, but Nan received daily flowers, candy, and gifts.

The Germans were great autograph hounds, waiting for hours with their albums. One afternoon Robin, Fred, and Jo went to a lunch meeting with the BBC. As Fred told it, "Robin was eating lunch one-handed, which he learned in America, and signing autographs. This young girl or fellow put the book down, and Robin opened it. His face didn't change, but he said, 'I don't *believe* it. It has taken me fifteen years to reach this standard, and look!'"

There was *Irene Higgs* written in Nan's familiar hand.

Robin was fifth in figures, behind Jan, David, Charlie, and Jean-Christophe Simond. The British judge, Geoff Yates, gave him his lowest marks.

"It's hard to live in the free world," Carlo quipped to a Soviet ISU member—a subtle reference to the national bias and rampant collusion that often characterized Eastern Bloc scoring. That isn't to say that Western nations were innocent.

Robin skated the last of twenty-two short programs. Breezing through a flawless performance, he caught his left toe pick at the end of a footwork sequence. Leaving the ice, he skated past his family and shrugged. Then he looked at Carlo, and both burst out laughing. Though he won the short program and climbed to third place, with only Jan and David above him, the trip cost critical tenths of points.

"It wasn't a mistake. I didn't chicken out. It wasn't a fall. Shit happens. It was just one of those stupid moments."

Some judges ignored it, while others were punitive.

Yet there was one thing no one could take away from Robin: except for the freak slip, it had been the best short program of his life. It might have been the best those judges had ever seen.

Jan skated a good long program. His sizable lead in the figures would surely hold up. When Jan's marks appeared, Carlo announced bluntly, "That's it. It's over. All you do now is go out and enjoy yourself." Knowing that he couldn't win, Robin skated his program as an exhibition.

"I threw in another triple loop that wasn't supposed to be there, and I had the most wonderful time on that ice."

More than a thousand British soldiers and dependents stationed at Dortmund, a large Bristol contingent, and the Granny Castles brigade all willed Robin to win. His goal was to better his Olympic performance, and he did. Five precise triples were incidental to the immaculate spins, quick footwork, airy delayed Axel, high kicks, Cousins slide spiral, and joyful musicality. It was a personal best and a wonderful note on which to exit.

Three 6.0s drew a wild ovation. It took more than five minutes to clear the ice of flowers. Cameras panned to Fred hugging Jo and Nan, one with each arm. Robin skated to Jo before leaving the ice and presented her with freesia and pink roses. As he stood on the second step of the podium, he blew a kiss to Nan.

"Dortmund was my favorite event. It was like being given a great present. Still to me, watching that on tape, with the flowers everywhere and my grandmother there, I couldn't have asked for any more."

At the competitors' hotel, protesters jammed the switchboard to insist that Robin should have won. The silver medalist himself demurred.

"I've had my share of championships this year. This is the first one out of eight I haven't won. If there is anyone I would rather have won it than me, it's Jan. I'm really happy for him. We go back a long way. When I used to take my naps to watch skating competitions at midnight, he was skating *then*."

Jan had given it everything he had at both Dortmund and Lake Placid. Toller dared to suggest that the results of the two competitions should have been reversed. (To be fair, his assessment was on technical grounds and didn't take into account Robin's artistic superiority.)

"Robin Cousins was the best skater in the world, the most famous skater in the world, and everything an Olympic champion should be—but, on the night, he did not deserve it. It was just one of those things. In the long program, which was the determining factor, he did not do a triple flip, he did not do a triple Lutz, and he put his foot down on a triple loop, whereas Hoffmann went out, in his Teutonic way, and did everything he could possibly do. On that night, Hoffmann outskated Robin.

"There was to be residue after that. I feel that Linda Fratianne was sacrificed and Anett Pötzsch was then given the women's title. Anett Pötzsch is the world's most forgotten Olympic gold medalist, a great talent that went wrong, thanks to Jutta Müller. Too bad she wasn't American.

"So Robin won. Then I think that the powers that be wanted to settle the score. As Olympic champion, Robin went to Dortmund. I personally thought he was better than Jan Hoffmann on that night, but it was a *quid pro quo* situation: I win the Olympics, so you might as well have the Worlds.

"Four years later, the same thing was to occur, but in a far more blatant way: the win of Scott Hamilton, which was, I felt, truly the crime of the century. There was a common denominator. If Robin Cousins was debatable, Scott Hamilton's win was conspicuous in its injustice, but if they didn't deserve to win the Olympics on the night, they deserved to be the Olympic champions because of their skating, their careers, and what was to come afterwards. They were the children of destiny. They became the great performers and entertainers and icons of their age, and the Anett Pötzsches and the Jan Hoffmanns were forgotten the second they stepped down from the podium. The children of destiny have vindicated themselves and have proven to one and all that not only were they great, but they were the deserving champions for that epoch."

As Brian Klavano saw it, "That's where somebody up there is putting it all in the right order: that a person that gifted was given an Olympic gold medal that obviously brought him untold wealth and gave him that ability to then broaden—and he's given it back. He's given enjoyment to so many people, as a performer and as an inspiration to so many young skaters coming up. He left his mark on the sport. He put the medal to good use. He's kept his image and his nose clean. He's played his role well."

Robin himself wasn't inclined to weigh it all up.

"The result's the result. You can't always think about 'What if?' I should have won this. I shouldn't have won that. This person should have beaten me here. I skated better than he did. It's not *about* that. I didn't learn to skate to compete. I'm not competitive against other people by nature. I just do everything to the best of my ability. I want to do it right, and I want to be the best, but not at someone else's expense."

Well said, but what a world of difference one night made.

5. Through the Hoops and into the Fire: 1980-82

*B*efore the saucer-sized, 22k-gold-plated sterling silver medal had settled around Robin's neck, headlines shouted <u>Ice Hero Looks to Jackpot Future: Now Robin Poised to Cash In</u>.

A man named Larry Parnes offered Robin and John Curry $75,000 each plus 10 per cent of ancillary rights to skate in a televised head-to-head challenge match in London, with an option for a second in the United States. Assorted entrepreneurs proposed novelty records, pantomimes, and television appearances. Robin wondered why an ice skater should become a game show guest. The lure of pecuniary gain had never been his *raison d'être*.

During the busy days after Worlds, he put matters in the hands of a management group and set out to fulfill his remaining obligations to the NSA and the ISU, embarking straight from Dortmund on the world tour.

In Bristol, preparations for a celebration hit a snag due to U.S.-Soviet tensions over Afghanistan. At President Carter's request, the American team had refused to take part in the Russian segment of the tour. When the ISU decreed that it was all of the tour or none, the Americans packed up and went home. The ISU prevailed upon Robin to save the union from embarrassment, so the celebration-planners hit high gear to bring it off a week early.

On Saturday, March 22, Robin flew in from Geneva for lunch with the Lord Mayor. An open-top bus tour began on Dingle Close, which bloomed with Union Jacks and bunting. One whimsical Sea Mills neighbor wanted to turn the tennis courts into a skating rink.

More than fifty thousand people—the largest local crowd ever to assemble—lined the route into the City Centre and showered the bus with bouquets. The spectacle reached Biblical proportions: people in trees, on balconies, atop walls, leaning out windows, lining bridges, following on bicycles, and craning from ladders. Traffic jammed as drivers waved and honked their horns. Soccer games stopped while players applauded.

The hour-long procession ended on College Green, where the Lord Mayor made a formal presentation. As he concluded his remarks, television host Eamonn Andrews ran across the Green and leapt onto the dais.

"Robin Cousins, today 'This is your life!'"

A bemused look spread over Robin's face. He wondered, "How can I be having a 'Life' when I'm still only twenty-two years old?"

During taping in the HTV studios, a parade of familiar faces passed in review: Jo, Fred, Martin, Nick, Pam Davies, Doris Nash, Joan Watson, Alan Weeks, Lynn Seymour, the Fassis, and an honor roll of British sports heroes. Throughout, Robin was nearly speechless, but the *pièce de résistance* sent him into a few discreet tears.

A week and a half earlier, a telephone call had awakened B.L. and Bob Wylie at 5:00 A.M.

"This is so-and-so from England. We would like to have you come over and be on the television show 'This Is Your Life.'"

"Yeah, sure," they said, suspecting a practical joke. "When are you going to send us the tickets?"

A reasonable voice on the London end replied, "I will call you back and confirm."

"Jolly well, it was for sure," said B.L. "They put us in a hotel, and we were not to come out. My husband got out and ran the next morning, and the people on the show nearly had a heart attack. They said only Americans would run."

At the studios, the Wylies met Fred and Jo for the first time. It didn't take B.L. long to win Jo's advocacy. B.L. was short for Betty Lu, which was short for Elizabeth Lucy. Elizabeth Lucy's teachers had insisted on calling her Betty, which she didn't like. She had changed her name to B.L. at summer camp. The "This Is Your Life" staff didn't want to duplicate the familiar initials of British Leyland.

"We can't call you B.L. on the air. That's a car name."

Jo "which is short for Edna" found herself in familiar territory. She turned to the staffers and decreed quietly but firmly, "If she wants to be called B.L. on the air, call her B.L. on the air. We won't discuss this any further." They didn't.

After the Lord Mayor's reception, there was a party at the Holiday Inn, where a margarine sculpture of Robin served as the centerpiece. Fame, as he soon learned, is a slippery thing.

In April, the Bristol Ice Dance and Figure Skating Club honored him with a dinner. A local artist gave him a portrait of himself. Then he made a presentation of his own. He gave Pam his Olympic commemorative medal, telling the large crowd, "She wasn't able to be with me in times of triumph, but, without her, I wouldn't have been able to do anything."

Later that month, he spent a two-week holiday in Sea Mills. His childhood bedroom overflowed with gifts from Dortmund, among them a portable television and three large teddy bears. Bears, giraffes, elephants: if they came in toy form, Robin received them. He passed some out to nephews and nieces, while others found homes at the local children's hospital.

On the television show "Pebble Mill," Toller Cranston was asked to advise the neophyte.

"The most important thing is to rely on your inside voice. It's your feeling and your perception of things that is going to, I think, carry you through. I thought, when I turned professional, that the Geniuses would fall out of the sky and help me do this and that, but I've found that the saving grace for me was in my own intuition."

Turning to the host, Toller continued, "[Robin] is really the greatest skater that the world has ever seen. He has an intuitive sense as to what is right for him, the kinds of music that he wants to skate to, the way he wants to be presented in a show, and I think that that should come from him, and he should tell people what it is that he wants, as opposed to having people dictate to him what they think he should be doing."

Robin sends on Toller's advice to anybody else who will take it, with the postscript that it should be followed without arrogance, and as long as one can justify one's opinions.

In May, Robin went home "for good." He began his civic duties with the first of many ribbon-cutting ceremonies. In June, he spent a week in Australia on the "Mike Walsh Morning Show." In July, he unveiled the plaque naming Avonmouth's Robin Cousins Sports Centre.

One day Robin went into town to meet Nick, who was running late as usual. While he waited, by chance, in front of a real estate agency, he noticed the photograph of a Tudor-style stone country house with mullioned dormer windows topped by half-timbered pediments, overlooking the Severn estuary in the nearby village of Almondsbury. Vine-laced pillars stood sentry in the foreground, flanked by curving stone terraces erupting in flowers.

As soon as Nick arrived, he and Robin drove to the address and toured the grounds. Then Robin arranged to view the estate with his parents. Jo was so overwhelmed by its magic that she "did her usual stupid thing" and burst into tears. Robin tried to calm her by saying, "We haven't bought anything yet. It might not happen."

By August, Fred and Jo were settled in the four-bedroom house with lovely gardens and a swimming pool. Baridon House, as they christened it, had sturdy black beams and a staircase, legend had it, from Bristol Castle. Robin liked its character and warmth—and the fact that it was thoroughly English.

"Robin always said he would buy us a house," Fred told a journalist, "but when it finally happens, you have to pinch yourself to convince yourself that it is true."

Robin did observe some mixed reactions.

"I have to say they loved it, but it took them a while to get comfortable with it. Face it, these were people whose lives were about to be changed. One of the fun things in all of that was seeing them happy and the family set for the next chapter of the book."

Overnight change, even for the good, roils the calmest waters and sinks a weak ship. Common sense and the strength of family bonds kept the Cousins boat on an even keel. While sailing through his own maelstrom, Robin looked out for his parents. He found satisfaction in their delight in Baridon House that tumultuous summer.

"When I won, I wasn't the only one whose life changed. That's something people tend to forget. It's not only you. It affects lots of people. It's jumping through the hoops and into the fire. It's a fairy tale dream and then the nightmare that comes with it. No one prepares you for either winning or losing. There is no finishing school where you learn to become an Olympic champion—and that includes the family."

Brian Klavano met Robin shortly after Fred and Jo moved to Baridon House.

"The thing that struck me about Robin is that when he became Olympic champion, he took care of his folks first and then himself."

Several years later, Jo took Brian on a drive.

"Let's turn up *this* road."

There was the modest house on Dingle Close.

"What a difference a day makes," Jo told Brian. One slip on a triple Salchow and none of the rest would have happened. She and Fred didn't take their good fortune for granted. Brian found that admirable.

"They were pillars of strength through all his struggles—and their struggles. Unbelievable sacrifices they made, total commitment, and do you know what? They didn't give him any more than they gave the other two. They never put him ahead because he might get farther."

Baridon House assuaged the inconvenience of celebrity. Heaps of mail arrived daily. At first Jo panicked, wanting to answer each letter immediately, but she and Fred had jobs outside the home.

Martin and Nick, despite full-time jobs of their own, pitched in and devised a triage process. They sorted the letters into categories: those with and without stamped, self-addressed envelopes; those that did or didn't request a photo. There were boxes all over the house. As much as a year later, the torrent continued unabated: on average, one hundred items per day. Nick realized they had made a mistake in thinking they could handle things themselves.

"Idealistically, we thought we could reply. Of course, we were totally besieged by the mountain of mail. I was only a small cog in the wheel, and I did what I could. My mum did the main part. We had a system that was basically *acknowledge* or *do not acknowledge* (for a congratulatory card or someone who hadn't left an address). If it was *do not acknowledge*, it went off to one side. I can't remember if Rob had one before, but certainly afterwards a massive fan club took off. The second category was those who wanted to join his fan club—which was, I suppose, about 40 per cent of the mail. Those had to be sent off to the fan club people in Blackpool. The third category was those who wanted a signed photograph.

"Some wonderful things were sent—dolls, pictures, school projects—so there was a fourth category for more than a cursory acknowledgment. In retrospect, we should have gotten secretarial help. You'd be halfway through, and the postman would arrive in his special delivery truck with the next lot."

Peculiar fan incidents occurred. Two Japanese girls turned up on Dingle Close. Learning that Robin had moved, they plopped onto the doorstep and began to cry. Neighbors phoned Fred and Jo, who invited the visitors to their new house and showed them Robin's scrapbooks. The girls departed happy, leaving Fred and Jo in puzzled disquietude. Brian recognized their challenge.

"You've sent your child off to training, and suddenly he's a celebrity. They enjoyed coming to shows and were supportive, always there, loving all the flowers and making sure they were shipped off to the hospitals afterwards. They took their role as an Olympic champion's parents very seriously and handled it well. You have to respect how hard that is."

The Worst Pro

It was in Biarritz, France, on Robin's twenty-third birthday, that he made a lasting impression on two new continuing characters in his life story. He stepped onto a small oval of tank ice, stroked around, did one big jump, and landed in the seats. Stephanie Andros and Brian Klavano looked at one other.

"I think we broke him."

As the artistic director/choreographer and the performance director of Holiday on Ice, Stephanie and Brian were in charge of the show's expensive new whiz kid. Although his first trick was more than their nerves could handle, before long he was one of their favorite people, and they were two of his.

Robin had gone first to Brian's company, Green Division, in rehearsal in Biarritz, surf capital of France. Brian's job was to work Robin into the show and acclimate him to the small, portable ice system. It was Stephanie's job to "shrink" the Olympic program for use as a cold spot.

The first day of rehearsal stuck in Robin's memory. It started with the wayward jump.

"I remember doing a huge Axel and landing on the other side of the header, *running* around the rubber, and jumping back on the other side as if nothing had happened.

"Then I had my birthday party. I remember getting drunk on champagne that they had backstage. Stephanie turned around to Brian and said, 'What are we going to do? We have to rehearse, and our star is drunk.' We weren't drunk, actually, but we'd been drinking, and Stephanie and I ended up having a whole conversation in Bs. Be bere balking bike bis ball bevening. It was Bephanie and Bobin."

Stephanie had twice met with Robin to discuss his role in the show. He wanted to play characters and skate with the ensemble. They next intersected in London and flew together to Biarritz, where Robin so impressively demonstrated the length of his Axel and his powers of enunciation.

Stephanie had a free hand.

"I know that Jo, Fred and even Carlo Fassi were all concerned as to how we would present Robin, what I'd do with him, because you can certainly do the wrong thing, and it was crucial when he had just become champion."

Her plan was to teach Robin the opening and finale; work him into Ted Shuffle's Silver Division show opening in Nice; and prepare him to rejoin Green Division when it reached Wembley in December. She oversaw his music, costumes, and choreography. He remembers her telling an adagio skater, desperation in her voice, "Teach him about makeup."

Robin thought, "Makeup?!" *That* was something new.

Whichever city was potentially the most lucrative was the one that Robin played. He spent extended periods in major cities. During his two seasons with the show, he rotated in and out of four concurrently touring companies. In all, he toured for thirty-six weeks, from August through March, with the occasional add-on.

Stephanie, who had worked with many stars, found Robin unique. First, he wasn't temperamental.

"I never had that with Robin. There were no clashes, no temperament, and I've had it with just about everybody else."

Second, she found him a quick study. If she made a suggestion, however elaborate, "He'd run it through, and he'd already remember it—and teaching him steps! There were numbers where he was required to skate with the chorus and the rest of the principals. I only had to run through it with him once, and he had it. He'd memorized it already. There are times that I've spent an entire day with a champion on maybe thirty-two bars of music—and they still didn't have it."

Third, he was willing to try anything.

"I've worked with a lot of champions, and Robin, to me, is the most versatile and certainly the most fun to work with. He doesn't wear horse blinkers. I've worked with Toller Cranston, Katarina Witt, and, going way back, with Olympic champions Trixi Schuba, Wolfgang Schwarz, and Sjoukje Dijkstra. They've all been good in their own right, but many of them balked at something I might suggest that they try to do. They'd say, 'Well, no. I have my image.' I used to tell them, 'Don't cut yourself off. You can still grow a lot more, even though you're an Olympic champion.'

"I didn't have to do any of that with Robin. If I said, 'Okay, Robin, we're going to put you in a big, fat, balloon-type costume and you're going to come out doing walkovers and back-flips,' he would say okay. Many people are afraid to ruin an image. This is because they don't have the talent, in my opinion."

Fred and Jo attended Robin's premier in Nice, a large city on the semitropical shores of the French Riviera, not far from Monaco. Carlo and Christa were there, too. Robin fell in his first-half Olympic number, trying to skate it perfectly—still, and forever, their student.

"I had a great time in the second half. I'd already fallen over. The shit had hit the fan. 'Now just go out and enjoy it,' Stephanie said. Between Katie and Geary and Atoy Wilson and Stephanie and Brian, I had the most wonderful time."

As a neophyte, Robin met new obstacles. Jumping through the hoops and into the fire took on a different twist. He had to reach an uneasy truce with his standards.

On the second day of rehearsals, Stephanie had told him, "You were the greatest amateur that ever lived, and now you're about to become the worst professional. It's two completely different worlds."

"That made it okay," Robin found, "because it was *so* different. The things I thought I was going to have difficulty with were easy, and the things I thought were going to be easy were the hardest. Skating under the lights, skating in a small, confined space—yes, it was difficult, but that wasn't where the real difficulty lay.

Performing what I wanted to do in the way I wanted to do it was the difficult thing, because I thought what I had to be was an Olympic champion thirteen shows a week. You end up trying to create what people already think you are, and that's brick-wall time. You're racing towards a brick wall going seventy miles an hour. You have to put the brakes on before you crash. You have to put it into a perspective that works for you.

"I spent the first three months on the tour agonizing over bad performances and stupid mistakes—until I realized that, although I was being announced as the Olympic champion, and I was doing a version of my Olympic long program, I could never in a million years try to repeat the euphoria that I had felt, and the performance that I had given, in Lake Placid."

Consistency was key. Robin learned to perform at 70 per cent technical output with 100 per cent enthusiasm.

"Then I could honestly say I had done a good job and know that I could turn that out on a daily basis with enough energy to be the same on a Saturday matinée middle show as I was on a Sunday afternoon second show as I would be on a Wednesday night. You always panic that one of those fifteen thousand people who came to see you didn't approve, didn't think you had done enough. You cannot please fifteen thousand people thirteen shows a week."

Brian and Stephanie helped Robin to understand that, but he still tried his best to please them all.

Robin's financial adviser, an Italian Carlo had recommended, suggested that, for tax reasons that Robin never understood, he should invest in a Monte Carlo condominium. He spent precious little time admiring his corner view of the Mediterranean.

"The only things I remember are the frogs in the hills. The most deafening noise—croaking all night! They started the minute the sun went down."

Brian and Robin became good friends during those heady days. While Princess Grace was alive, Monaco was cheery and bustling. Starring in Holiday on Ice gave one entrée to a succession of dinners, parties, and wine receptions, all in an atmosphere of lush tropical opulence: a lifestyle that neither Brian, the son of a Calgary veterinarian, nor Robin, the motor clerk's son, was accustomed to—but they were willing to get used to it.

Skating in Nice was nice work if you could get it: feasting on barbecues; tanning in the sunshine; winding along the corniche to Monte Carlo. It was a change from the daily training grind, although Robin was never comfortable *not* training. Only in recent years did it occur to him to wonder, "What am I training *for*?"

It was in Nice that Robin met an American couple, fellow principals Katie and Geary Baxter. Katie was a former pairs skater. Geary was a barrel-jumper whose act concluded with a leap through a burning hoop.

If Holiday on Ice was a family, Geary and Katie were two of Robin's favorite relatives. For years, they had lived out of suitcases.

Then, like many others, they had bought a trailer to haul from city to city. To establish a sense of permanence, they hung pictures and decorated for holidays. In Nice, the trailers stood in a row in a dry river bed dubbed "the sand pit." The skaters all lived like Gypsies, lounging in lawn chairs in the soft, fragrant Mediterranean night, laughing, talking, listening to music, and enjoying postshow barbecues featuring Geary's Buffalo wings.

The Baxter trailer became the hub of Robin's social life. For months on end, he camped on its foldout couch. His hosts found that hilarious. There he was, on his way to millionaire status, sleeping like a derelict on their sofa.

Robin loved to listen to Katie talk about the places she and Geary had traveled.

Katie remembers, "We'd get into talking about life, and ways of life, and spend many hours trying to unravel the world—why it was the way it was at that time. We'd all been around, so it was fun to delve into those things."

They went to Berlin before the wall fell. They rode on trains behind the Iron Curtain, thousands of passengers in dead silence. It was a different world from the one they had grown up in. Suddenly they were in countries at war. When bombs fell in Israel, they couldn't help wondering, "Why does the world have to be like this? We're just out doing a show, having fun, trying to make people happy."

Katie found her work's purpose in the wonderment on faces in the crowd.

"It gave you an uplift. You'd think, 'Oh my gosh, I can't do the thirteenth show this week.' Then you'd get out there and try as hard as ever, because you'd see some soul smiling back at you."

She couldn't help laughing about one idiosyncrasy of the Czechoslovakians. Before each show, the skaters emerged from their trailers and entered the rink through the back door "into the ugliest building with the ugliest dressing rooms in the ugliest pit you've ever seen." For this brief ritual, the Czechs dressed in Chanel suits and high heels. Of course, they immediately donned costumes and worked up a sweat. Then they climbed back into their cocktail suits to leave through the grubby rear exit. The public never saw them except on the ice. Who appreciated their efforts? The Americans wore blue jeans and sweatshirts, but the Czechs had their pride.

The personalities within the show fell into two groups: the doers, the fun-makers, the sightseers, the partyers; and the ones who did none of the above. Many of the none-of-the-aboves led unhappy, alienated lives, while the doers formed strong bonds. They were all ultimately strangers in a strange land. They worked like slaves, played hard, and laughed often.

Atoy Wilson saw stars come and go, stars who had been adored as amateurs.

"All of a sudden they came to Holiday on Ice, a United Nations from all different parts of the world. You'd go from palaces to bull rings. It was eclectic. Those young men and women came into the show as strangers to the whole little world. They had to say, 'Listen, I'm into this. There are sixty people who are all different varieties and characters, and they're not all the *crème de la crème* of skating. I have to deal with them, because that's my life. I have to travel with them. I have to eat with them. I have to sleep with them. All of it.' It's people like Robin, and people like Toller and Denise Biellmann, who had a definite aptitude for just hanging and having a great time."

Many of the highest achievers were down-to-earth. Their focus on attaining youthful goals had kept them from becoming full of themselves. When Lenel van den Berg heard that Robin was coming to his division, he thought, "Oh, well. You get these stars, and they don't remember people." Robin surprised him by picking up where he left off at Skate Safari.

Stephanie found Robin "a congenial, easy guy to get on with—as long as you're serious about your work. He doesn't tolerate someone who is either flaky or full of excuses. That's when he'll go a little cold, because he's a very hard worker himself."

He knew he was fortunate in his colleagues.

"I'm drawn to people who are passionate about life and about their jobs. I was lucky, inasmuch as some of the people who were in the show when I was at an influential point in my professional skating career were passionate people. They were proud of their jobs and proud of what they had to offer the show. I loved all that. A dream for me would have been to get as much applause at the end of my Olympic number as Katie got for doing spirals down the ice. There I was, working my ass off for four minutes. She did fifteen seconds, and they loved it."

Katie had seen Robin compete in Dortmund. She made a ritual of watching his adapted long program.

"We weren't allowed to, but I sneaked into the top

rows, close to the set, every night. I don't think I ever missed watching him skate, night after night. He was such a wonder to watch."

Katie was his partner in production numbers: classics, jazz, Dixieland, sultry ballads, and comedy. She played Marilyn Monroe to his Elvis Presley. With their matching strokes and good natural rhythm, they began practicing pairs routines. They put together a Neil Diamond number and auditioned it for company president Skee Goodhart.

Stephanie loved to watch them together.

"Katie is one of my favorite female skaters, and what a beautiful stroke *she* has. She did a lovely ballad, 'I've Got It Bad and That Ain't Good.' Atoy came out and did 'Ain't Misbehavin'.' That left Atoy and Katie together. Suddenly Robin came charging out. There was a little battle between Robin and Atoy. Atoy took off in a huff, and Robin skated. Then he and Katie skated together. They were marvelous. Katie was very talented as well. *She* didn't have horse blinkers on. It's a great feeling to get with kids like that on the ice. They want to do everything there is to do and have fun doing it."

Robin hopped from France to Switzerland to England, then back to France again. Halloween found him in Marseilles with Kirk Wyse.

"Robin went out and watched every show: the kiddy numbers, the production numbers, the opening. Already he was saying, 'I'm going to do a show someday.' He had a drive to produce, direct, and choreograph shows, and he tried to learn everything he could. Most of the other superstars we worked with were so above it. 'I'm here. I'll do my guest spot. I'll make my money. Don't bother me.'"

The Queen's Loo

In November, Robin put on his Olympic tie and went to Buckingham Palace to become an MBE (Ordinary Member of the Civil Division of the Order of the British Empire). It was one of the proudest moments of Fred and Jo's lives.

His only visual memories are of immense rooms and many columns, but the atmosphere was unforgettable.

"You didn't want to touch anything or move out of your spot. It was like a glorified doctor's office. You were shuffled from this room to that room until it was your turn to go to the *big* room. I guess there were probably a good couple of hundred people who were being honored. You wait in a rather large anteroom where you are instructed as to what you have to do when your time comes. Make sure that you're standing exactly on the line, so the Queen doesn't have to lean forward. If she puts her hand out, you shake it. If she speaks to you, you respond. It's all very formal.

"You start to panic a little bit. You think, 'She can't speak to everybody,' but I had, from what I remember, quite a lengthy conversation with her. My Olympic performance had been shown here live at something like three o'clock in the morning. What she said was—I remember the gist—'We're very proud of you and excited that it all worked out, but I have to say that we were not one of those who stayed up until three o'clock in the morning to watch. However, I do think I was the first one to my newspaper the following morning.'"

The day had a humorous twist. Jo and Fred had promised some friends to bring them a sample of Buckingham Palace toilet paper. Jo plunged into the loo, expecting elegance. Instead there was a wide, dark-brown wooden shelf with a toilet bowl in the center. It reminded her of the outhouses of her great grandmother's day.

"Here we were in these antiquated toilets. The toilet paper, which we thought would be very fine, was plain old garden variety government issue, as hard as you can get. There was no way I would bring that back to friends."

The Queen had met Robin on three previous occasions. One of those had also involved his mother and a loo, as Jo explained.

"He was asked to skate along with the other British champions of the time at the opening of the Gillingham ice rink. They already had quite a new toilet for disabled people, but because the Queen was going to be there with the Duke of Edinburgh, they had to redo it for her especially. I thought that was just terrible at the time. We got there in the morning, when the receptionist was going out to buy all new equipment: a nail brush, a flannel, and the very best soap you could buy, plus everything else which had to be absolutely new and untouched—as did the toilet.

"The conversation the night before with the owner of the rink was 'How do you ask the Queen if she wants to use the loo?' I said, 'Don't be silly. Her lady-in-waiting will have already ascertained where it is. You will not even know she's disappeared.' In any event, she didn't even use it—and guess who got to use it first."

A month after the MBE ceremony, Robin was a finalist in the BBC's Sports Personality of the Year viewers' poll. The winner was to be announced during a live telecast. In his excitement, Robin forgot Fred's birthday. He phoned on the way to the studios to apologize for not sending a card.

The two other finalists were runner Sebastian Coe and decathlete Daley Thompson. When the winner's feats were enumerated, Robin didn't recognize himself until the host referred to millions who had stayed awake until three in the morning. Robin was the second skater (after John Curry) to win the award. Fred and Jo, watching TV, toasted his victory with homemade wine.

Home at Wembley

The two-month stint at Wembley Arena was Robin's national homecoming. Since London was the only English venue on the schedule, people arrived by the busload from all corners of the country. The entire Cousins family attended the December 19 opening. As the Olympic rings flashed on the curtain and the ice, the crowd kept time to Robin's music and showered him with flowers. There were shows on Christmas Eve and Boxing Day, but Robin spent Christmas Day by a log fire in Bristol—the first time in three years.

Members of the Holiday on Ice entourage were invited to meet the Duchess of Gloucester. Betty Goodhart, Skee's wife, basked in that august company wearing a diamond with more carats than Bugs Bunny. Geary noticed that dye from the blue program had rubbed off on her fingers. He commented slyly, "It must be the cheap jewelry." Fred Cousins doubled up royally with laughter.

Atoy Wilson related the saga of Doris, the bag lady of Wembley.

"She was a stereotypical English eccentric, a person who probably was brilliant but had gone over the edge. She adored Robin. She stood there nightly in the cold.

Sometimes they let her in, just by the doorway. She had a high, unique voice, and you'd hear her get excited about Robin. 'Where *is* he? He hasn't come to see me, and I need to have him come and sign my autograph.' She asked for an autograph every day. The thing that was touching about it was his humanity towards that lady. I think one day he took her out for tea. She was a bona fide eccentric. Clinical. Might be in a hospital now. I thought, 'Wow, he really feels for people.'"

The Flip Side of Celebrity

One night Robin, Brian, and Katie headed into London to see *Pal Joey*. Robin, being typically frugal, suggested, "Let's take the tube."

"No, no. Let's take your car," said Brian, being typically sedentary. Robin owned a blue Jaguar, one of his few luxuries.

"No, we'll never find parking."

Brian was familiar with Robin's levels of tolerance.

"He doesn't like crowds in that regard. He doesn't deal well. If there isn't a parking space, he's not very patient. He's better off to ride public transit. By the time we got into town, we were running late, so we couldn't go out for a cool dinner at Peppermint Park. We ended up having to go into Burger King."

"I did not come all the way into London to go to Burger King," Brian protested.

"It'll do," Robin said, his Denver tastes coming back to haunt them.

The girl at the cash register started to take their order.

"What would you—?"

She looked up and froze. Robin Cousins was at her Burger King counter. The color drained from her face. The manager walked her away and took the order himself.

"You're just so aware. Everywhere he walked,

everybody was stopping and turning and nudging. You start to feel like a freak."

Katie and Brian thought it was hilarious, but Robin walked in those shoes every day.

"You forget who you are to others, because you are not any different, but you've changed instantaneously to everybody else around you. It was strange within the first six months or so, understanding that there were certain things I just could not do that I had taken for granted before."

One day, Robin noticed a woman following him in the grocery store.

"It is you, isn't it?" she asked.

"I don't know. That depends on who you think *you* is. Jack Nicholson, no. Robin Cousins, yes."

"What are you doing *here*?"

"I'm shopping."

"Don't you have it sent 'round?"

"No, I don't."

The woman left confused.

"Your lifestyle doesn't suddenly change. People just assume that it does. It's not what you are, it's how people perceive you that changes. The English tabloids have a picture of Sharon Stone shopping in jeans and a T-shirt. Well, why shouldn't she wear jeans, a T-shirt, and a base-ball cap? Why should she have to look like the Sharon Stone they expect to see in the movies? She didn't ask to be photographed. We are plebes like everyone else. That's all we are. I wouldn't want to see someone on the stage or screen and then come out and see the identical persona on the street.

"I liked to do the same things that I always did be-fore I won and continue to do so now. I have seen how megastars have to act, and the one thing I'm thankful for is that it was never that bad. I know what it's like to be bothered in restaurants when you're eating. People start talking to you, because they're so used to seeing you on television. You do find them following you, staring at you. You think, 'Is my fly open? Are my clothes on backwards?'

"Another thing that happens is that people will start talking about you. Because you can't hear them on television, they think you can't hear them on the street. It's nice that people still recognize me. I can't say that we all don't love it when it happens. If someone says, 'You must get bored signing autographs,' I answer, 'The only time I would get bored is if there weren't any to sign.'"

Occasionally, people have asked Robin, to his chagrin, "Who did you used to be? Didn't you used to be the ice skater?"

Robin was always patient with his fans, Brian found.

"Hours and hours of signing and posing and handing out pictures. He accepted the role incredibly well, whereas I've watched others fight it. There were times when he said, 'Can't I slip out the back door?' I'd say, 'No, there's a little girl down there in a wheelchair who's waited for forty-five minutes.' You knew darn well that he wouldn't have slipped out, but it's tedious. It's a job."

Stories of stalkers and emotionally-disturbed admirers abound in the skating milieu, as in other highly-visible substrata. Robin was lucky to have loyal, respectful fans, but he wasn't unfamiliar with the other kind.

"I have some die-hard fans who are wonderful, and I've had some fans who are frightening. There's no other word for it. Figure skating is far too accessible to its fans. At Landover, you have every Olympic and world champion in one hotel, and the fans are right there knocking on your door. I hate the idea that we have to be segregated, but unfortunately there are those people out there who do believe that you belong to them. If they are your fans, as much as they adore you, you owe them. That's a scary thought."

Robin was sometimes a soft target. In accepting the

role of Olympic champion, he had to learn to be guarded against his natural inclination to look only for the good in those around him.

Last Wishes

While fame and wealth offered opportunities to do good, there was a commensurate responsibility that exacted an emotional toll. At Wembley, Robin encountered a girl whose dying wish was to meet him. She arrived on a stretcher. After spending time with her, Robin went backstage and burst into tears.

Once, he received a letter from a woman with cancer who planned to attend his show. On the night, Nick went to find her.

"Robin says would you like to come backstage?"

The effort was almost too much for her. Robin gave her flowers and posed with her for photos. Her death not long afterwards deeply affected him. He sent flowers to her funeral.

It was humbling. How could Robin do enough, or be enough, to justify such longings?

There were happier cases. One fan, confined to her home by agoraphobia, an abnormal fear of crowds and public places, permanently mastered her fear in order to see Robin perform.

I Love You, Good-bye

During the last Wembley finale, Atoy vied with Robin for Katie's affections.

"It was tight choreography. I'm doing something with Katie. She's falling, but she falls into *his* arms. He lifts her up. I catch her. There's a point where Robin and I are nose to nose, eyes to eyes, hands on the hips, looking defiant, as Katie's goofing around. All of a sudden, Robin goes nose to nose and plants a big, wet kiss on my lips as if to say 'I love you' and 'good-bye.' I was absolutely mortified. I'm an African-American, and I probably turned *white*. We had a riot about that."

Paris

Robin closed in Wembley on a February Sunday and opened in Paris two days later with a different division. There was something magic about Paris and the Seine. London and the Thames just weren't the same. He walked the quais past Notre-Dame and explored the Latin Quarter, speaking bad conversational French: what he had learned at Henbury wasn't spoken on the streets. His facility for picking up accents made him authentic-sounding, if not grammatical.

The skaters parked their trailers in the Bois de Boulogne, too thick with *filles de joie* to be safe and inviting. Most of the cast rented apartments. Robin's was a short métro ride northwest of the Palais des Sports, an arena at the bottom of the fifteenth *arrondissement,* just above the Périphérique. They frequented the Alcazar and the Paradis Latin, striking up friendships with the dancers.

Not everyone was grateful to be in Paris. Robin found that cast members, especially Americans, were with Holiday on Ice either for two weeks or for twenty years. If the less hardy were in Switzerland without McDonald's or in Paris *sans* Wonder Bread, they wished to go home. Robin couldn't understand North American attitudes towards Europe.

"You have all these wonderful cheeses and fresh breads. What do you want Wonder Bread for? Why do you need McDonald's when you have a French bakery or a *charcuterie* with fresh meats? They didn't *get* Europe."

It was during the Paris run that Amanda Rayner, an English student doing a project on life behind the scenes, made her début in Robin's life. On three-performance days, the shows were sometimes shaved to save time. On one such day, Amanda interviewed Robin in his dressing room.

"He was in the usual jazz pants, a T-shirt, and a pair of dance shoes, chatting away. You always have the music coming in. Robin suddenly looked up. 'Oh, my God! I'm on in thirty seconds.' I was getting him down the stairs, dressing him as we went. I've never seen him put his boots on so fast. There was also the day that I managed to be part of his downfall. He asked me, 'Could you put my boots away?' I put the guards on instead of the toweling covers. The next day, when he went to put the boots on, the blades had rusted. *That* was a good moment."

King of the Back-Flip
When Robin became a professional skater, he gleefully burst the shackles of amateur restrictions. There was a world of movement waiting to be explored. As you might expect of a man who spent his childhood upside down, one of the things he wanted to try was the back-flip.

His opportunity came in the late spring of 1981, during the Holiday on Ice hiatus. He went to Santa Rosa, California, to appear in Charles Schulz's show Love Is Here at the Redwood Empire Ice Arena. Nick had taught Robin the basic form on land. The man who helped him put it on ice was Lloyd "Skippy" Baxter, the back-flip-on-ice pioneer (and Geary's uncle). Not only did Skippy invent the move; he arguably performed more than anyone else. That entitled him to spell the word as he liked, and he liked it hyphenated.

Skippy had been a U.S. novice and junior champion. In 1940, he won the senior men's silver medal and qualified for world and Olympic pairs competition as well. World War II forced the cancellation of both events that year (and for six to follow).

Skippy served as a ski trooper with the U.S. Army's Tenth Mountain Division, a volunteer unit that included twenty-eight professional ice skaters. After the war, he traveled the ice show circuit, skating in the Sonja Henie revues with his brother Meryl, Geary's father. Skippy was a straight man, while Meryl was part of an ice comedy team, the Three Rookies. During his sixteen years with the show, Skippy never missed a performance. He calculated that he launched 100,000 back-flips—and missed only three.

The first mistake occurred when Skippy's unit was about to ship out. Although he knew he wasn't ready for the leap of faith, he made the attempt and luckily wasn't hurt. The other misses came early in his performing days.

"I hadn't done the back-flip enough on that small stage to get it down cold. I landed on my shoulder, but I got up. I really didn't hurt myself."

That must have scared the spectators.

"Well, yes, and the orchestra, too. I almost fell into the pit. I think that's why I opened up."

Later the brothers ran their own rink in Santa Rosa. Eventually Charles Schulz (of "Peanuts" cartoon fame) offered to build a bigger rink if the brothers agreed to manage it. Meryl went on to other things, but Skippy stayed and continued to teach skating.

Near the end of the run of Love is Here, Robin asked Skippy to teach him the back-flip.

"If you really want to learn it, you have the physical ability, but you also have to have the mental ability."

It was a question of mind over matter. In the back-flip business, he who hesitates is lost—"dead meat," as Robin put it.

On Saturday between shows, Robin thought he was ready. Skippy didn't have his harness with him, so he tied together two bath towels. He and a skater from the show wrapped the towels around Robin's waist. Each held one end and skated alongside. If Robin failed to complete the full revolution, he would land softly on his feet, supported by the towels.

During the twenty or thirty minutes that they worked, Robin executed a dozen assisted back-flips.

"Maybe we ought to wait until tomorrow and start again," Skippy suggested.

"Couldn't we do some more now?"

"If you hurt yourself during the run of the show and Mr. Schulz finds out I was helping you, we'll *both* be in trouble."

Skippy bought a wide cartridge belt at an Army-Navy surplus store and looped a rope through each side. With that contrivance, they started fresh on Sunday. The ropes extended three or four feet out from Robin's sides. He was more comfortable with the extra maneuvering room.

"Well, Robin, I think you're ready to solo it," Skippy told him. They circled in tandem. In case something went wrong, Skippy wanted to be nearby. Twice Robin made the necessary rotation, if not with perfect form. Then Skippy left him on his own, instructing him not to try the back-flip if he had reservations. Robin circled the rink twice but felt uneasy. Skippy gave him a pep talk.

"Okay, I think I'm set."

"By gosh, he went around and he did it," Skippy reported. "Then he did two more."

He told Robin, "Great! When you get on a large sheet of ice, you can make it bigger and better. Don't put it off for a week or two. You may lose the rhythm."

Skippy taught the back-flip to a number of other skaters. A few, like Scott Hamilton, began at Santa Rosa and caught on elsewhere. Others weren't "hungry" enough to learn it, or feared injury.

Most skaters assumed a tuck during rotation. According to Skippy, Robin's full layout was more difficult.

"You have to get higher, and you have to have more speed, because your rotation is slower."

Werner Groebli, Mr. Frick of the ice comedy team Frick and Frack, often went to the Center Theater to watch Skippy perform. His back-flip was the best, according to Groebli, but Robin's was second to the master's. Their secret, in his opinion: the long glide out.

Skippy celebrated his seventieth birthday with a back-flip. He hasn't done one since.

"Not on purpose!"

The back-flip that rang in Robin's second New Year at Wembley was less suave than usual. Overcompensating for New Year's Eve indiscretions, he added an extra oomph and wiped out—the first and only time. Backstage the word flew from one dressing room to another. Robin fell on the back-flip! Everyone feared he had landed on his head. Luckily, he had fallen on a less sensitive anatomical feature. His tailbone still hurts when he thinks about it.

"I do remember yelling some kind of expletive. Holiday on Ice was probably more concerned about an expletive coming out of my mouth than about me falling out of a back-flip."

Michael   Crawford

During the second-season Wembley run, Michael Crawford, star of *Barnum*, arranged for Robin, Brian, and Kirk to see the show from house seats. Arriving late, they found the inside doors closed.

"Oh, well," they thought, "we'll have to wait for intermission."

An usher approached deferentially.

"We were waiting for you, Mr. Cousins."

He led them to their seats. Then the show began. Kirk and Brian's jaws dropped wide open. After the performance, Crawford invited them to his dressing room. It was decorated from floor to ceiling as a circus tent.

Years later, at *Phantom of the Opera* in Los Angeles, Robin invited Crawford and his daughters for a getaway weekend on Lake Arrowhead. Showing them the Blue Jay rink, he realized that Joanna Ng's repertoire included "The Music of the Night."

"Quick, Joanna, do it," he urged. It was a hit.

Elton   John

Elton John's associates approached Robin about skating in a video spinoff of the album *21 at 33*. Robin flew to Nice for a breakfast meeting at the Negresco Hotel. There was Elton, in shorts and a T-shirt, in his suite overlooking the Promenade des Anglais. Over scrambled eggs and toast, they discussed his idea: Robin would skate to "White Lady White Powder," dressed in scarlet on a pure-white set.

"To this day—which is funny, because I'm an Elton John fan—I have not heard the song. The album did not spawn a lot of hits, and hence there were not a lot of videos made, so that never happened, which was a shame.

"I've always admired both his and Bernie Taupin's work. The music he writes is so poetically right for skating. Contrary to what people believe, you cannot skate to just *any* kind of music. There are certain classical, modern, and rock 'n' roll composers who write music that is all conducive to skating. He is one of those."

The Best Man

Robin's contract with Holiday on Ice expired in the spring of 1982, when he left to pursue his own projects. In the meantime, there was family business to attend to. Robin played several pivotal roles in Nick and Helen's wedding, not least of which was designer of the bridal gown.

Helen, with her long arms and back, had tried many ill-fitting dresses. Robin suggested a dressmaker he knew, and the three formed a partnership. Through give and take, they agreed to the details: pin tucks down the front, a bow in the back, a combination of overdress and under-skirt, a stand-up collar. In stages, Helen whittled down the massive theatrical collar in Robin's drawings to something less reminiscent of Snow White. The only difference be-tween what he drew and what she wore was that the final version was softer and less dramatic.

Helen was from Belfast. As Nick said, "I had always assumed that Rob would be best man at my wedding. There were lots of factors that contributed to the fact that we were married in London, but one of them was that it would have been very hard to get Rob to Northern Ireland at that time. It was difficult terrain because of terrorism."

The wedding took place in the Dulwich chapel.

As best man, Nick recalled, Robin was in a position he didn't relish.

"Although he's a gifted and articulate responder to questions, I don't think he particularly enjoys speech-making, but he was extremely amusing. It was a fun wed-ding, and he was instrumental in that."

It appealed to Robin's love of family and his sense of theatre. Helen's dress was not his final foray into nuptial *haute couture.*

6. The New York Years: 1982-86

After his second season with Holiday on Ice, Robin bought a New York condominium at 70 East Tenth Street, a *pied à terre* in the land of skating opportunity. As Americanized as he was, he was comfortable there. Moreover, as Brian Klavano explained, "I can't remember what he paid for the place, but if it was a quarter-of-a-million-dollar condo, in England that quarter of a million dollars would have purchased maybe a little two-bedroom apartment, whereas in New York it got him a palatial Broadway villa. It was one of his dreams, theatre and entertainment being in his veins. We fantasized that we would get a show mounted on Broadway."

Meanwhile, a different opportunity arose.

Gloria Ciaccio was Radio City Music Hall's public relations director. One December day, she received a visitor.

"Hi. I'm Robin Cousins. I'm going to be starring in a show at the Music Hall called Ice. If you want me to do publicity for the show, if there are interviews that need to be arranged, here's my home phone number. Please feel free to call me."

Gloria was taken aback. Most stars were "really bitchy."

Robin was on the road when Gloria needed publicity shots for the posters to fill the show windows along Fiftieth and Fifty-first streets. He called his building superintendent and had her let into his apartment. While he gave her instructions over the phone, she rifled through his drawers.

In January, Gloria got to know Robin even better. Everyone involved with Ice was summoned to rehearsals at the Olympic Center in Lake Placid. The year before, Gloria had toured the United States with Radio City's fiftieth anniversary show. She was used to jumbo jets. The Lake Placid trip consisted of two short hops on planes slightly larger than the Wright brothers'.

Gloria left the first flight green around the gills and plopped into one of the plastic seats that stood back-to-back in a tiny terminal in the hinterlands. She dropped her luggage and publicity materials onto the next seat and went to find chicken soup and saltines. In sitting back down, she knocked a window card onto the floor. When the man behind her turned around to discover the cause of the thump, he noticed a poster labeled "Robin Cousins."

"Oh, hello," he said to Gloria.

"Hi."

"Do you remember me? I remember you. You're the publicity officer."

"Yeah, I am, and you're Robin, right?"

After flying all night from London, Robin wasn't

getting the reaction he expected.

"What's wrong?"

"The plane that I was on was so small—"

Just then, the clerk asked for their tickets.

"Why don't you give me your ticket, and I'll go check us in?"

Gloria stated her intention to handle the matter herself. She wanted to be assured of an aisle seat.

"No, no," Robin insisted. "Give me your ticket. You just eat your soup and crackers. I've been to Lake Placid before, and I'm used to this."

"No. I'm nuts about getting an aisle seat."

"Look, woman, give me your f—ing ticket!"

When Robin returned from the counter, there was a checkmark on Gloria's ticket.

"I wanted an aisle seat."

"Mmm-hmm."

"How big is this plane?"

"Well, *everything's* an aisle seat."

With that, they climbed aboard the eight-seater.

"You have two choices. Either hold my hand—and I realize I don't know you well—or take a look at these nails. They could be permanent fixtures in your knee."

"No, no, no. I've had knee surgery."

As Gloria's hands grew clammier with each air pocket, Robin invented songs to distract her. Each time the airplane shuddered, he launched into a chorus of "Stairway to Heaven," "It Ain't Got That Swing if You Don't Got a Wing," or "Don't Let a Plane Go Down on Me."

Just before they reached Lake Placid, he thought of another diversionary tactic. The tiny terminal at the end of a driveway pretentiously labeled "Airport Road" was a house with fifties-style art deco doors and three steps descending to the runway. He could picture producer Bob Shipstad's expectant face in the door's round window.

"Let's give Bob Shipstad a real scare. You take my

skate bag and all your stuff. I'll just carry the window cards. I'll put my arm around your shoulder, and I'll limp. We'll see how fast we can see the whites of Bob's eyes. Then we'll see if he touches any of the stairs on the way out."

Unbeknownst to Robin, two male principals in *Ice* had already been injured. Robin and Gloria were the last ones off the plane. They could see Shipstad's eyes peering out. As Robin limped across the runway, the door flew open. The producer's feet barely touched the ground. He arrived, stammering, before them.

"What, what—"

Robin burst out laughing.

"Fooled you, didn't I?"

Shipstad was livid.

"I chilled some wine for you. I had steaks for dinner. Forget it. I'm dropping you two off at McDonald's."

When the rehearsal period ended, the company was bussed to New York. Robin immediately threw a cast party. Forty skaters trooped through his wide glass front door and across the chandeliered lobby under the stern gaze of uniformed doormen. (One of the doormen is still there and remembers the colorful young tenant and his friends.)

Robin shared top billing with Toller Cranston and Peggy Fleming. Ice was a high-quality production with a live symphony orchestra, one of the best ensembles in history, choreography by Sarah Kawahara, and lavish sets. The most lavish of all was the finale set. The stars were pushed onto the stage, standing in skates on white grand pianos. (During the dress rehearsal, Robin fell off.)

Next came an ensemble number.

"Sarah Kawahara's choreography is precise to Sarah. I got it. Peggy sort of had it. Toller wasn't even close. He was never going to *be* close, so he made things up. I laugh when I see the tape. He's just bopping around in his own world. It's fabulous."

Robin and Toller then vanished momentarily.

"I think Toller would concur that the finale entrances he and I had would be hard to top in any show. The Rockette staircases had been made into plastic ramps, so after we'd done the number on the ice, we both had to race up and around to the staircases. I slid down one, came around the corner, and back-flipped. Toller zoomed down the other, swung around, and did a back spiral. Peggy stayed serenely on the ice."

It was a tossup which was the more dramatic: Robin's full layout back-flip or Toller's excruciatingly-extended back spiral.

Toller skated brilliantly in Ice—thanks to Robin, he claims.

"Robin and I had great camaraderie. He had his third of the show and I had my third. I quivered and quaked before the curtain. In the opening number, he had to do an upbeat thing, and I had to do a classical thing. I listened for his applause to see if he landed his jumps, which always galvanized me into doing that myself. If he went down, I was going to go down, too.

"Yet my experience in Ice and his experience in Ice could have been Mars and Pluto. I never saw him, and he never saw me. I was doing my little thing, and he was doing his little thing. They were completely autonomous. I was never in the same orbit, yet the circles overlapped occasionally, and overlapped with respect, love, and friendship."

The Blizzard

The weatherman predicted six inches of snow for Friday of the production's maiden week. When Robin stepped outside between shows, the weather was cold and wet but not threatening. By the interval of the second show, snow was falling. At the final curtain, the city was under a thick, white blanket. Loudspeakers in the streets blared warnings. All the taxis had vanished by the time Jo and Fred, visiting from England, tried to leave the theatre. They slept in Toller's dressing room (his boast that his was the best may have clinched the decision) while their son strode home, engulfed in swirling snowflakes, from Fiftieth Street to Tenth, forty blocks. Toller walked to his room at the Warwick Hotel.

Dozens of people stranded by the storm spent the night at Radio City, most on mattresses in the basement. In the morning, Fred and Jo encountered an unusual cabby.

"He was making his homeward journey, picking up anyone who wanted to go on the main road. He filled his taxi up to the brim and overflowing. I'm sure we gave him a tip, but there was no payment asked. I ruined my lovely boots, and Fred ruined his lovely shoes. I had never seen such snow. The clearing people had gone down the center of the road and whooshed the snow either side, so all the cars which had been left there to be picked up later couldn't be. They were great mounds of snow that looked like cars."

For two days, the blizzard pelted the Eastern Seaboard. Wire service reports called it the most ferocious in forty years, with its fifty-mile-per-hour winds, accumulations of one to three feet, and freak episodes of thunder and lightning.

The Blizzard of 1983 killed off business. Ice didn't extend. New York shows build by word of mouth. By the time everyone was talking about Ice, it was due to close.

The reviews were some consolation. The *New York Times* proclaimed, "Miss Fleming has wondrous grace. Mr. Cousins is a fantastic leaper, who finally overwhelms one by an incredible back somersault. Mr. Cranston is as skilled as a ballet star, with a lithe, catlike facility that is coupled to a passionate personality. . . . [Ice] has all the sharpness of a new blade, clean and tingling and enjoyable."

Peggy's Practical Jokes

Robin loved what Ice offered: the size, scope, and atmosphere of Radio City; a live symphony; and, not least, the practical jokes he shared with his costar.

In the spring of 1980, he had débuted professionally with Peggy Fleming in "The Big Show" for NBC. In awe of her lofty stature, he didn't expect her to possess a sense of humor. During Ice, he learned that she did, and it matched his own off-color wit.

"It makes me laugh just thinking about it. We had all sorts of things going on during that show. It was Peggy who started it. She probably wishes now that she hadn't."

They skated a romantic duet in Peggy's Currier & Ives vignette. One night she had a mischievous idea.

"Peggy batted her eyelids at me, and she'd written 'Eat me!' on them, one word on each eyelid, in eyebrow pencil."

The contest had begun. The challenge was to keep the pranks secret from the audience. Like so many labor pains, they increased in frequency and intensity. Peggy arrived on the darkened stage in a sleigh. When the lights went up, there she sat like a demure Victorian lady in a bonnet and fur-trimmed coat. The sleigh proved the ideal vehicle for jokes. Once, Robin left cheese in it overnight. Another time, it was fish. He and some friends cut up pornographic magazines and decorated the interior with naked men.

"The lights came up and Peggy *screamed*—in delight, I think—and then had to proceed to be terribly regal, not able to cast her eyes in certain directions."

Robin's dresser and Gloria padded the bustline of Peggy's Victorian coat. She made a quick change and rushed onto the stage as the realization dawned that her chest had expanded to sixty-eight inches triple D.

"The padding of the coat was one of his most excellent jokes. There was nothing I could do about it. The dresser just wrapped the coat around me, and off I went. I thought, 'Oh, I can't even see my skates.'"

The *pièce de résistance* was Robin's final prank.

"Peggy had always said that she loved the idea of a live orchestra. She'd always wished she could play an instrument. At the end, having heard Peggy say I don't know how many times that she wanted to play an instrument—I couldn't do it, but one of the kids in the show went to a sex shop and bought a rather phallic black vibrator which we put into the sled for the last performance. The caption I wrote for it was, 'Here, Peggy. You keep talking about playing instruments. Try this for a mouth organ.'"

Determined to win the competition, Peggy balanced a bucket of flour and confetti over Robin's dressing-room door. He opened the door and was buried in an avalanche of pastel-colored dots and fine white powder.

"It made quite a mess," Peggy crowed, "but I didn't have to clean it up. I got the first laugh and the last."

When the company disbanded, Toller told Gloria, "Being in the Ice performing company has been like going to summer camp. I'm kind of sad to see us all leave."

The pranks have continued on a limited basis. Peggy attended Robin's fortieth birthday party wearing a molded-plastic naked *derrière*.

With a View of Broadway
Three months after Ice closed, Brian Klavano took up residence in the guest suite at 70 East Tenth Street. He had a bed, a hard foam sofa bed, and a desk that he bought at a street sale for ten dollars. The desk wouldn't fit through the door, so he paid some enterprising Puerto Rican youths to dismantle it.

"The building was a whole city block, and we were the only people under the age of—dead. It was the building where Leon Klinghoffer lived, the man in the wheelchair who was killed on the Italian cruise ship the Achille Lauro.

Robin came home one day from a trip, and the place was surrounded by police cars and press. It was just bizarre. So it was a building of some repute—but a nice location, right on Broadway and Tenth Street."

Housed in a tall, light-grey building, the apartment had an unusual floor plan. Each room jutted farther out than the last in a staggered arrangement that provided corner windows in most rooms.

"I used to look out at Grace Church. There were soap opera weddings, lots of weddings there. It was quite a pretty little church."

Robin was lucky to have a view of the airy Gothic Revival jewel. His fourth-floor windows were exactly the right height: low enough to look out onto the treetops yet high enough for a panorama that included the church, a clock tower, and the Chrysler and Empire State Buildings, bathed in colored spotlights that changed with the season.

The living room was off the foyer, with huge windows on two walls. The dining room jutted out from the living room, with a similar window configuration. Robin treated the two rooms as one, rearranging the furniture to suit the circumstances.

Then came a small kitchen. Brian's room, with private bath, protruded beyond it. (As Robin said, "He had to be near the kitchen; that was where the food was.") Brian placed his desk in the corner and enjoyed a diagonal view of Broadway.

The last suite was Robin's, in a soothing chocolate-burgundy, with a wall of windows above the Great White Way. From their lofty vantage point, the two young optimists looked out onto their future.

Toller once remarked that Robin's one flaw was a terrible color sense. The earth tones that Robin favors are as dull as dirt to the Canadian *artiste*.

The apartment was professionally decorated. Off-white walls and window treatments set off light-cinnamon carpeting and ceilings. Willowy stylized peacocks adorned the two beige, taupe, cinnamon, and charcoal couches. Behind the larger of the two was a pyramid of elongated Japanese nature prints. Glass and chrome tables, wicker-backed cinnamon velvet chairs, exotic plants, and old skating posters rounded out the décor of the central living area. Robin's own artwork decorated the bedrooms: highly detailed sequined birds and peacocks, executed in Holiday on Ice dressing rooms.

Jo and Fred have a fire screen that began as a doodle. Robin worked between shows until it became a giant embroidered peacock whose structure and proportions reveal an analytical mind and fastidious attention to detail.

According to Nick, "If Rob has a weakness, it *is* his fastidious attention to detail, which sometimes can border on the paranoiac. The peacocks, the fire screen, are not simple pieces. They involve intricate lines, lots of lines on the page. His choreography is always anything but simple in production, but in his own conceptualizing, I think there is that simple line and form."

Celine McDonald was intrigued by Robin's artwork.

"It all came very naturally. He would sit down at the

dining room table and start doodling and doing figures. He was collecting a lot of skating posters at the time, and I think that inspired him. He has a talented eye."

Robin's apartment became the entertainment center and nurturing hearth for a close-knit group of friends. Vincent Cippola, a writer, and Celine McDonald, a nurse turned photographer/painter, were a young married pair who had struck up a friendship with Robin without knowing he was an ice skater—let alone that he was any good at it. Robin liked that about them. On Thursday nights, Gloria, Celine, Vin, and Brian gathered with him for dinner and "Dynasty," making sport of the show's bad dialogue and excessive wardrobes.

"It was just fascinating," Robin found. "Very American. I'd never seen anything like it."

Gloria wasn't enamored of the menu. Usually Brian made his special corn-laced spaghetti or Robin whipped up pineapple chicken, a recipe acquired from the Holiday on Ice chef. The alternative was Lean Cuisine.

When "Dynasty" wasn't on, there was music. Sometimes Robin got inspired by whatever was blaring through the stereo. He pushed the furniture aside and performed impromptu choreography while his friends contributed opinions.

Robin invited Trish Bernays to visit New York. She was amused to find that he had copied a number of details from her London flat.

"His home was charming, in the middle of Greenwich Village: a proper apartment complex with two or three uniformed doormen. We all looked like tramps going in and out. I don't know what they all thought. It was quite a drab lot of rich people and then young Robin with his gang of weird, artistic-looking friends.

His taste was quite fun, not boring—totally different from his mum's. I don't know where it came from. He liked unusual things."

Amanda Rayner also turned up in New York. Robin and Brian wouldn't let her pay for anything, so she cooked them a proper roast beef dinner. Her Yorkshire pudding was slow to rise. Robin opened the oven door suspiciously.

"You call that Yorkshire pudding? My mother will be ashamed of you."

Before it was done, the pudding rose so high that it bore the imprint of the upper oven rack. Amanda called that evening "the kind that you want to wrap up, put in a box, and take out now and then" to enjoy all over again.

Amanda accompanied Robin to Tiffany's to inquire about replating his Olympic medal. Frequent handling had worn off the gold.

"He walked in in his oldest jeans and his tatty old T-shirt. I remember the lady at Tiffany's giving us a filthy look, trying to work out why he had that medal. They thought he had pinched it."

"Do you have it with you?" the clerks inquired.

"No."

"Well, why don't you just post it to us?"

Robin left and never heard from Tiffany's again.

There were two special closets in the apartment, one for costumes and the other for music. The large walk-in closet off the entrance foyer contained records, cassettes, and tapes by the thousands, alphabetized within categories: Broadway, West End, soundtracks, compilations, vocal, pop, rock, and classical. Robin often returned from London with an extra bag full of European releases.

He was no less compulsive in New York. According to Brian, "If he vanished for an entire day, chances are he was at Tower Records."

Brian sometimes arrived home to find the apartment pitch black except for the light in the music closet. He'd peer in, and there would be Robin in a headset, cutting music. The speakers were outside in the living room. Robin sometimes banged on Brian's door at three o'clock in the morning.

"You have to come out here and listen to this. I've got it. This is the perfect piece."

Robin loved New York for its cultural opportunities. He studied films and live theatre: lighting, set design, sound, music. He analyzed what worked and what didn't. That was his sponge theory at work: soak up ideas. They'll be useful when you least expect. He viewed the apartment as a base of operations for his expanding professional career. Although he had an active social life, it wasn't one that admitted permanent attachments.

"New York was very much a transition period. It wasn't somewhere that I thought I was going to be forever. It was a place to be for the time, doing what I wanted to do, where it all worked. I could get where I needed to. It was a central place for the rest of the world, as it were, at that point."

New York, in Robin's memory, consisted of training, traveling, and sitting in the apartment. Brian Klavano recalled a more colorful epoch.

"All he liked to do was bound around Manhattan."

"There's a great little place up on Thirty-third," Robin typically announced.

"Let's take a cab."

"No, come on."

Walking with Robin was just like walking with a sprinter.

Brian called the New York years "the most decadent, wonderful phase. We were working towards that Broadway goal, so we had a press agent on retainer. We had producers trying to get a show going. Robin was invited to every single Broadway show, movie opening, little off-Broadway opening—a lot of which came with the limousine and the party afterwards, because he was a star. People wanted him at their openings as much as he wanted to go."

If Robin expected to be out of town, Brian responded, "Mr. Cousins regrets that he is unable to attend, but Mr. Klavano shall represent him. Please have the car there promptly at seven."

"It was a hoot," Brian laughed.

The ingenuous youth from a farm in western Canada was living in a realm that had previously been the stuff of dreams. He and the erstwhile boy from Bristol found themselves at trendy night spots watching Jack Nicholson fall off bar stools.

They decorated a charity Christmas tree, bough to bough with Elizabeth Taylor's family. With its clear glass icicles made by a prop shop, Robin's tree raised almost as much as Taylor's.

Robin liked Christmas. He had managed to hold on to his childlike spontaneity and infectious sense of wonder. They were among his most engaging qualities—and perhaps the impetus for much of his creativity. He was a frequent featured skater at the ceremonial lighting of the tree at Rockefeller Center.

In 1985, Lily Tomlin was the celebrity hostess, sitting in an oversize rocking chair in the persona of Edith Ann, her precocious, bratty five-year-old character. The rehearsal was a disaster. Whenever Lily heard feedback, she brought the proceedings to a screeching halt.

The show went without a hitch. Dressed in red pants and a white jacket, Robin performed to Bruce Springsteen's "Santa Claus is Coming to Town," then glided over to kiss the hostess. After the Rockettes, the skaters, and the choral groups performed, Edith Ann announced, "The show's over. Now I'm going for a ride on Robin's back."

The sixty-five-foot spruce in Rockefeller Center is among the most famous in the world. By decree of the gods, rain, sleet, or snow accompanies its lighting. That was the case the next time Robin performed.

The Manhattan skies dumped rain by the bucketful.

The Rockettes danced on a wooden platform in front of the gilded Prometheus statue. Water splattered everywhere—like *Singin' in the Rain.* After skating through an inch of water, Robin joined Liza Minnelli on a sopping bench. For some reason, they started laughing like teenagers.

"It was probably the fact that everybody was panicking about the show—except the people who were in the show. Because of the rain, we hadn't gotten to finish the dress rehearsal. I thought, 'Either I fall down or I stand up. No rehearsal is going to change that.'"

Nine months after Vanessa Williams won the 1984 Miss America title, her nude photograph appeared in *Penthouse* magazine. Stripping her of the crown and sash added fuel to the fire of celebrity.

One evening, Robin and Brian attended an opening-night party at Limelight, a fashionable disco. They were standing by the bar when Vanessa entered the room. Everybody rushed to her side, gushing. Robin and Brian stayed where they were, telling each other, "Oh, there's Vanessa Williams." They were careful not to let their excitement show. Then *she* spotted *them.*

They could see her saying, "Oh! Is that Robin Cousins?" She parted the room and went straight for him. It was her turn to gush while the paparazzi fluttered and flashed. Robin was completely taken aback that Williams knew who he was. He had forgotten that television put him in *everybody's* home. He would never have approached her, yet it was fun when she took the initiative. A framed photo taken that night is one of his favorite New York souvenirs.

Robin enjoyed the bouts of celebrity, but not without mixed feelings—an ambivalence characteristic of fundamentally reserved people who achieve fame. He enjoyed moving about in public unnoticed, dressed in jeans and a T-shirt, yet was flattered to be recognized.

"I always find it strange. It's nice that people know who you are, but I guess you never see yourself the way you see other people."

One day he headed towards the door, bound for a seminar in Colorado. Fixing Gloria with a melodramatic look, he delivered his exit line with British grandiloquence: "I must go be *Olympian*."

Acting "Olympian" was a suit he put on for special occasions. He normally wore something more casual.

The Longest Pro Skate

Between March 1982 and early 1985, Robin competed in Pro Skate, a series similar in some respects to the pro tennis and golf circuits.

"If Pro Skate were around now, the amateur skating world would be shivering in its boots."

Elva Oglanby was its executive director. Her partner David Spungen and promoters Steve Leber and Michael Cohl were also involved in production and development. Elva invented Pro Skate as a vehicle for John Curry's exhibitions. While inspired by John, Pro Skate was made for Robin. During one long streak, he won everything in sight from New York to Tokyo to Sapporo and back again.

"That was an intensive period," said American competitor Allen Schramm. "A lot of skaters had a lot of work."

The greatest virtue of Pro Skate was its judging system. The panel included experts from the skating, theatre, dance, and music worlds who evaluated aspects of technique, the use of music, choreography, artistic impression, and overall performance. The average score of ten "public judges" weighed in as the ninth mark. Skaters generally felt that created fair and balanced judging. Because each judge focused on his own area of expertise, critical judgments were based on knowledge and experience. The overall result didn't favor one dimension over another.

One particular episode amused Toller Cranston.

"Robin and I participated in what was to become, historically, the longest skating show in the world. There wasn't a single professional alive who wasn't in that competition. It started at four o'clock. As the early crowd was stampeding out the door, the late arrivers were coming in at seven and eight o'clock. I never did find out how long it lasted. I left in the middle and was on the plane while it was still going on.

"Elva Oglanby had created the skater-of-the-I-don't-know-what award, and John Curry, who was being managed by her at the time, was the recipient of this self-created award.[12] John went out on the ice and announced to the public that he was dedicating his award to Elva for all her kindness and help. Robin and I collapsed laughing. We said, 'Just you wait, 'enry 'iggins. Just you wait.' We knew it was only a matter of time."

"I don't know about collapsed laughing," Robin countered, "although we probably did, I have to say, and I'm just too embarrassed to admit it."

Toller's mirth was gallows humor. His own dealings with his one-time companion had left him in high dudgeon (and Toller in high dudgeon is glorious to behold). In *Zero Tollerance*, he portrayed himself and Elva as a pair of marauding evil twins.

Just before John Curry's death, Toller dryly quipped to John's brother, "I do not regret losing the Olympic Games to John Curry. I do regret meeting Elva Oglanby."

Evelyn Kramer

Robin trained at Sky Rink, an Olympic-size ice surface on the sixteenth floor of an office building at 450 West Thirty-third Street between Ninth and Tenth Avenues. It was there, on the only indoor rink in Manhattan, that he first worked with Evelyn Kramer, who taught a gifted youngster, Kyoko Ina.[13]

One day Kyoko and Robin practiced on the same ice. Evelyn and Robin fell into conversation. She already felt a connection to him. Carlo Fassi had visited her on his way to Lake Placid.

"Can you imagine? You're going to do it again," she

---

[12]Not to be confused with the American Skating World Professional Skater of the Year award, first presented at Pro Skate and later at Landover.
[13]Kyoko, with Jason Dungjen, was the 1997 U.S. pairs champion.

had told Carlo. "You're going to have another Olympic champion."

"I don't know," Carlo had said in a moment of acute honesty. "I'm not so sure."

"I know you will," Evelyn had assured him.

Robin was the most magnificent skater she had ever seen. Her faith in his ability was absolute.

Some time after their first conversation, Robin phoned Evelyn to ask her to work with him on competition programs. She possessed a rare virtue: the willingness to offer criticism. Evelyn was one of the first coaches to work with a top-level professional. Nowadays the arrangement is commonplace. Then, coaches were for amateurs. Evelyn was careful to stay in the background.

Her approach with Robin was entirely different from her approach to training amateurs. She never attempted to advise him on technique. She helped him with strategy, scouted the judges, served as a critical pair of eyes, and helped him avoid pressure by establishing a competition routine.

Working with Robin changed Evelyn's life. Other professionals flocked to her door. Robin was both the first and the best, in her opinion.

"Robin is a rare bird, and the more distant I get from him, the more I deal with other professionals, the more fabulous he becomes to me. He becomes more and more of a champion. He's more special than anybody I've ever worked with, in every single way. He does not make things difficult for himself. He doesn't go through the same traumas that anybody else goes through—and I know them all now, how intense they get. I don't have the same relationship with Scott Hamilton, but I think both of them are grand champions. Both of them are Olympians in a sense that's higher than any medal."

As Toller saw it, "What happened was that both Robin and Scott accomplished one of the secrets of life: they grew into the people they were destined to become. Robin, and Scott, too—this, to me, is extremely important—had such an understanding of self and the vocabulary and style that they worked with that they became grand masters."

What set Robin apart, in Evelyn's book, was his infectious enthusiasm.

"He can make anything work. He believes in what his work is, and therefore you believe it. Now he does this crazy stage stuff. He gets all excited about this and that. After a while, you can get tired—but *he* doesn't."

Toe Shoes or Blades?

Katherine Healy was a dance and skating prodigy. Her coach, Glyn Watts, introduced her to Robin at a Superskates show at Madison Square Garden. When she was eleven, Robin appeared at Sky Rink. The two went to the stereo at the same time.

"He's never, ever going to remember me," she told herself, her heart pounding—but he did.

Ever the ballerina, Katherine practiced what she did best: layback spins and luxurious spirals—fluid arabesques. She wasn't as enthusiastic about jumps, particularly double Lutzes. One day when she was twelve, Robin scolded her.

"*Why* aren't you practicing your double Lutz?"

She stared at him, unable to summon an answer.

When Robin noticed Katherine's sit-spin form, he "hit the ceiling."

"If he was at the rink, it seemed that he always made everybody want to practice harder and skate better. Just that he was so good made everybody else on the session work harder."

Katherine had skated at Sky Rink since the age of two years and eight months. Although she had her own coach, everyone at the rink pitched in. Evelyn helped. Robin helped. In extreme situations, "They'd get on my case together.

"I needed the other kind of help. Most people need help with line; I was exactly the opposite. I had my line and my spirals down pat, but I'd be having trouble with double flips—things that most skaters, especially now, can do without thinking about it."

She was surprised that Robin took an interest in her, since it was well known that she was John Curry's protégée. At Pro Skate at Madison Square Garden in 1982, Katherine, John, and Peggy Fleming were pitted against Robin and Dorothy Hamill. At thirteen, Katherine was un-accustomed to skating in a spotlight. When she took the ice, the lights went out, leaving a follow spot. She fell twice.

"I went out and blew it, basically."

"I'm sorry," she apologized to John.

"No. It wasn't right, what they did with the lights."

John jogged across the ice in gym shoes and told the referee, "I never saw her fall before. How could they do this with the lights? It's not right if they don't rehearse it that way. She has to have a reskate."

Katherine, backstage, wished she could crawl under a rock.

The lighting change had been a last-minute switch to suit television needs, so Katherine skated again, and her team won.

"John and Robin both wanted me to have a reskate. Robin was the captain of the other team, so it was bad for him if I did. I never forgot that, because it was generous."

Katherine began performing with the London Festival Ballet. In the summer of 1985, she danced *Romeo and Juliet*. Robin sent a bouquet of flowers with a poem he had written—Fred's legacy. Robin had never received a card signed just "Mum and Dad." There was always a witty poem enclosed. Whenever Katherine won a competition, earned a role, or had a gala opening, Robin was among the first to congratulate her.

There was a time when Katherine might have chosen to skate rather than dance—an agonizing decision—but
members of the establishment opposed her artistry. They
told her in so many words, "The artistry has to come out."
Years before Oksana Baiul, Katherine wanted to "use *Swan
Lake* music and have *Swan Lake* costumes and make little
Swan Lake gestures," but the hierarchy frowned upon
such things—the very things that made her special. Skating eventually began to borrow from ballet and contemporary dance through the use of characterization and
emotion, yet Katherine couldn't wait for the evolution.

Robin was in New York on and off until Katherine
was sixteen. By then, she was rarely there herself. Her
ballet career had exploded; skating had taken a back seat.

One of the few times since those days when Robin
and Katherine joined forces was during the 1989 filming of
the first "Symphony of Sports."

"What if you dance and I'm skating and I partner
you?" Robin suggested. He choreographed a *pas de deux* to
"Lean On Me."

Katherine's first reaction was, "What does the floor

look like?"

For a dancer on pointe shoes, the floor had to be just so. It amounted to a rug over a spring floor.

"I had a great time. I was practicing all my jumps, because the floor flung you up in the air."

However, it was not ideal for pointe shoes.

"What if you just wear flat shoes?" Robin said helpfully.

If you take yourself seriously as a ballerina, you don't appear on national television without pointe shoes. Katherine chose a soft satin pair—treacherous if she should step onto the ice.

Friends asked, "Aren't you afraid without skates on?"

"No, because it's Robin," she said.

"Symphony of Sports" was taped before a live audience. What amazed Katherine was the intensity of the crowd's reaction to "Lean On Me." She had done thousands of *pas de deux*. It was just one more, she thought. At the end of the show, that number alone was retaped, through no fault of the skaters. Katherine wasn't as thrilled as the audience. She had removed her pointe shoes, untaped her feet, changed her costume, and laced up her skates. Back the process went in reverse.

"Lean On Me" had one more outing: in Star Spangled Ice at Blue Jay, California.

On the day Katherine arrived, she and her mother had dinner with Barbara Underhill, Paul Martini, Judy Blumberg, and Michael Seibert. Katherine didn't feel well, but she put it down to jet lag and a difficult junior year at Princeton. The next morning, she woke up with raging chicken pox. Paul flew into a panic, thinking that he'd never had the disease. The skaters all checked their medical histories. Luckily, everyone was immune.

Katherine told Robin that she would perform despite her spotty appearance. She thought he would say no, because she looked "pretty horrible."

"If you feel up to it," was Robin's answer. During the rehearsal, he practiced Katherine's introduction: "With us tonight is Freddy Krueger."

Five months later, Katherine ran into Paul. "Well," he asked, "do you have any other communicable diseases?"

Katherine's story had a surprise ending: in 1997, she married coach Peter Burrows and returned to skating.

A Landover Retrospective

Candid Production's annual invitational World Professional Championships arrived at the Capital Center (later the USAir Arena) in Landover, Maryland, in December 1980, early in Robin's first season as a professional.[14]

Several of the less recent Olympians feared risking their reputations, so Dick Button instituted team scoring. Robin brought down the house with "Bilitis" and the Holiday on Ice version of his Olympic program. In 1981, he skated to "Let It Be Me" and "Morning Rain"/"The Jellicle Ball" from *Cats*.

Despite the group format, competitive juices flowed in that field of thoroughbreds. Button labeled the teams All-Stars and Pro Stars.

Landover offered a paycheck after lean amateur years. Randy Gardner called it "pretty good. Even though they advertised a certain amount of prize money, most of us had appearance fees, which is the case now still, so you never really knew what anybody was getting in the end."

In 1982, Robin signed an exclusive contract with Pro Skate. It was in effect for three years, until the series fizzled. In the interim, Dick Button added individual competition. Charlie Tickner won Landover in 1983. In 1984, Scott Hamilton took the honors.

---

[14] Although Dick Button hosted an event in Tokyo in 1973, the annual World Pro competition began in 1980. Its sister event, the Challenge of Champions, with no fixed venue, was inaugurated in 1985. In 1997, "Landover" moved to Washington, D.C.

The last hurrah for the team format came in 1985. The All-Stars showcased Robin, back from Pro Skate, with Toller, Tai Babilonia, Randy Gardner, Dorothy Hamill, Linda Fratianne, Judy Blumberg, Michael Seibert, and Oleg and Ludmila Protopopov. The Pro Stars were Scott, Norbert Schramm, Elaine Zayak, Rosalynn Sumners, Jayne Torvill, Christopher Dean, Kitty and Peter Carruthers, Barbara Underhill, and Paul Martini. The total declared purse for that pantheon of skating gods was $210,000. Tickets cost between ten and twenty dollars.

Robin won the individual event with "Horizon" and "Satan Takes a Holiday," which earned a full set of perfect 10.0s. Rosalynn skated to Cousins-choreographed "A Song For You" and "Beauty and the Beast" (from an obscure film version of the classic).

Scott wrested back his title in 1986. Then Robin won in 1987 with "Street Music" and "Machinery." Toller perceived some mutual envy.

"If Robin Cousins resented Scott Hamilton's diminutive appearance, Scott resented Robin's statuesque, leggy appearance. If Scott resented Robin's lyricism and poetic quality, Robin had a certain disdain for Scott's hokeyness."

If Toller was right, Scott didn't let on.

"We had a good rivalry going. Robin would win it one year. I'd win it the next. He'd win it again. We'd tie. We'd be very close. The first year we competed against each other, I did a short version of my Olympic long program and Robin did 'Satan Takes a Holiday.' That was a fun year—the first year I did a back-flip. Then 1986 was exciting, because he got 99.9 and I had to skate after him. I had gotten a 50.0 on the first program, and he got a 49.9. In the second program, he got a 50.0. That meant I needed a 50.0 to win. That's kind of tough, but I won the competition."

Scott performed "Flight" in the technical event. Robin interpreted *Country*. Then Scott trumped "Out of Mind, Out of Sight" with "Battle Hymn of the Republic," wearing, in essence, the American flag.

"One thing I didn't like about Landover," Scott admitted candidly, "was that I went through two different times. When I was doing four triples, Dick wanted it to be an artistic competition. That favored Robin. If that's what Dick wants, that's what is going to make me want to be stronger artistically. I moved things around and focused more in on the program. Then when I do that, Brian Boitano turns pro. He comes in, and all of a sudden Robin and I aren't as competitive anymore.

"The day Dick decided to go technical, the rivalry was gone. Robin was doing triple toe and double Axel. I had three different triples, and I'd repeat one. Boitano was doing four or five in his first number. All of a sudden, the competition changed. It was written for Boitano. It was tough to compete with him. Robin and I were both very competitive in the second number, but we always fell far behind after the technical program. There was no way we could catch up.

"In a one-mark system like Landover is, the judges have to react to the triple Axel, while everybody else is a tenth or two or three behind. In the artistic number, there's no way you can make up that kind of ground. I don't think a one-mark system works at all. There's too much inequity. You can't recognize somebody's skating ability in one mark. There are different strengths. So when he went from artistic, which favored Robin, to technical, which favored Brian, I was stuck in the middle. I was second five times in Landover."

Scott had a point. That was why skaters found Pro Skate judging so far superior.

Ironically, during the early 1980s, Robin had no technical rival, though Toller's artistry occasionally nosed out his own.

Brian won in 1988, when Robin skated injured to *The Warsaw Concerto* and "Where Do We Start?" In 1989, still licking his wounds, Robin won the World Cup in Ottawa with *My One and Only* and "The Music of the Night."

Michael Rosenberg had asked Evelyn Kramer to judge. She hadn't worked with Robin in some time. One day, she asked him on the phone what music he planned to use.

"The Music of the Night."

He had skated several years earlier to the original version, released in the U.K. as a single before *The Phantom of the Opera* opened on the West End. Hearing his choice, Evelyn thought, "That's dumb."

"Brian Boitano skated to that."

"I know."

Robin waved his magic wand over the Civic Centre, plunging it into profound silence. Evelyn got goose bumps. The crowd broke the spell with a delayed standing ovation.

That year at Landover, Rosalynn fanned the Cousins flame with "The Power of Love." What she had planned for her second number is lost to history. When a major East Coast snowstorm buried the capital, she pulled out a piece Robin had sent her, "White Christmas." Some rated that as her finest performance, the one that should have earned her the elusive "turkey platter."[15]

In 1990, Robin returned to Landover with "The Music of the Night" and the London Symphony Orchestra version of "You Really Got Me," a *Bolero* sound-alike after his unorthodox editing, finishing a strong second to Brian.

The 1991 round went to Brian, with Scott second over Robin by .1. Robin demonstrated line as the essence of art with Rachmaninoff's Concerto No. 2, then blew away the artistic field with a 50.0 for "Blue Serenade" by Manhattan Transfer. *American Skating World* named him Professional Skater of the Year.

---

[15] The name Rosalynn and her mother jokingly awarded to the large silver tray bestowed upon winners in each division. In 1993, Rosalynn was given one of her own to commemorate ten consecutive years at Landover.

Robin was busy elsewhere when Brian won in 1992. In 1993, Robin's ninth Landover appearance over a record span of fourteen years, he skated to k.d. lang's "Busy Being Blue" and to his own reading of the Wordsworth poem "On the Frozen Pond." Some thought the latter a *tour de force*, while others found it pretentious. Paul Wylie, fresh from the Olympics, nudged Robin aside.

When Scott and Robin won in alternate years, many fans suspected "fixed" outcomes. Brian Klavano disagreed.

"No, I absolutely, 100 per cent, believe that the competitions are not fixed—having now judged the U.S. Open. It was much harder than I had anticipated. Honestly, you're swayed by the audience a lot."

The judges had agreed to set the standard at 9.7, with 10.0 reserved for an "incredible" performance.

"As soon as a judge was booed for an honest mark, tens started popping up. There were Joe Druar and I, the only two with the audacity to stick with the true results."

Brian sat beside Tamara Moskvina, who planned to award a 10.0. When Brian wrote 9.8, Tamara peeked over and whispered, "You are brave." Then she leaned closer and added, "But correct."

"So, no way could Dick Button be saying, 'Okay, kids, this year we'd kind of like Scott to win' or 'It's Robin's turn this time'—although, based on the fact that most of the judges are going to wimp out and give tens all the time, all you have to do is control one or two, and that's going to control the outcome. But, no, the truth is that they lose their concentration. The audience pressures the judges tremendously. It's really just down to luck that one gave you a tenth of a point more than somebody else did. The competitors are so equal that it's really not controllable.

"I keep my ears open, because I, too, would have had that opinion. But, having had the opportunity to get into a judges' room with a lot of those people, I firmly believe it's not fixed. That's kind of nice. Part of it was refreshing, and the other part—that people wimped out and gave all those tens—was disappointing. But stand there and get 18,000 people booing you! My tuxedo was getting wet."

It was traditional for Rosalynn to share a good luck dinner with Robin on the night before Landover. Then they went to the Georgetown Mall. In 1985, he took her to her first ballet, the Joffrey's *Romeo and Juliet.*

"I was so young and new at all this. To be hanging out with him, and then to see the ballet—my eyes were *this wide*. I sat next to him and thought, 'Oh, my god, this is Robin Cousins I'm with.' We had become buddies, but, at the same time, I was still in awe of him. At Landover now, the skating is unbelievable, but it's just not the same without Robin. It was never the same without Dorothy, either. There were a few skaters who *were* Landover.

"They loved him there. It didn't matter what place anyone got. He was always the highlight. Every time he stepped on the ice, he gave it everything he had. That taught me so much. In my career, when I had ups and downs, he was always there, never saying much, but never giving up on me. He doesn't have to say a lot. It's how he treats what he does and loves what he does that spreads to everyone around him."

The Choreographer

Much of Robin's choreographic ability sprang from his feel for music. The response was inborn. Beyond that, he absorbed images from his environment—visual, auditory, tactile, kinetic—becoming a sculptor of living clay.

Simone Grigorescu understood the creative paradox.

"Most people think that it drops from the sky, but it doesn't. Creativity is not sitting in a dark room imagining that God will put his hand on your head and you will be endowed with creative genius. Creativity is drawn from other creative people and sources. We inspire each other, and we model."

On Robin's birthday one year, Gloria Ciaccio took him to a Manhattan Transfer concert. He loved the swing-era numbers the group performed in oversized coats and neon-colored ties. As he and Gloria walked home from Radio City that crisp late-summer evening, he created a number in his head: conceptualizing, choreographing, costuming, and dancing all the steps. Gloria could tell that he was excited. His British accent became more pronounced.

Robin often walked to trigger ideas. He analyzed productions with bad reviews to judge what might have been done differently. He listened to music, studied art, and noticed people, machines, and nature. The fragments lodged in his brain like shards of glass in a kaleidoscope. When the kaleidoscope turned, neurons fired, and a novel response emerged. It was that simple—and that complex.

Where does choreography start? Ask Randy Gardner.

"It can start with an element; what you selected for music; the story, what you're trying to say. Each process is different."

Sarah Kawahara explained that she drew inspiration from nature and sculpture. First she assessed a skater's vocabulary of movement, hoping that he would listen to his music and become part of the orchestration, rather than putting it on externally like a garment.

Sandra Bezic found reasons for movement. If she had a mental image of what she wanted to express, the ideas spilled out. She saw each program as a role: the dancer's approach. When she and a skater stepped onto the ice, she rarely began at the beginning. She just began.

For Robin, choreography started in the car. Having chosen a piece of music based on the mood he wanted to convey, he played it on his car stereo and left himself open to inspiration. Rather than working directly on the ice, he often choreographed in the abstract—in three dimensions.

Perhaps that had something to do with his innate spatial perception.

"Absolutely. If I can't see it, it can't happen."

What he put together in his head translated to the ice with few or no changes.

"It's almost like being channeled. I don't want to get metaphysical, because I don't believe in all that, but it almost feels like the music goes on and what I've dreamt in my head, or what I've seen in my head while driving the car, then goes straight to the feet and misses the brain mechanism in between."

David Santee, a Curry skater, worked with Robin several times.

"They were so totally different in their approaches. John was a genius, very intense. Robin was laid back. He was brilliant, too, but you certainly had a lot more fun putting the programs together because of his sense of humor. It definitely was all business with John. I think what makes Robin a great choreographer, as well as a great skater, is his versatility. Ask of him, or expect to see from him, just about any style."

As Allen Schramm viewed the essence of Robin's work, "It's a special way he uses movement that goes through everything he does. It's big. It projects well. It's extended. It touches people. For me, that's the real key."

The big moves, the jumps and spins, organized themselves based on the music. Then came improvisation. Robin had a clearer picture, needed to improvise less, when he watched someone else as opposed to creating for himself. He worked by repetition until movements remained the same over time. If he couldn't remember what he had done, it hadn't been right in the first place.

Jo often said, "You should write that down."

"No, I don't need to. If it's a good idea, it'll still be in my head six months from now. The good stuff I remember. The bad stuff disappears."

Robin believed that one of everything was enough. Giving oneself more than one chance to perform a move meant allowing oneself the option to miss it the first time.

As a professional, he rarely created a program for himself with the intention of including a specific element. He wasn't embarrassed to skate a number with one open Axel, as long as it was interesting to watch.

Evelyn Kramer studied Robin's evolution.

"In many ways, he got better and better. I knew he was a wonderful skater, but today, when I watch any of the men skate, nobody has what he has, and nobody had what he had. When he believes in a piece of music, it's amazing. No one can do with a piece of music what that man can do. It has nothing to do with a back-flip, double Lutz, or triple toe. He feels it inside of him."

Robin strove for choreography that didn't compete with the music. Sometimes he found a piece too powerful.

"If it has too much to say in its own way, I defy anyone to try to alter it by performing it."

That's what he feared was true of the k.d. lang piece.

"She has such a performance in her own voice, in the way she attacks lyrics. If you can't balance that with what you're doing, it becomes a counterbalance. You end up fighting with the music. *Phantom* was another piece like that. It's so majestic that if the choreography didn't exactly work, then I was not going to be skating *with* it; I was going to be fighting *against* it. I felt there was nothing to do with the k. d. except to go with the exact phrasing of the music; use her breathing points as pause spots within the choreography."

Some music lent itself to playfulness. Robin liked to choreograph on the underbeat, hit every other beat, or work in double time. He rarely listened to anything without skating to it in his brain. That marriage of skating and music dictated what he enjoyed, a "character flaw" that he readily acknowledged.

"My biggest problem with music, and with my acceptance of different styles of music (whether pop, rock, jazz, fusion, classical, or opera) is that if I cannot hear a melody, if I cannot count a beat, if I cannot feel a flow or skate to it in my head, it's instantly dismissed as a piece of garbage—which I know is pompous. Certainly I have an appreciation for the people who perform it, but I'm not going to sit through it, just because it's good, if I don't like it. If it doesn't have some form of motion in its formation, I can't follow it. Therefore I can't understand it. I don't understand why it was written. I don't *get* it, and if I don't get it, I don't want it. It's not that everything has to be in sixes, threes, and eights. I quite like syncopated stuff.

"Phrasing is important. When a phrase matches skating, it's very nice (and *Phantom*, a lot of Andrew Lloyd Webber's music, is written that way). I had this conversation with Carl Davis. He writes lyrical phrases that match dance and skating. You don't skate to music just because you like it. If you can't improvise to it, you can't skate to it. You can't make it fit."

On the other hand, editing cajoled some music into compliance.

"It's even more fun when there are lyrics involved, like 'Blue Serenade.' I made a whole new song out of that one."

Brian Boitano asked, "What album is that from?"
Robin told him.

"I listened to that, and I didn't find anything nice."

"Well, it's been changed around a lot, and I speeded it up a little bit here and there."

Robin thought, "If Manhattan Transfer ever hear it, they're going to die."

His *City Slickers* number was an edit, but not an edit-down. He added a bit. What he did was tantamount to composing with existing music.

"Yeah," Robin agreed irreverently, "or recomposing

or decomposing. I do have a problem sometimes with the idea that if so-and-so had wanted his concerto to be four minutes long, he would have written only four minutes."

Robin was annoyed by lack of attention to editing by phrase.

"I go down to the absolute phraseology of the music in creating a seamless piece. It is so jarring to go to a competition and watch someone with Gershwin's Concerto in F, which is simple to edit to whatever length you would ever want to, but they still cut in the middle of a bar. 'Oh well, we finished the choreography here, so let's cut the music.' No, don't!"

Robin looked for material that inspired letters saying, "We loved your program. What music was that? It was so different."

Jo was the barometer whose approval he sought.

"She has seen everything I could ever do but still can't tell you one jump from another. If she remembers something, I know it must work. My dad's always non-committal. He'll like anything that I do. My mother knows what she likes and what she doesn't like."

Jo didn't always recognize music by title and composer. She identified programs by costumes or distinctive moves. If Robin pulled together her favorite moves and set them to the right music, he knew she'd be happy.

Fred and Jo particularly liked "Scherzo," Malotte's "Lord's Prayer," "First Approach," "Satan Takes a Holiday," and "The Flower Song" from *Carmen*. On the other hand, Jo thought *Country* sounded like a saw. She had a similar aversion to William Lloyd Webber's "Aurora"—Robin's "suicide number." Toller was another of its critics.

"Robin had created a scenario where he pulled out kind of a box and the portrait of some dead girl, and he tried to direct the number to her memory. It might have been in the name of being progressive, but neither the audience nor I got it. If you're the Olympic champion, you're allowed to do silly things and get away with it. A couple of times, I've seen him do numbers that were really the biggest yawn, but you're allowed to make mistakes in the name of Art."

Jo hoped that Robin would skate to Frank Sinatra's "My Way," Fred's favorite song.

"He always did things his way. Still does. But I knew, as soon as we saw Charlie Tickner do it, that Robin would *never* do it, even if it was in our back garden."

Much of Robin's best work wasn't professionally preserved on videotape or film, including Electric Ice, Ice Majesty, and "Pie Jesu" from Andrew Lloyd Webber's *Requiem*. Networks that taped numbers without televising them later destroyed some of the footage. Unlike books or paintings, skating programs can't be enjoyed on demand. What remains is a general sense of the performer. With some, one remembers the "big" move: Boitano's 'Tano triple Lutz; Ito's triple Axel; the Biellmann spin. Notwithstanding the Cousins slide spiral, his high tuck Axel, his layout back-flip, and bidirectional spins, in Robin's case, it is the mood that lingers.

Toller confessed to a sliver of jealousy.

"When I think of Robin Cousins (and I've judged him many times), I have not seen anybody—and I actually always hated him for it, because I knew I never had it myself—who had an ability to cover the ice more quickly and in such broad strokes that no one can compare. If he took one stroke, I had to take ten. He also stepped on the ice and became larger than life, and, because of his appearance, became even taller, even leggier, even bigger. He understood, too (and it would come out years later, particularly now) that he had a propensity for light entertainment, almost like British song and dance, exquisite matinée entertainment similar to the mastery and genius (yet not the classical approach) of, say, Fred Astaire."

For Evelyn, the quiet moments were the best.

"I don't think it's a move that makes Robin Robin. Yes, he has beautiful moves, but it's what he does with a piece of music—and with his hands. If I think of moments that have really affected me, it's his hands."

Tubular Bells

Robin's head had always brimmed with ideas for his own show. One night during the Nice run of Holiday on Ice, he and Brian Klavano, the two young men about town, having gone to the Sporting Club show and out to dinner with friends, sat on a bench on the jetty in Monte Carlo, looking out over the yacht basin. As the Mediterranean Sea glistened under a full moon, Robin kicked around ideas for a theatrical skating production.

"I have this great idea to do Mike Oldfield's *Tubular Bells.*"

"Who's getting the ideas organized? Who's going to put you on the West End?"

Robin was the first Olympian Brian had met. Brian assumed that producers stood at Robin's elbow, ready to make his wish their command.

"Well, nobody."

"That's pitiful. Somebody has to start doing that."

A few months later at Wembley, they resumed their conversation. Then Brian's parents visited London, and he took them to see *Evita*. Inside the program was a biographical sketch of producer David Land, the man who had sponsored Tim Rice and Andrew Lloyd Webber. Brian read, in essence, "David saw some good ideas and brought them to reality" and "David has visions." Eureka, he thought.

Leafing through the program the next morning as he drank his coffee, Brian noticed Land's business address.

"Well, David has these visions. David works at Wardour Street. It's Monday morning. I'm going to go knock on his door."

The receptionist entered the inner sanctum and

pitched Brian's idea. A few minutes later, Land himself flung open the door and said, "Come on in. Sit down. Let me hear more." Coincidentally, Land had just attended Holiday on Ice. Brian realized that if he had appeared a week earlier, Land might not have seen him. Two weeks later may have been too late.

"This is all fascinating," Land said. "I have to dash off, because we're opening a show in Australia, but I want Robin to call me."

Eventually Robin had a lunch meeting with Land, who put him in touch with his future coproducer, Bill Kenwright. For a long time, nothing happened. By the end of the summer of 1982, Robin was jetting between Bristol and Manhattan. Brian returned to Europe from his vacation in Canada, ready to leave on his 1982-83 South American tour. When political upheaval delayed the Mexico City opening, he found himself with an extra month off. He visited a friend in London, then phoned Fred and Jo.

"Why don't you pop up for the weekend?" they suggested.

Baridon House buzzed with Robin's ideas for a show. He would build it, in part, around *Tubular Bells*, a piece known imperfectly from its association with *The Exorcist*. Robin's fascination with the music dated to the 1970s.

According to Brian, "We got a piece of cardboard, and that was going to be the stage. We started building little pipe cleaner scaffold structures, which were going to be the set. We discussed how we'd have a band flying up and down on a piece of truck. We were having a heck of a good time. Each day we'd be doing this, and Robin would play music. He basically conceived enough material for four productions."

Robin sat in the living room and skated each step in his head. He verbalized the movements to Brian, who committed them to paper. The material all ended up in a large workbook, recorded by a system of notations that most resembled the schematics of football plays.

Fred and Jo loved almost every minute of those energetic days. Jo had one pet peeve: Brian's habit of using the word *shit*. One day she cornered him in the kitchen and laid it on the line.

"You know, I quite like you. I'm quite enjoying having you around, but I have to tell you that there's one word you use that I'd really rather you didn't."

Brian promised to clean up his act.

They all grabbed tape measures and trooped to the Hippodrome to get staging ideas. One challenge they discovered was the rake of the stage. Most older ones slope towards the audience, so when actors move upstage, they climb an incline. That doesn't work for ice. The stage would have to be leveled and extended over the orchestra pit.

"So you learned all this stuff," Brian said. "It hadn't even occurred to me that this existed. We had nothing concrete going on. It was just 'This would be a great idea. How do we get it to happen?'"

Suddenly it was two weeks later. Brian left for Argentina and Brazil. The winter and spring of 1983 came and went. Then one June night in Rio de Janeiro, Brian received a call from the Holiday on Ice office. There was a telegram from Robin: "The show is on. Call me."

After finishing his own tour, Robin had gone to America to skate in the Schulz show Perhaps Love. He was staying at the rambling California ranch home of the parents of local skater Bob Bowles, where he had been housed as a young competitor when he went to training camps in Santa Rosa.

Brian phoned.

"You become oblivious to time zones, so it was at some obscene hour that I called and got Mrs. Bowles."

"This is Brian. I'm calling from Brazil. Is Robin there?"

"Well, no. He's sleeping!"

"I'll try to call back."

It took Brian three days to reach Robin and hear the news firsthand: Electric Ice was going into rehearsal.

Before he left Brazil, Brian phoned Jo and Fred. When Jo answered groggily, Brian swore at his own stupidity.

"Oh, shit! Is it three o'clock in the morning?"

"That's the word I don't like," said Jo. She didn't miss a beat, even at 3:00 A.M.

Brian flew to San Francisco, where a thief took his wallet and credit cards. Somehow he rented a car and drove to Santa Rosa. Mrs. Bowles opened the door to the light-skinned blond.

"Hi. I'm Brian from Brazil."

Her face was blank. She had been expecting a Brazilian.

Brian and Robin spent several days in heavy but heady discussions. Robin hoped that Brian would serve as the linchpin of his show, even though it wouldn't be easy for him to give up an excellent job with Holiday on Ice.

"Brian said yes straight away and then only afterwards thought, 'Oh, dear'—which is not dissimilar to what I do. I always say yes and then think, 'What have I done?' But it was great. He was a good friend to the company. He was a good friend to the business of what skating is all about, and he remains that. To be in a position of having hired somebody who you know will give you an honest opinion (whether you ask for it or not) was important. I was lucky."

Brian went home to Canada for a few days, then flew to New York to begin his duties as resident manager of the newborn Electric Ice Company.

Sunny Fredonia

It was Elva Oglanby who had jump-started the show. Robin isn't certain how that happened.

"I had spoken to Elva during Pro Skate, and to Steve Leber also. We were sitting around having drinks, as you do after a competition. They asked me, 'What do you want to do next?' and of course I spilled everything out. The next thing I knew, it was going to happen. I didn't ask where the money was coming from or what the money was. It was just, 'This is what's happening,' and it was great. I thought it was that simple."

Of course, nothing ever is that simple.

Elva then phoned Robin in Santa Rosa to announce, "I have the dates set for rehearsal."

"I was absolutely ecstatic. That's the dream: your own ambition coming to fruition. Many people in the company were already doing Pro Skate: Bob Rubens, Brian Pockar, Angela Greenhow, Allen Schramm, Simone Grigorescu. They all loved the idea. We were a unit. There were a couple of extra spaces to fill in. Tami Pennington was engaged to Allen at the time. I saw her skate, and even if she hadn't been engaged to Allen, she was the perfect foil for the other girls: more of a showgirl, not a competitor, and certainly tall enough. Her legs went to the armpits."

Three people Robin tapped for his cast were in the Schulz show: Elina Viola, Keith Green, and Reggie Raiford. Robin paired Keith and Elina and began working on their material. He added Keith's bride, Dianne Green; Michael Shinniman from Ice; Sally Anderson from Holiday on Ice; and former amateur competitor Editha Dotson.

Elva lined up a late-summer tryout at the Paper Mill Playhouse, a well-known repertory theatre in Millburn, New Jersey. Meanwhile, the company needed rehearsal ice.

Elva was immersed in John Curry's projects. Two months earlier, she, John, Mark Hominuke, and Patricia Dodd had toured the facilities at the State University of New York at Fredonia with an eye to establishing a resident repertory company. Dean and Mrs. Douglas Carter hosted them for dinner. There was excitement at the prospect of the Curry company joining the college community, but John, ever gloomy, felt otherwise. When Robin's project came along, Elva's production group remembered Fredonia and the new rink that was empty until fall.

In July 1983, the fledgling company gathered in the town of 11,000 in rural Chautauqua County's grape belt. The skaters lived in dormitories and walked wherever they needed to go—sometimes to local "watering holes," where they drank beer to wash down the Buffalo wings.

Amanda Rayner arrived in New York City from England one day, expecting to visit Robin, but he had gone to Fredonia, leaving friends to instruct her. She had to return to the airport and fly to Buffalo (on a ticket he had bought her).

"There was a message left on the coffee machine. Could I bring the fourteen or fifteen sweatsuits for the entire company? I had my own stuff. I had my cameras and all that. I also had a magnum of champagne, so I had bags for days. It was a 7:15 P.M. flight from La Guardia to Buffalo. Brian was going to meet me. Editha was due to fly in from somewhere else, so Brian only had to do one run to the airport to pick us up.

"I hailed a cab at about 5:15, me and the baggage. It was a big Checker Cab. Twenty minutes later, we'd done two blocks. At about six o'clock, we were in the Midtown Tunnel when the cab overheated. The driver was Brooklyn-born and bred. It's unusual to find a cabby who is actually a native New Yorker. I had all the bags on the floor, and I ended up lying across the back seat with my feet hanging out the window. I was singing good old-fashioned English music hall songs to my cab driver, who was singing Vaudeville back to me.

"As we came out of the tunnel, it had gotten very grey, and an electrical storm had started. When we reached the airport, it was 7:15. The cab driver said, 'Don't worry. Nothing will take off in this.' At that point, the heavens opened. I virtually drowned. I went up to the desk, and they said, 'You have five minutes. It's gate nineteen.' The champagne, the bags, everything—I gathered it all up and legged it, screaming at the top of my voice, 'Get out of the way. I'm coming through.' They were closing the door as I fell onto the aircraft.

"We sat in a queue of fifty-seven planes, and I think we finally took off at nine o'clock. By the time I arrived in Buffalo, Editha had been there for ages. She and Brian were sitting there gassing. I do remember getting into Fredonia. Robin was going potty. He thinks of me as thoroughly inept. I walked into the room and dropped the whole lot onto the floor. The rest of the company was there, and I said something along the lines of 'Cousins, you are an absolute bastard, and if you ever do this to me again, I will kill you.'"

It was Simone who looked up and said to Robin, "*That's* an English lady?"

Amanda didn't know that Robin had told everyone, "Oh, you'll all adore Amanda. She's so English. Such a lady." She had blown it with the first words out of her mouth.

Amanda's two-day visit lasted five. New York would always be there, but rarely could she watch a show come together. She happily spent nearly half of her two-week holiday sitting on the ice taking photographs.

There was a bonus in the Fredonia location. Katie and Geary Baxter had left Holiday on Ice to live just outside Jamestown in a house overlooking Lake Chautauqua. Katie taught with her sister at the Jamestown Skating Club, founded by Lois Walker, their mother. After years of dining out and hosting barbecues, Geary ran a restaurant, the Inside Edge—and it was all happening forty minutes south of the college. Robin spent weekends with the Baxters, reliving his nights on the foldout couch in Nice.

Katie's parents owned a house farther up the lake shore. The skaters arrived to water ski and laze in the sun—

a thrilling change from days in an indoor ice rink. Robin proved himself an intrepid water-skier, while Brian developed a particular fondness for floating aimlessly in an oversized inner tube.

College officials asked the cast, "Do you mind if we open rehearsals to the public?" That offered the welcome chance for feedback. Area residents arrived in droves with local produce and homemade baked goods.

Meanwhile, the campus also hosted the Buffalo Bills' summer training camp. Hulking linebackers, sweaty from calisthenics, had their own idea of sightseeing: visiting the rink adjacent to the gym to admire the female skaters.

One morning, Simone and friends set out along the sidewalk that led from their dorm to the rink. The football players lived in a neighboring hall. One of the Bills, in workout clothes, broke away from his teammates and ran towards Simone. Her first thought was, "These guys could probably kill me." He threw her over his shoulder like a prehistoric cave man selecting a mate, then ran in the direction of the dorms.

"Stop! Turn around," Simone ordered. "If you're going to run with me, run me to the rink."

Some of the Bills sneaked out to meet the women at night. When their coaches caught them, there were heavy fines for breaking curfew.

The skaters, who tended to be short and slight in spite of their musculature, sometimes used the Bills' physiotherapists.

"Those were pretty big guys," Allen thought. "It was intimidating, especially going through the locker rooms."

The skaters' athleticism surprised the Bills and provoked a sometimes grudging admiration. Trainers and coaches occasionally joined the company for meals. One of them had a crush on Sally and often brought her flowers.

Robin had assembled thirteen of the best skaters available. He wasn't interested in their reputations but in their diversity and basic skating.

"I have to say that with Electric Ice I was blessed with one of the greatest ensembles of complete skating that ever existed. Certainly Allen brought something to the show that I could never have brought to it. Everybody had something to offer, so that without that person, the show would not have been what it was. That's such a joy."

Stephanie Andros had worked with other skaters who created their own shows.

"They made sure that whoever they took on couldn't do quite as well as they could do. Robin took on extremely talented skaters, both male and female, and let them do everything that they did well. He didn't say, 'Oh you can't do that. *I'm* doing that.'"

Brian Klavano agreed.

"As incredibly talented as John Curry was, when there was another skater or a pairs team getting close to his applause, they weren't in the next city."

John could hold his own with anyone, but Robin had more self-assurance.

"I'm a firm believer in the philosophy that just because you're on the ice on your own, that doesn't necessarily make you a star. You can be on the ice with twelve other people and still be the star of the number. I'm quite happy to have other people around me. It doesn't diminish my worth, and I think that works in reverse. The chorus isn't there to back up a principal. The ensemble is there to augment."

That was Robin's sensitivity to an entertainment package. It took humor, athleticism, and artistry to please an entire audience. Naturally, he had a healthy ego. He wouldn't have made it to the top without that conviction and focus on self, yet he was able to subjugate it to the good of the whole. Prima donna flashes were rare.

How Electric Ice fell together became one of Simone's "most treasured memories."

"There was something incredibly special that was created there, without us being aware of it happening. That was a wonderful small company. I always knew Robin wanted to have something that he could create himself. From among his former acquaintances, he handpicked all the members of the company. What better way to establish great rapport among people than to pick all the personalities and talents that you want to have around you?"

The group felt like a family. There wasn't the intrigue, gossip, or backstabbing that sometimes existed in large companies. Still, Simone prized their individuality. Allen Schramm, for example, had a style completely different from Robin's.

"He has a wild and earthy quality. You don't know where it comes from or where it's going. The audiences loved him. He was like an animal that was released, trying to eat up space around him with his movement, whereas Robin was lean and tall and controlled and had more of an otherworldly quality."

Allen didn't see himself as unusual.

"I love to skate, and I love music. It's fantastic to be

able to combine them."

That was the common denominator. Again, Robin had gravitated to people with a passion for what they did.

Angela Greenhow and Allen were a team, two wild spirits on the ice. Eventually they married and had two daughters.

Brian Pockar was charismatic, with smoldering sensuality and masculine beauty. Off the ice, he was reserved and refined, a real gentleman. Bob Rubens was the brooding artist. Sally Anderson was elegant and soft. Michael Shinniman was playful. Simone's skating was emotion-charged; lyrical, with power.

What they found satisfying was contributing to the choreography, putting a piece of themselves into it from the ground up. The goal was unprecedented: to combine contemporary dance movement with figure skating in a full-length theatrical production based on the sustained development of a theme. Permutations of the ensemble interpreted the pieces as a corps de ballet presents themes and variations.

Each half had one musical reference point. The first was Vangelis, including *Chariots of Fire* and *China*. The second was Mike Oldfield, primarily *Tubular Bells*. Oldfield's personal arranger helped Robin adapt it.

"There had been another version of *Tubular Bells* that Mike had done live: a lot funkier and more rock-oriented than the recorded version. The live version was what our piece was based on, which subsequently was added to two other pieces that made up the encore.

"We experimented. In the middle of the second week, the cast all suddenly realized what we were doing. It was unique: forty-seven minutes without stopping. No breaks. No one left the side of the stage. Five of us were on the ice for twenty-two minutes without getting off, but nobody thought about that. It was just an involving piece."

Trouble in Paradise

Brian was amazed at the first run-through to find the show virtually identical to what Robin had described in his living room in Bristol.

As long as Robin was in control, things ran smoothly. Jef Billings of the Elizabeth Courtney Costume House designed and constructed the costumes and flew to the campus for preliminary fittings.

The first-act outfits were Lycra leotards for the women, trousers and sleeveless shirts for the men, in hot colors with space-age flourishes. Billings had the idea of decorating them with snap-on Ping Pong balls—one idea that didn't make the final cut. When the balls were nudged, they flew off and bounced on the ice.

For the second act, there were sleek black unitards with swirls of crystalline glitter, androgynous except for the women's cutout backs.

Meanwhile, Robin thought that Elva was busy in New York. Unbeknownst to him, she had flown to London. Elva was a great talker. She started talking to Bill Kenwright, David Land's contact. Kenwright was an up-and-coming English producer with a number of successful shows including *Joseph and the Amazing Technicolor Dreamcoat*. He had the nerve to try something different. In fact, he had already been working on Electric Ice when a theatre opened up. Instead of playing New Jersey, the company was London-bound.

Elva met with Jo over lunch and wrote out the budget on a napkin.

With what joy and shock Robin learned that the producers had summarily dismissed the Paper Mill Playhouse. He was off to the West End, to the Victoria Palace Theatre. His mood alternated between exhilaration and sheer terror.

Brian thought in his droll way, "That's convenient. I can go to London, phone Skee Goodhart, and tell him I may not be coming back to work."

While the company rehearsed in Fredonia, Electric Ice set a box office record. First-day ticket sales exceeded all previous West End records for single-day sales. Elated, Robin flew to England to complete arrangements while the other skaters extended their two-week commitments.

Then a few rain clouds began to gather. Elva, attractive and flamboyant, made lavish promises but occasionally fell short when practical considerations reared their heads. She announced that the producers couldn't afford to send Billings to London for final fittings. The Courtney people took issue with her position. If they couldn't send Billings, perhaps they shouldn't send the costumes either. Lawyers talked to lawyers. Elva declared that the producers were running out of money—already, and Robin had an inkling of trouble in Paradise.

"That was the first time that we ran into money problems. Jef and I had got on very well with Ice, and he was doing me a favor in being involved with Electric Ice. We certainly weren't able to pay the fees that they would normally have commanded. Then we were not going to be in New Jersey. We were going to London. The producers wouldn't pay for him to come to London. They would find somebody in London to do the fittings.

"Of course, the stuff didn't fit properly—and Bill, the London producer, didn't like any of it and didn't agree with my vision. The second act costumes pretty much stayed the same. The first act costumes were used for a while, but Bill didn't like their formality. He certainly didn't want me wearing the same as everybody else. I liked the idea of being an ensemble. So things were changed around, and Jef got not necessarily swept to the side, but left behind— and there was nothing I could do about it."

There were other small glitches on the production side that Robin was blissfully unaware of. He was all the more surprised, then, when he heard a knock on his apartment door many months after Electric Ice closed. He was summoned to give a deposition in a suit being brought by the London Marriott, the hotel that had lodged the cast. Thousands of pounds hadn't been paid, and it was Robin's name on the show. He told the court what little he knew and heard nothing further.

"I have since quite happily stayed at the Marriott in London, so obviously things were cleared. I think I lucked out, by all accounts. The Marriott was the only incident, although there were probably lots of peripheral things that collectively added up to what could well have been a big disaster.

There was a humorous dénouement to the whole affair. Many years later, Elva invited Amanda to lunch—at the London Marriott! Amanda had close business ties there and let them know that one of the Electric Ice producers was due to appear. The lunch passed without incident.

Perhaps Amanda put it the most colorfully: "We have a saying in my family about the cow that gives the best bucket of milk and then kicks it over. That's what Elva would do."

Elva knew a good idea when she saw it. She was a great supporter of artistic skating. More to the point, would Toller, John, and Robin have done what they did without her? What a loss if they hadn't.

Robin spoke for all three: "As artists, we generally are so easy, so pliable, because we all want desperately to do what we do. When somebody comes along who has a voice that you believe—that was the thing. Elva was articulate. You maybe only heard what you needed to hear, and she only told you what you needed to hear, which is not a bad thing if you're a producer. I didn't know any better, and I'm sure Toller and John didn't. At that point, the only three people who wanted to do something creative and different were John, Toller, and myself. It is kind of strange that the only person we had in common—who helped us do what we wanted to do—was Elva Oglanby.

"She didn't have any preconceived notions. It was, 'Whatever you want, you've got.' She never had the visions we had, but she knew the people to organize them with. Yet I think that what she really knew was how to make us feel the way we needed to feel—which was great, because that's how I got the rehearsals in Fredonia, and that's how I got the show together. I have to say that there's a lot of it for which she was responsible that I absolutely do not regret."

Elva left Electric Ice in Bill Kenwright's hands and continued to promote John Curry's projects. Robin had only one additional dealing with her (with the exception of Pro Skate): "losing Editha Dotson from Electric Ice and having her cry for hours in the dressing room because she didn't want to go to John's company. Elva had contracted her to John and informed me that she had found a replacement for Electric Ice: Wendy Burge. Wendy was fabulous in the show, but I had hired Editha for a reason, and I wanted her to stay. I'm sure if John had known—but she was dragged by the skates."

On the West End

Robin painstakingly edited the tape reels for Electric Ice, only to find that not only was the company going to London; it would have live musicians: union rules. He said, "Why not, I guess." In the end, it was a great success.

Two contrasting events summarized the runup. Amanda's mother was a grande dame, an English combination of Dear Abby and Dr. Ruth. By the time Amanda returned home, her mother had invited half the media in the country to a party for the cast: a Sunday afternoon of cucumber sandwiches and proper English tea.

Bill Kenwright had hatched a plan that was hardly geared to the cast's true talents.

"He had a vision of us skating to 'Rockin' Robin.' We all had to go to a recording studio and sing it. I remember putting it wrong on purpose, I was so against it. It was just

very tacky. The audience loved it. Everyone was so enthusiastic, except for the skaters."

It was at about that time that Brian thought, "This is
looking good." He called Skee Goodhart. Fortunately, Skee
was in Europe, which avoided the time zone problem. Brian
promised to meet Skee in Le Havre to launch Holiday on
Ice. That would give Goodhart time to find his replacement.

Brian was a former chorus skater and line captain
who had climbed to performance director. After the Electric Ice opening, he crossed the English Channel by ferry.

"With Holiday, as a performance director, I always
kept my skates, because you're rehearsing on 150 feet of
ice. When I watched Robin's choreography, I said to myself, 'Oh, no. I won't be needing to get on the ice and do any
of *this* stuff. This is way beyond my abilities.' It was time to
move solely into management. I went over to the edge of
the ship with a glass of champagne and buried my skates at
sea."

Brian had never worked in the theatre before, but
he was clever enough to bluff.

"When we first started working in the theatres in
England, the theatre people were so nice to me. They
thought I knew my stuff, because I wouldn't say anything
too incredibly stupid, but they assumed I just didn't know
the British terms for upstage, downstage, and prompt side.
They needed to help me with the terminology. I didn't have
a clue. Later, when we started working in the American
theatre world, the Americans thought, 'He obviously knows
his *British* stuff, but we'll teach him the American terms.'
You get the nerve to go in and try it. Hopefully, you'll get it
together."

As the days ticked down to the gala opening, Robin
asked Amanda to take the women shopping. By opening
night, they glittered. Never mind that those were beads of
sweat. The Electric Ice premier was on August 31, 1983,
possibly the hottest day of the year. The theatre (typical of

England) wasn't air conditioned. The glitterati would suffocate in tuxedos and evening gowns.

Meanwhile, the night watchman's replacement hadn't shown up, so the chap had turned everything off—including the ice refrigeration—and had gone home.

Robin was devastated. He didn't want to open, but there was no convincing Bill Kenwright, who had never missed an opening night in his life. Electric Ice wouldn't spoil his record.

"The ice was mushy and horrible, but I thought, 'I'm not going to compromise.' My opening move was a big flying sit spin. The blade landed, cracked the ice, and stayed there. I did a break dance on my backside. It was a letdown, because the previews had been phenomenal. I couldn't wait to get to the opening night. The opening had to be, I would say, 45 per cent of what we had been doing for two weeks. The day after, we were back to normal again."

The critics attended the opening. The grumpiest of that breed complained of "disco" music at "maximum decibels" and a "barrage of lighting effects," comparing Electric Ice unfavorably to Curry's balletic offerings.

The reviewer from the *Daily Mail* heaped upon Robin the ultimate indignity: "The long and gangling athlete cannot, of course, be blamed for the fact that he brings to the star spot a countenance that would look more at home gazing out helpfully from behind the cheese counter at Sainsbury's."

Years later, Robin met that reviewer at a party. Jack Tinker asked, "Have we not met?"

Robin answered with a smile, "No, but you have written something about me—but that's another story which we shan't get into."

Rosalind Carne, of the *Guardian*, was more in tune.

"The title is perfect. If ever a sheet of ice radiated power, it must be this one. . . . One of the strong points of the display is the way in which it makes good use of the inherent mystery in the material. Instead of bright lights and spectacular effects, we get grey mists, pink dawns, and forms looming out of semidarkness. Mr. Cousins himself is responsible for staging and choreography and a single artistic vision is most apparent after the interval when the company don black cat suits and move through a single piece of music with something akin to dramatic form. As the rhythms grow insistent they stagger in a line, arms falling around their heads like puppets on a string.

"Later they take their places one by one under colored spots, slaloming among the standing figures.

"Then the soloists take over, the elfin British Angela Greenhow, the graceful, confident Romanian Simone Grigorescu or the Canadian Bob Rubens, effecting extraordinary turns on two feet as well as on one. It is impossible to name them all here, but then the wonderful thing about the occasion is that no one usurps the limelight, despite the outstanding qualities of the star."

Robin took the good and the bad with a grain of salt.

"I think the reviews, by and large, were quite glowing, especially in terms of what British reviewers can do to a show. It's difficult for theatrical reviewers, who know theatre inside out, to review something they know nothing about. You need to be a skating aficionado or a skating critic to critique skating.

"John's company was very much ballet on ice. That was what he wanted it to be. It was what he set out to do with ballet choreographers. I think that some people were not objective about John's show, either. Dance critics shouldn't have critiqued that, any more than they should have critiqued my show. People get it or they don't get it. At the end of the day, it's the audience that decides."

The opening-night party was at Stringfellow's, a well-known London club. The next day, the papers reported an unsuccessful gate-crashing attempt by Princess

Diana's brother.

Mike Oldfield, an opening-night guest, confessed to Robin that he had never heard his music played by anyone other than himself; nor had he imagined performers interpreting it. He found the experience strange and magical. Before long, all over London, people were asking for Oldfield recordings.

Vangelis liked the show so much that he kept going back for more.

Rock 'n' roll keyboard specialist Chris Parren was one who had tended to dismiss figure skating. "My learning curve went up quickly," he admitted, when he came face to face with live performance and its attendant sweat, grunts, groans, and occasional flesh wounds.

Chris and four other "hardened studio musicians" formed a rock band that played on a raised stage with multiple spotlights beaming downward. The motorized platform ascended from the ice like the mother ship in *Close Encounters of the Third Kind.*

Chris credited Robin with good musical instincts and knowing what he wanted: accompaniment timed precisely the same, night after night, with the help of an electronic sequencer. The cutting-edge technology wasn't flawless. Once, only one of the platform's two motors worked properly. As one side rose more quickly than the other, the equipment edged towards Chris. The piano didn't actually slide off and crash onto the skaters, but it might have. Another time, an electrical surge shorted out both the platform and the musicians. The pulleys had to be worked manually, with all the attendant clanking of chains that would otherwise have been masked by music.

The whiz-bang technology depended on computer programming. When a gremlin infiltrated the works, Robin and company did some fast thinking.

"There was a click track on the synthesized part of the music that could run for only X number of minutes before it needed to be changed. That was fine for Vangelis, because they were individual pieces, although it was one act, but the Oldfield was straight through, and on the rare occasion (as it did happen) that they couldn't change the click from A to B quickly enough, we would improvise.

"Chris Parren, the lead piano, improvised at one point for eighteen minutes. I went on and improvised. Then I presented Allen, who came on and did the same. Then somebody else came on. It was great. We were watching each other improvise in front of a live audience that didn't know there was a problem. Chris was playing the most beautiful versions of, I think, just three key changes of Oldfield music where the transition came. You could tell, once Chris got going, whether we were in for a long run with the click or not. The minute he started to wind it down, you knew that whoever was supposed to start up the next piece needed to get out there quickly, but there was never a performance of Electric Ice when, from the opening chord of the very first song to the finale of the second act, anybody left the side of the stage."

Electric Ice had a way of transforming its audiences. Fredonians became lifelong skating fans. Dancers developed new perspectives. The establishment reevaluated members of the cast. Then there were people like Cindy Moyers who left frustrated. A dancer and Holiday on Ice skater, she saw a medium she desperately wanted to work in. She returned to her job in profound misery.

"I spent the rest of my career making up for the fact that I didn't get to do Electric Ice."

The show was a homecoming for Robin. Jo was there, mothering all "the kids," just as she mothered her own. They referred to her and Fred as "the Cuzzos."

Trish Bernays got into the act, too.

"I was trying to hold down a job as well as see Electric Ice most evenings. Because Robin was with a show, we could go to other shows free. We all had a delightful

time. I think that was the era I look back on with the most
fondness, rather than when he was struggling. It was such
a relief when he'd made it and didn't have to do the
competitions."

Amanda Rayner worked nine to five, then headed
for the theatre. One evening, Robin became ill.

"If you knew the show as well as I did by then, you
knew that something was a bit off. To everybody else, it
looked fine. Elva was standing with me, stage right, up in
the dress circle. I looked at her and said, 'Watch center
stage. I promise you that, as those lights and that curtain
come down, Robin's going to hit the ice.'"

Amanda had seen Robin collapse at the end several
times before. He bore out her prediction. He had gotten
through the show, and that was it. Elva panicked.

"Oh, my God! Get an ambulance! Get an ambulance!"

"No, Elva. Just take him home, feed him, and get him
to bed. He'll be fine tomorrow."

On Guy Fawkes Day, Amanda helped to organize a Bonfire Night party. That same November, she hatched a combination charity benefit/publicity stunt at which the skaters set *Guinness Book of World Records* marks at the Richmond ice rink. During the televised event, Robin achieved an Axel measuring nineteen feet one inch in length; an eighteen-foot back-flip; twenty consecutive split jumps; twenty-seven pull Arabians (with Tami Pennington); and a thirty-nine-revolution one-foot upright spin. By performing the show on small ice and training on large surfaces, the cast became disciplined and versatile.

Electric Ice was originally scheduled to run for seven weeks, but it extended until almost Christmas, when the skaters disbanded to honor other commitments. In early December, many of them went to New York to compete in Pro Skate. Robin won the men's event. Allen placed second. Angela won the ladies' competition, with Simone third behind Denise Biellmann. Keith and Elina finished second in pairs. It was a near sweep by the Electric Ice Company. Some of the cast members had finally received the recognition they deserved, in Robin's opinion.

"Angela was someone our association had allowed to slip between the cracks. She was more of a rebel than I was in terms of free skating and ideas. At the junior championships at Billingham, she skated her long program to *Jesus Christ, Superstar.* She wore a beautiful white dress with a big silver sequined cross. I remember people being absolutely gobsmacked and aghast that she was skating to freaky, weird music. She loved all that stuff, and I thought she was fabulous, but it wasn't 'right.' She was the best thing that ever happened to women's figure skating in England that nobody's ever heard of—another great champion who never really was, through no fault of her own."

Allen had risen no higher than seventh in the U.S. with the fluid, *outré* improvisational style that Electric Ice showcased so well.

Home to the Hippodrome

In January 1984, Electric Ice set out for Perth, Australia, through the kindness of Bill Kenwright, who had a show opening in Melbourne. Brian told his local contacts, "I've heard from Ice Capades and Holiday on Ice that you have salty water."

"No, no, no. We've had that corrected."

Brian tried to make ice. Salt water freezes at a much lower temperature than fresh water. The resultant slush had to be drained and replaced by water trucked in from the mountains. Meanwhile, the company had several days off. Kenwright made a generous gesture. He flew the entire cast, including the musicians, all the way to Melbourne for the opening night of his show.

Winter in America and England was Australian summer. As soon as the skaters returned to Perth, they hit the beaches. Within an hour, they had burned to the shade of Tami's hair.

In the spring, Electric Ice marched triumphantly on Bristol. The Hippodrome at last! Brian wanted to make a splash.

"It has to be like Hollywood premiers. We have to get the searchlights going. Won't that be great?"

After hunting for days, Brian found that the Royal Air Force had klieg lights left from the war.

"Okay," said the RAF. "What time is your show?"

"The house will open at six-thirty."

"It doesn't get dark until eight."

Brian had found lights for a daylight opening.

On April 11, hundreds queued in the rain to see their hometown hero. Two days later, there was an extra matinée so that he could treat sixty-five Sea Mills pensioners, his grandmother among them, to an afternoon of fun.

A week or so into the run, Robin woke up feeling ill. He fulfilled his morning engagement, the inauguration of an open-top bus service in Bath, but near the end of the matinée, he collapsed offstage, in acute pain and burning up with fever. He went to Saint Mary's Hospital with the presumption of appendicitis.

"My parents are not people to hang around, but my dad was coming to meet me between shows, so he happened to be in the Hippodrome. The stage door is the same level as the stage, with a set of swing doors between. He had just walked in and was standing at the side of the ice, watching the finale. I got off the ice, and that was it. The next thing I knew, I was on the floor. Bless her heart, Amanda Rayner found the only florist that was open and sent flowers."

In truth, Amanda found a florist that *wasn't* open and still managed to send flowers on behalf of a distraught cast who refused to believe that England screeched to a halt at Easter time.

Robin spent two days in the hospital with a severe stomach virus. On the day after his release, Easter Sunday, he gave a thank-you party for the cast at Baridon House. The following night, he sat in the audience and watched his show for the one and only time.

"Fabulous. It was great. Not my show, but what those kids did—what Allen did—in my absence. They all shared bits. The show does go on, and they gave the audience their money's worth. I was sad not to be in it, but I've never felt so sick. I think it was exhaustion and tension and trying to do a million things. I had survived the opening. The body then said, 'Hello. Enough!' But I was sick as a dog."

A Near Miss

In the late spring, Electric Ice went on to Manchester, Birmingham, and Liverpool. The crowning achievement was to come in October: playing New York's Virginia Theatre.

Broadway producers visited the show and committed to the project. They asked Robin to name a collaborator. He suggested Michael Peters, choreographer of "Thriller" and "Beat It" and cochoreographer of *Dreamgirls*.

Within twenty-four hours, Peters had phoned. Then he flew to Birmingham for discussions.

"Michael was great. He understood the vision. He was able to throw me new curves choreographically: 'I know that's what you can have in England, but on Broadway it can be bigger and better.' People have always said that you have to go for the top and maybe cut from there, rather than make something fit parameters. With what shows were costing on Broadway, Electric Ice was nothing."

When Robin returned to New York, he and Peters went to see Harold Wheeler, a well-known musical writer and arranger, to discuss giving the show a Broadway edge. Theoni Aldredge, a top costume designer, drew sketches.

"We were close," Brian figured. "If it costs $200,000 to mount the show in London, it costs $2 million to mount it in New York. There's such a vast difference in the commitment. As modest as we kept the show—we had the costuming, the ice people, all the elements—by the time you pay the union labor, the union rates on lighting, and everything else, *and* add in publicity, it's so unbelievably high. It added zeroes to the budget."

The prospectus projected weekly operating expenses of $187,000 before royalties and theatre expenses. The $2 million budget was to be capitalized in fifty units of $40,000 each.

Robin wrote to his fans' newsletter, "We have decided to delay the production until the New Year because of other commitments, and need less-interrupted time to make it exactly the way we feel it should be in order to take Broadway by storm!!"

Those exclamation points were wishful thinking.

"All these skaters," Evelyn Kramer said, "they're artists. In terms of business heads, we don't have them. We trust everybody. You take care of it. Let me just skate."

Garnet Ostermaier seconded that analysis.

"I don't know if I should say it or not, but I think people have taken advantage of Robin in the past, because he is an extremely generous, trusting soul and didn't always see through the outside of people who were trying to use him, or use his money, or use his success for their own benefit. He always had that kind of heart where he didn't think that way. People did take advantage of him, I think, more than once—more in America than when he was in Europe. Broadway woke him up a bit. I think that was when he started to realize, 'I have to watch people more,' but he still found it a real struggle. He was always the first to lend a helping hand, and he never asked for anything in return."

Trish observed a related phenomenon.

"A lot of people in America promised him the world but never produced. He used to get really upset about it until he realized that the Americans bullshit a lot, particularly in New York, trying to impress you with all the money they can get. Then nothing happens. He used to be heartbroken about it all, and then he started growing up a bit. He was kept in an isolated, sheltered little world, and I think it was a bit of a shock when he had to come back to reality. We all protected him too much. We're all guilty of it—keeping the real world away from Robin."

Robin was less naïve than he sometimes appeared. His enthusiasm shouldn't be confused with a lack of wisdom.

Brian took a pragmatic view.

"It's weird, the Broadway production world. There are people who do nothing but back shows. It's a political and networked game that we didn't fully understand, and that we probably won't—ever. You need to align yourself with one production group, which we did. They were young, sort of the new Bill Kenwrights. While you're networking, you might have another producer say, 'Let *me* do that. I can do that quicker and better.' But if you switch your alignment, you look fickle. We were too green and dumb to know, 'Should we jump ship and go with *these* people, or should we stay with *them*.' They were making promises. They'd pick him up in limos.

"Up at Sky Rink, we did 'Body Moves,' and the potential backers who came to that audition gave it a standing ovation.[16] The only time that group of jaded New York money people had ever before jumped to their feet—and they were in the cold of Sky Rink, sitting in those horrible aluminum bleachers—was at the backers' audition for *A Chorus Line*. Generally they'd sit there and go 'Clap, clap, clap. Cocktails!' We were just so jazzed."

Then it turned out that the backers were hesitant to risk their money with a young production team. The who's who of the theatre world raved about the audition, but

---

[16] On December 10, 1984, the cast presented a sample of numbers from both *Electric Ice* and its successor, *Ice Majesty*.

none wrote checks.

"Maybe we should have gone with the older guy who was making other promises. Who knows? There hadn't been a big, successful ice show. Ice at Radio City had failed because of the blizzard. Toller's show had not succeeded economically. John's shows were artistic triumphs but financial disasters, so why were we going to be any different? We were just another British Olympic skater with nice ideas. It's hard to get backers on your team. Who knows how close we got, or by how wide we missed?"

Robin believes, "Electric Ice on Broadway would have been the breakthrough, the ice show to end all ice shows, with the talent and the people who were behind it."

Falling short of Broadway was due to a complex tangle of factors. Was it misplaced trust? Business naïveté? Lack of a story line? The economic failure of similar ventures? Bad timing? All of the above? Within a week of the backers' audition, Robin knew in his heart of hearts that Electric Ice would not play New York.

"People all wanted to know what the story was, what the book was. It wasn't a book show, any more than Bob Fosse's *Dancin'* was a book musical. You never knew whether those people could really be that stupid, having just seen two hours of it. It was like going to see Baryshnikov or Fonteyn and saying, 'But what's the story?'

"It wasn't as if Electric Ice or any of the things that we were doing was that difficult to follow. I can't believe that at the backers' audition, four hundred people gave it a ten-minute standing ovation without meaning it. I found it all hard to comprehend, but I did know that, with anything, people are fickle. If you don't catch them then, you're not going to catch them at all. The moment came and went—and it really was a moment.

"My heart sank when Brian and I went to the theatre and there in *Playbill* was an advertisement for Electric Ice at the Virginia Theatre. They had to lay out

Playbill so much ahead of time, but that was the moment that hurt the most: sitting in a seat to watch someone else's show, looking at an advertisement for my own show that was never going to happen."

With most of his resilience intact, Robin looked ahead to a new project. Viewing his life to date on balance, it's hard not to conclude that his optimistic naïveté has served him better than hard-boiled cynicism would have.

Geckos and Shark Meat

In the Baridon House living room in the days of cardboard and pipe cleaners, Robin had conceived enough material for a repertory ensemble. As Electric Ice wound down, the company learned new numbers. Ice Majesty was born.

It was more diverse than Electric Ice, which pleased those who felt that the first show had been too much of the same thing. Others preferred what Electric Ice had offered: the sustained development of a theme. Electric Ice was for young, cerebral theatregoers; Ice Majesty appealed to a broader base.

The new show had its first chance at life thanks to a conversation over a beer.

According to Brian, "A fellow came and saw Electric Ice at the Hippodrome and loved the show. He was a soccer person who was taking teams to Kuala Lumpur, Malaysia, and through that was connected with Nestlé, the sponsors of the tournament. The guy said, 'We're looking for other entertainment to bring to Asia.' He latched onto our show. It's weird how a little conversational thread can actually mount a show. You just happen to mention it to the right person, who happens to have two million dollars at his disposal, and off you go."

Something similar happened once to Brian Orser. The stranger seated next to him at a banquet asked, "What are you working on, Brian?"

"I have an idea to take a tour of skaters up through

the Yukon, but we can't afford to get them there."

"Well, I'm the head of public relations for Canadian Airlines. Do you think I could help?"

Thus was born the Canadian Airlines Northern Lights tour of the Yukon and Northern Territories. Orser had no idea that he was talking to the man who could say yes. As Brian Klavano knew, "You could spend two weeks on the phone, trying to get through to somebody to tell you who to talk to."

Ice Majesty went to Kuala Lumpur in early 1985. The cast often took the bus to a small private beach, scrambling to an elevated spot that became an island at high tide. At mealtime, they ate in the streets. Robin had been told to avoid hotel fare.

"I wasn't that keen on having shark, but we found one little place where they cooked everything out in the open on grills over the gutters. They scrubbed the grills, and at least you could see what was being prepared. They cooked the shark steaks on aniseed leaves. I think we could feed the whole company for about $3.50."

There was culture shock on both sides. What the promoter had sold and what the cast delivered were two different shows. The audiences were expecting Michael Jackson, not the classics.

Kuala Lumpur was hot and humid. The show venue was an enclosed basketball stadium ringed by narrow ventilation slits. Only in the expensive seats was there air conditioning—little round vents of the type seen in airplanes. Geckos overran the set.

Brian asked the arena staff if there was some way to cool the building and keep the ice better refrigerated. It got hot overnight, as opposed to during the day. He and Robin walked in one morning and found that the custodians had placed portable oscillating fans around the edge of the ice. Where the fans had blown, there were pools of water scalloped around the perimeter. It looked great but cut down the ice size.

Flawed posters dotted the city. The graphic designer had forgotten one of Robin's blades. There he was, in a butterfly, wearing one skate and one shoe. He had the poster framed for his future amusement.

Frequent Flyers

While Kuala Lumpur was an interesting detour, the goal was the Hippodrome. By late spring, that prospect shone a few watts more brightly. Brian became a globetrotter in earnest.

Pan American had just introduced business class and the first frequent flyer program. By virtue of flying to Australia on Pan Am, Brian had accrued "a bazillion" of their miles. He could take a helicopter from the heart of Manhattan straight to Kennedy airport and check in half an hour before flight time. What was bizarre was that he could buy an economy-class ticket for $300 and upgrade it to business class with 10,000 miles, but the airline credited him 10,000 miles for flying business class. Pan Am hadn't figured out that it should credit only 3,000 for economy.

"*I* wasn't going to tell them," Brian concluded with impeccable logic.

While launching Ice Majesty, he went back and forth between New York and London three times a month.

"It was hysterical that it was ultimately cheaper for me to go back to New York—business class with the helicopter—than it was to stay in a hotel in London for two extra nights."

Garnet

By the time Ice Majesty reached England, some of the original company members had left, and their replacements had arrived. Allen, Angela, Simone, Sally, Tami, Michael, and Reggie were joined by Jean Yun, two-time Korean champion; Donald Bonacci, American ice dance champion and adagio pairs skater; John Rait, Canadian ice dancer and veteran of the Curry and Cranston shows; and Garnet Ostermaier.

One day in May, Fate called on Garnet. She hadn't seen Robin for two years. A coach by then at the Paramount rink in Los Angeles, she was lounging by the pool at the Professional Skaters' Guild of America convention at Las Vegas when she noticed him.

"Robin, do you remember me? I'm a woman from your past."

Robin took one look and shouted, "Garnet!"

Evelyn Kramer was within earshot.

"This is the girl I was telling you about. She needs to be in your show."

Garnet had thought about joining a show, but she was making a good living coaching—not easy to do.

Robin cajoled, and Garnet relented. Her parents were furious.

"What are you talking about? You're leaving to join an ice show? You've spent the last three years building up your clientèle. You have an apartment."

Garnet parceled her students to other coaches, with the understanding that her position wouldn't be available when she returned. She gave up her apartment, put her worldly goods in storage, and went to Europe to join Ice Majesty. She realized later that it was the smartest decision of her life.

On July 7, Robin flew to New York, intending to do his laundry and repack. The airline lost his dirty clothes en route. They eventually followed him across the Atlantic, where they ended up at his mother's feet.

"Dirty washing, a whole mound of it. My washing machine will be going nonstop," Jo chirped to the *Evening Post*. A heap of laundry was a happy indicator of a Robin returned to the nest.

While the Hippodrome was being refurbished, the

cast rehearsed in an abandoned bus station in Avonmouth—
"a raunchy, remote-looking place," according to Garnet.

"We had four weeks of rehearsals. Every single day,
Jo and Fred showed up with trays and trays of food for fifty
or sixty people: fried chicken and baked chicken and
everything for the girls who were dieting. Jo was everybody's mother."

One day Garnet got a haircut. By the time she left the
coiffeur, her auburn hair had been bleached almost white,
cut short, and spiked in the mode of London punks. She
looked in the mirror and thought, "They're going to fire
me. What have I done?"

Robin was at the far end of the bus station when she
arrived. He took one look and shouted, "I *love* it. It's going
to look great under the lights."

Jo was another story. Her quiet tones conveyed dis-
approval.

"Garnet, I don't think your mother would like that."

Garnet watched in fascination as Robin created the
show.

"I wouldn't want to blow up his head, but it was really genius level. He heard a piece of music. For a couple of
seconds, he stood there. Then he started moving his feet.
All of a sudden, he got a step, but instead of just finding the
step to the music, he would, in that time, have correlated
an entire cast of skaters, the formations and patterns. He'd
look up and say, 'Okay, Brian, this one there, this one
there, this one there,' and he placed everybody. Brian had
to read his mind and try to remember, because Robin
thought so quickly. The material just came out of his head.
Then, surprisingly, when he showed it to everybody, it always worked right off the bat. I've worked with a lot of
choreographers, but his work was always the quickest to
come together. I don't mean to say that the steps were
simple. They were difficult, but somehow their formation,
timing, and coordination jelled with the skaters quickly."

When Robin demonstrated step sequences, the cast grumbled, "Oh, great. He *is* an Olympic champion. How are *we* supposed to learn that?" By the time he had broken down the material and taught it step by step, everyone was saying, "Ha! We're doing it."

While the ideas flowed, a good assistant was invaluable. When Robin turned to ask, "What did I just do?" somebody needed to know the answer. Brian had enough experience that when Robin came along with his "whole new plateau of choreography," Brian understood it. He learned how Robin's mind worked and kept notations as best he could. Much of that was intuitive.

"I've seen and worked with practically every ice choreographer in existence (and certainly a lot of dance and stage choreographers), and I think that he's probably in the top two or three. He hears it, and I'm sure he sees it, too. Then it channels down to his feet. He'd half explain it to me, and I would see the other half with him. I could almost hear the end of the music coming, see what he was building to. It's a gift, a gift that few have, or that some may have but never get to realize."

The Juice Ruse

Handling the show's expenses brought Jo into contact with Brian—someone who was up at the crack of noon. When Jo arrived at his hotel room, she always noticed an empty juice glass. Brian confessed to Robin, "If your mother phones at ten o'clock in the morning and says that she's coming over, I don't want her to think that she's waking me up." He drank the juice, hoping the empty glass would convince Jo that he had been up for hours.

A Sour Note

A disagreement with the Musicians' Union marred the runup to the premier. Robin accommodated Ice Majesty's diversity with a full-length audio tape, but the union claimed that taped music deprived its members of work. They "compromised": Robin could use tape as long as he hired ten musicians to play before the show and during the interval.

"I hadn't put Ice Majesty together to put anybody out of business. I had put it together with music that I had paid for. We bought the rights to use the songs, the most expensive one being Frankie Goes to Hollywood, because it was the most current. We had done everything by the book. We had gotten copyright permission. I thought, 'The musicians playing on the tape are being paid. It's all legitimate.' Unbeknownst to me, it was an unwritten law within the theatre that you don't put in a musical show that doesn't have live musicians.

"Ice Majesty was a huge hit and was subsequently booked by the same cities we had done the Electric Ice tour with—who then had to back down because the Musicians' Union told them, 'If you take the show in, we will not allow our musicians to perform in your theatres for other shows.' What that did was point out, 'This is why we don't see Alvin Ailey. This is why we don't see Dance Theater of Harlem. This is why we don't see the Joffrey.' They couldn't afford to pay musicians. Taped music was used widely worldwide, but not in English theatres."

Holiday on Ice faced a similar dilemma. It hired union musicians to play along with recordings but sometimes passed their leads under carpets and didn't plug them in. The musicians played, oblivious that no one could hear them.

There was another twist, odder still.

"Because Holiday on Ice was a traveling tour, Equity would let the regular performers stay in the show for only X number of weeks. If the show extended, it had to employ British skaters regardless of their standard. Stephanie ended up changing choreography on more than one occasion in order to accommodate certain British skaters. We had one who could only stop by dragging her toe pick behind her. We had to slow down the pinwheel so she could catch it. The only time she put on skates was when Holiday on Ice came in. Competent performers sat on the side in order to accommodate union card members."

Body Moves
Ice Majesty offered a range of styles, motifs, and emotions: drama, robotic contemporary movement, comedy, and a sultry forties mood, with music that ran the gamut from John Williams to Herbie Hancock. "Body Moves," with a score by Kitaro, was spellbinding. It explored movement through ever-shifting emphases: on the arms, the edges, the lean of the body, the footwork. It was Robin's favorite of the hundreds of pieces he had created.

"I started out with the full company, then separated them and did the basic moves, the stretches and so on, that make up skating movement. Simone and Angela did the same thing but in different styles. The pair worked. Then we worked in a trio. Then we worked in a sextet. The beginning was the wake-up, the dawn. Then we went into the duet that was like two lovers waking up. Angela was bright sunlight in the middle of the afternoon. Allen was stuck in the twilight zone."

Having analyzed, Robin synthesized, then analyzed again: simple to complex to simple; variations of bodies in motion.

A few years later, he created a series of spray paintings called "Body Moves." Like the choreography, the large canvases represented the essence of skating movement. In adapting them to a line of T-shirts and sweatshirts illustrating a male, a female, and a pair, he reduced the human form to outlines. There lay a paradox. He heeded detail yet reduced things to their essence. How did the T-shirts relate to the peacocks? Where was the detail in "Body Moves"?

"One requires it and one doesn't. The human form is simple to me. It's basically a trunk and four branches with a head stuck on the top. It's only what you do with the trunk and those four branches that then gives it its fluidity. In doing the skating bodies, the original idea was to create shadow forms. You would see the outlines and curves only where the light hit. I ended up doing a bit more detail, but that's all you need to convey the essence of the motion, to capture the beauty of what we do."

Whether in skating or art, "Detail always comes later. Whereas other people start with detail and build on that, I tend to start with the core of the steps. Detail is the stuff that makes the steps tell the story."

Robin is a brisk walker.

"I get from A to B. I don't dawdle. It's all placed, though not consciously."

He has an internal rhythm, a restless energy, that demands expression: fluid, harmonious, efficient. What doesn't flow from his feet flows from his hands.

Celine McDonald saw that connection.

"There's a certain flow in skating, a certain line of the figure, that he carried on into the drawings. When he was doing his choreography in the living room, it was all about the arm being up and then looking to see if it balanced with the leg. To me, every position was sharp, even though, on ice, it all flowed together. The drawing was the same way. It was about thin, strong lines."

Dance critics and dancers reacted enthusiastically to "Body Moves." Because Robin hadn't put himself in the piece, he watched in nightly fascination—"the quickest twenty minutes" of his life.

Street Heat

"Street Heat" opened the second act. Robin noticed that John Rait's mood-setting bit during intermission grew a little longer each time he performed it.

"We had a garbage can at the side of the set, and John was an old man rummaging for something to eat. Every night there was a sandwich, cold pizza, or yesterday's bread. We put in things that he'd expect to find as a tramp, and he'd eat them. (We're skaters. We're not proud.) He'd sit on his bench, and he'd look at the audience and pick his nose or fix a knot in his shirt, as you see people doing. It did set up quite an eerie beginning. It got the audience laughing, but then you always laugh when you are uncomfortable."

The tale of warring gangs, lost innocence, love, abandonment, and sacrifice was set to a jazz-based Michel Colombier score. Robin played a pimp. When people asked him, "Where on earth did that number come from?" he told them, "I haven't got a clue."

Angela and Allen were the antagonists. Simone played Robin's love interest. ("Typecasting. Shades of Denver.") In the fight scene, she threw herself in front of Robin to save him from Allen. She was stabbed. Once, Allen got carried away and stabbed her five or six times.

Angela rushed onstage and dragged Allen off while the other skaters stood horrified in the background, then faded into the wings. Simone and Robin, left alone, acted out Simone's death scene. It took her forever to die—three and a half minutes, because that was the musical timing.

"Robin skates with me, and I'm dying, I'm dying. My ideal as an actress was to make the scene work and surprise Robin in the process. I was reaching out to the audience, realizing I'd been stabbed. Robin stood at the back of the stage, frozen, waiting to see what I would do. The first time we performed that, I managed to make myself cry. I turned and looked at Robin. He was truly taken aback. I'm sure he didn't know whether there was really something wrong with me or whether I was doing a good acting job."

Letting Go of the Dream

The agreement with the Musicians' Union applied only to Bristol. For the planned transfer to Liverpool, the union would not budge. Robin and Brian had taken a risk with Ice Majesty. Having severed their ties with the Electric Ice production team, they didn't have a producer doing the funding. Their own necks were sticking out, albeit well-protected. As upset as they were when the tour fell apart, they weren't in a financial position to fight the union in court.

When Robin's twenty-eighth birthday fell just before the closing, Amanda found a way to make it memorable.

She and her friend Lucinda Bird always tried to make the company laugh during the encore. They stole some spare leotards and tutus and wore them under their coats, preparing to reveal themselves from the back of the auditorium at the end of the matinée. As Amanda confessed, "There was a lot more of me in those days." When Robin decided to cut the encore, Amanda and Lucinda buttoned up. Jo was disappointed.

"You *have* to do it at this evening's show."

That night, Jo handed Amanda and Lucinda an inflatable birthday cake and a bunch of plastic flowers.

She said, as only Jo could, "'Go and give them to Robin."

"Jo, we're not going to—"

"Do as I say! Go give them to him."

Amanda and Lucinda looked at each other and muttered, "What the hell." With a loud whoop, they barreled down the aisle. Robin saw them coming.

"Oh, my God, no. They're not—!"

At that, they handed him the flowers and cake. The audience sang "Happy Birthday" while balloons and a giant greeting card fell from the flies.

Robin returned to America without regrets.

"I was the producer, director, choreographer, and star. I did the shebang, the whole bit, and learned many a lesson. I'd do it all again. Just find me the money."

There was still a slim chance that his show, in one of its incarnations, would land on Broadway. The cast stayed available. Until then, most skaters of Garnet's level— artistically superb but untitled—would have worked with Holiday on Ice, Ice Capades, or Ice Follies. Robin's show (like Curry's before it, and Cranston's to a lesser extent) offered a different sort of release in a more artistically satisfying vein. However, the new work wasn't consistently available. The skaters made more money when they made it, but they didn't make it as often.

Garnet admitted, "We were all really upset. None of us wanted to find another job. A lot of us held off for months, hoping something would come up."

She went to live with her German grandfather for a year. Michael Shinniman turned down work with Dorothy Hamill. Allen and Angela stayed in New York and took most of the year off.

Allen had been in New York with Robin during consultations with the creative team.

"It was just a question of the money, the money, the money. I think it was an idea a little bit before its time."

Garnet called it a terrible shame that Electric Ice

and Ice Majesty weren't produced in America.

"I always thought that was the biggest loss. (I don't want to call it a failure.) Somebody in his circle blew it and didn't get the right people interested. That wasn't Robin's cup of tea, going out and finding backers, but the people who were around him at the time, managing him and all of that, blew it, because they had a great product. The show was ready to go, with a few adjustments. The format was there. He just needed somebody to give him a chance. I think that, at the time, the failure of the Curry show was still in a lot of those theatre-owners' minds. I do think that was a detriment to Robin. Somebody should have been able to make that thing work."

One September night, Brian and Robin went out for pizza. It was late as they walked back towards West Tenth Street, discussing their options.

"It doesn't look good. We shouldn't have the Garnets and the Allens and the Angelas hanging on. They should take other jobs. We don't want them, through blind loyalty, waiting and turning down work. It may take yet another year. Things move so slowly in that $2 million league."

Brian concluded, "I should probably move out of the guest room and go back to Canada, so Fred and Jo can come visit."

For the two years Brian had worked out of the apartment, there hadn't been a guest room.

"The intent when Robin bought the condo was that his parents could come, and that would be their New York home—again, that wonderful ability of his to put them first."

Robin told Brian, "You know, you're right. I should start thinking of what to move on to next. Call me if something comes up."

They entered the apartment and found a message on the answering machine. Kirk Wyse had phoned Brian from England, where he had been skating in the summer show

Hot Ice II at the Blackpool Pleasure Beach.

"Call me no matter what time you get in."

It was midnight in New York, 5:00 A.M. in England. Brian, the king of long distance, dialed the phone.

The German producers of a dreadful show called The Merry Widow on Ice had just shown up in Blackpool with a proposal to remount it in a musical variety format. They had spent $2.5 million on an ice floor and equipment and were willing to refinance the show if they could recruit the right talent. One of the Blackpool principals had offered to choreograph.

"I'll be in the show," Kirk agreed, "but not if *she* is doing the choreography."

He made a pitch for Robin, but the producers said, "We can't afford him." They had already checked with his management.

"Well, then, you have to take his assistant."

Kirk convinced the producers that Brian would charge in on a white horse and save their show.

"Where are you?" Kirk asked Brian. "I'll have them call you in an hour."

By evening, Brian was ensconced in first class on a flight to Hamburg, having spent less than twenty-four hours unemployed.

The Island Interlude

Simone starred in the new show, Fantasy on Ice. Kirk and Lenel van den Berg skated as principals, while Kirk doubled as company road manager. Following rehearsals in a storybook German Alpine town, the troupe set out to tour in a tent. They planned to bring cancan and waltz productions, ice comedy, and Kirk's Charlie Chaplin routine to towns that weren't normally on the circuit.

Then the wind kicked up. The tent nearly blew away during Simone's first performance.

"There was a severe storm. We had to stop in the

middle of the show. I was considering the fact that I had perhaps made a big mistake."

Eventually they ended up in Greece, in a white marble amphitheatre in the harbor town of Piraeus. Their terrace looked out over the Acropolis, the Athens airport, and the bay. There they sat, amidst glorious decadence, wishing it would last forever, but it didn't. Brian, Kirk, and Lenel saw the promoter leave for the airport with a bag of money. They quickly removed the costumes and other portable items, but the city of Piraeus then put a lock around the building, trapping the scenery and ice floor inside. The final cast payday was tearful.

Then the German producers asked, "Would you mind staying until we can solve the problem with the theatre and get the ice floor out?"

The three musketeers remained briefly in Athens, then announced their intention to head to the islands, checking in every few days.

"We'll keep you on salary," the producers promised.

"We'll go live on the islands, you'll keep paying us, and we'll phone in? Good-bye!"

Along with Kirk's dog, Scrapette, they spent an entire month that way. Eventually even Brian got tired of reading and working on his suntan. He called the producers, who were then in Linz, Austria.

"We'll wait there, then fly back to Athens when you give us the green light."

They walked into the producers' offices in Linz only to hear, "You can go back and clean out the theatre now."

Brian hired laborers sight unseen.

"I was getting on a plane to go unload an entire show on the hope that the Egyptian on the phone had understood that I needed sixteen men tomorrow. They were lined up and waiting. It took me a day to get it all packed up."

Transitions

Robin had remained based in New York, continuing his own peripatetic existence. He did the odd guest appearance or competition, then flew home to Europe for Christmas. At the end of January 1986, he was scheduled to headline Ice Capades.

According to Evelyn Kramer, "He was skating to some dreadful piece of music. Nobody would tell him that it was a bomb."

Lee Mimms, Robin's manager, called Evelyn from California and said, "You have to go to New Jersey and make him change his program."

Evelyn announced, "Robin, this program doesn't work. Why don't you do 'Over the Rainbow'?"

He reluctantly agreed.

"'Rainbow' had been a great number, but it had *been*. However, it worked—for the amount of time I ended up doing it."

Evelyn never explained her sudden appearance in New Jersey. She didn't want to hurt Robin's pride.

"I was protective of him. This I've found: the greater they are, the more insecure they are."

Robin played a few dates in New Jersey and Long Island, then opened in Manhattan on January 29. Disaster struck during the very next matinée.

"I did a flying camel, and it felt like my leg had flown to the other end of the building. It was like a karate chop. I'd never felt pain like that. The adductor tendon had ripped, which is the one that attaches to the hip. It's in the groin. I had warmed up. I was ready. The physio said I had done everything I needed to. It just had gone. *Boom*. There was little they could do."

Expecting to be back in shape in a matter of weeks, Robin languished off the ice for three months. As time dragged on, and the acute pain persisted, he tried every remedy he could imagine.

Evelyn empathized with his frustration.

"Somebody who is such a great athlete and artist has no time for pain. It's in your way."

Robin began to face his athletic mortality. By spring, Electric Ice and Ice Majesty were effectively dead and buried, and his injury had left him uncharacteristically morose. Even after it healed, prospects seemed grim.

"Things were slowing down. Nothing had come of Pro Skate. A couple of Ice Capades guests dates, a couple of TV appearances—there wasn't a lot happening, I have to say. Who knew what direction skating would go? There wasn't a lot around for me to do."

Meanwhile Robin had been taking voice lessons. On April 20, he made his solo début at *A Night of 100 Stars*, a variety benefit at the Shaftesbury Theatre, London. He sang "Love or Money," but neither love nor money could revive his repertory company. Where skating was concerned, his spirits were at a low ebb.

It would be a romantic exaggeration to say that he was brooding, but there was evidence of at least somber introspection when he introduced "Good as Gold" at Skate Aid, the English benefit for African famine relief. Composers Richard Currier and Jim Piazza had based Robin's number on the Oscar Wilde story of the prince on a pedestal.

"He sees everything going on around him, but he can't do anything about it. A little bird comes and sits on his shoulder, and he tells the bird what to do. They wrote the song based on something that was apt for me: when you don't think you can do any good, sometimes you *can* do something, just by being aware."

Robin told his audience, "Not everyone has the chance to do it all, and not everyone has the encouragement to make it work. Sometimes Martin, Nick, and I even take it for granted. Maybe that's why this project is so important to me: my chance in front of millions to show we care and that there's hope one day that all the world's people will wake up with a family like mine to love and friends like mine to trust."

Six weeks later, he spoke in a similar vein at an Ice Castle show in California. Linking the message of "Good as Gold" to freedom, self-expression, and "the ability to do what you want when you want," something he had sorely lacked of late, he told the Blue Jay crowd, "I was injured in January and February and March and had three months to sit and think about what it was like when I was unable to perform. I was always very grateful that I was in a position to do what I wanted, to travel and to meet other people in various parts of the world. Three months off the ice made me understand how fortunate and lucky I am. There are a lot of people around the world who are not so lucky."

Face to face with the finite, Robin was grateful for what he had. He would never take skating for granted.

At about the same time, the New York group felt the urge to go elsewhere. Their centripetal force turned centrifugal. New York was expensive. Celine wanted to paint landscapes and raise a child in a clean environment. Vin hoped to start a business in Massachusetts, where he and Celine had been high school sweethearts. Gloria wanted to go home to Chicago.

Robin entered the summer of 1986 feeling vulnerable.

"That was probably when I was at my lowest in terms of what I could and couldn't do, skating-wise, and in terms of whether or not I was in a position to carry on a lot of touring and a lot of performing."

Evelyn Kramer remembered it differently.

"I think that's his emotion talking. He never did what he couldn't do. When it came time to take out a triple jump as the years went, he took it out. I feel that he's talking from his heart and not from his head when he's telling you that."

Perhaps so.

Perhaps the Phoenix needed to die before it could rise from its ashes.

"Very likely," Robin sighed when he read that analysis.

7. California Dreamin': 1986-94

The Ice Castle, an open-air rink in the San Bernardino Mountains, was the brainchild of Carol Caverly Probst and her late husband, Walter. When they broke ground for their dream home on Lake Arrowhead, there was a small, defunct rink in Blue Jay, a hamlet named for the Steller's Jays that populate the evergreens. The Probsts went to one of the town fathers to offer help in reopening the rink where Carol had skated as a child. They learned that the county had closed it for lack of parking space. The official walked them to a potential building site just a block away— "The only level ground in the mountains," Carol suspected.

Although the Probsts built their rink with a vaulted roof, they left its sides and far end open to the woods.

Robin skated at the charity launch in 1983. The beauty of the setting and the training altitude of 5,100 feet became the facility's prime selling points.

One day, Robin rode with Carol and Walter on the private tram that descended the slope from their house to the water's edge. Turning to Walter, he announced, "When I stop competing, I'm going to come to Blue Jay. This is where I'm going to live someday." Carol exchanged a look with Walter that meant, "Yeah, right. He probably says that to everybody."

"Here was this wonderful man we had seen win the Olympics. I remember watching him through my field glasses. He was so happy when he won. Now here he was at our house, saying that some day he was going to come back and live at Blue Jay. We didn't believe him."

Carol and Walter's long-term goal was to establish a two-rink international training center where skaters worked with top coaches under ideal conditions. In early July 1986, all they had was one rink and a dream. Robin spent a week there teaching a seminar. Then he agreed to return for the August carnival. After celebrating his twenty-ninth birthday in New York, he flew to California and climbed the hairpin curves that were carved into the San Bernardino granite. Beyond the precipice, the L.A. sprawl receded into smoggy haze and distant memory.

Someone asked Robin what he had been up to in New York. It struck him, "*This* is one of my dreams and ambitions, and here it is, being put together as a fledgling idea."

The Ice Castle perched above 845 acres of serene water ringed with luxury homes, among them the Probst mansion. Walter was a self-made man, the chairman of Essex International. Until his death in 1994, he was a well-known philanthropist, an avid golfer, and the owner of the world's largest collection of American cut glass crystal, but his greatest passion and indulgence was his wife. Robin loved hearing how they had met.

"Movie-of-the-week material. Carol Caverly was a star of Ice Follies. During her summer vacation, she went down to Palm Springs and modeled in an exclusive women's boutique in the days when they had runway shops.

Mrs. Probst, Walter's first wife, used to come to the shop and insist that she would only buy the clothes if they were modeled by Carol Caverly. When she passed away, one of her wishes was that her wardrobe would go to Carol. Cutting a long story short, Walter thought, 'This woman must have been pretty special to my wife.' He met Carol, who initially had resisted the meeting. They ended up having lunch. Then they ended up having a date. Then they ended up getting married."

Carol and Walter wanted Robin to be vice president, head coach, and director of the Ice Castle International Training Center. Together, the three of them would realize Carol's dream. Robin stayed at their home during the show.

Over dinner, they discussed the nature of skating and their mutual ambitions. Robin explained what he wanted from the sport and what he thought one could (and should) give back in return.

"It was then just sort of handed to me on a plate, and I thought, 'How can I not?' So I did."

Robin was surprised that the Probsts had made the offer to him rather than to an American.

"I think it was that Carol and I matched on the emotional level. We had all these grand designs, and Walter would say, 'Yeah! You two plan it.' He said that to the wrong two people at that point."

Robin flew back to New York and informed Gloria, "There's something I have to tell you." At the same time Gloria said, "Robin, there's something I have to tell you." A similar scenario played out with Vin and Celine.

"It was one of those times when we all wondered how the others would feel, because we were very much family. It was strange when we got together and suddenly realized we'd all made the same decision, pretty much within a week. We were all moving on. We said, 'Whew.' Then, boom, everybody went."

Robin closed the door on one phase of his life as he opened the window on another. In December, he skated in the original Stars on Ice five-city tour, competed at Landover, and continued on to the Challenge of Champions in Paris. Then he went home to England for Christmas, calling 1986 "a weird year."

Intersecting Trajectories

Brian Klavano was no stranger to the mountain. In October 1984, there had been talk of rehearsing Ice Majesty at the Ice Castle. Robin had called Carol to make the arrangements.

"I'm going to send Brian to look at the rink and the accommodations, to see if we can work something out. He'll be there on Friday."

"Oh, we've closed the house. We're moving down to the desert. The staff are already down there."

"We'll put him up in the hotel."

"No, no. Walter and I will stay up here for the night."

Brian drove with the Probsts to their estate.

"We'd gotten a coffee cake that we were going to have for breakfast. Walter went around the corner, and the thing fell off onto the floor of the car and squished in its box. So there was our tired little coffee cake in the bazillion-dollar house. I came into the kitchen the next morning, and there was Walter, going through the cupboards. 'Goddamn, where the hell did you put it? Who designed this place?' He couldn't find the coffeemaker. It was just so funny to see that incredibly powerful, wealthy man lost in his own kitchen."

The coffeemaker dripped from an upper cupboard to a hot plate on the counter.

"Unbelievable, the home. No matter how much glorious decadence you'll ever imagine, it doesn't come close to that house. They had just finished building it about a year earlier. There were switches that made windows, curtains, and skylights open. Televisions popped out of the wall. Fireplaces came on. Wet bars appeared. Unbelievable, the array of switches. I stayed in the Blue Room. I got all settled into bed. I was watching TV and playing with the curtains when Carol came banging on the door."

"Let me in quick! Don't touch anything!"

Brian put on a robe as Carol rushed in.

"I forgot to tell you. That is the Secret Service button for when the President visits. Don't hit that one. We'll have helicopters here."

Brian glanced at the signatures in the guest book. Bob and Dolores Hope. Jimmy Carter. Gerald Ford. At the end of his visit, as the car wound down the hill, Carol asked, "Did you sign the guest book?"

"Well, no, actually."

He hadn't wanted his name below presidential signatures. Carol was ready to make Walter turn the car around.

Ice Majesty ultimately rehearsed in Vail. The show came and went. Brian and Robin parted company on the occasion of the Manhattan pizza and Kirk's phone message. By the time Brian reached his Greek Islands phase, he was in the mood to resume some semblance of normalcy.

His parents had meanwhile moved to Edmonton. One day, he phoned his mother from Greece. She told him, "Brian Pockar is trying to get in touch with you. Something about the Olympics."

Pockar had been named artistic director of the 1988 closing ceremonies. "Listen," he told Klavano, "they're putting together the team to handle the ceremonies at the Calgary Olympics, and you, a Calgarian with your show background, would have a foot in the door."

Brian packed up in Piraeus in the spring of 1986 and went to New York to gather things he had stored at Robin's apartment. Fred and Jo were in town. Brian found that "his" room had a new color scheme and carpeting.

Seeing Fred and Jo reminded him that he hadn't visited his own parents in a while.

"So I decided to go home and spend time with my folks and see if I could nurture the Olympic thing with Pockar. It's kind of nice to be young and have nothing. I had no car, no condo, no payments, so it didn't matter where I hung out. All I had was my Visa bill. I did my good-byes in New York, knowing that that chapter was over, that decadence—and you don't want to stay in New York and pay for it yourself."

Kirk Wyse had found a job in Willy Bietak's show at Busch Gardens, Williamsburg: four performances a day in a theme park, the most humid, horrible summer of his life.

Although Brian had never heard of Bietak, the new producer of Ice Capades, on Kirk's suggestion he wrote a letter of inquiry. He mailed it on a Tuesday. On Wednesday morning, his phone rang.

"Hi. This is Willy Bietak."

"The Canadian post does not work that efficiently. Did you get my letter?"

"What letter? I've heard about you, and I want to have lunch with you."

"I have some free tickets left on Pan Am. Would next month work?"

"No. I've sent you tickets. I want to have lunch on Friday."

Bietak, nine-time Austrian pairs champion and skating impresario, hired Brian as his production manager. Brian immediately phoned Robin with the news.

"I'm going to be moving to L.A. Isn't that cool?"

"Yes. I just bought a house in Lake Arrowhead."

"You're kidding. This is hysterical. We're both going to end up in California."

Robin had put his condominium on the market. The Probsts found him a home to buy in a gated community overlooking Lake Arrowhead. The architecturally stunning A-frame with omnipresent decks and sliding glass came fully furnished. The owners had simply cleared out the closets and left.

Its sleek, masculine décor suited Robin to perfection: a glass dining room table set on concrete antlers; black Mikasa dinnerware; a large, curved sofa in the sunken living room; multiple beds in the four basement-level guest rooms, plus a family room complete with fireplace. At the top of the house was the master suite, "bigger than anything I've lived in," Brian certified. "It was its own one-bedroom apartment with a huge bathroom and multiple terraces. The house was woodsy yet modern, a perfect 'Come on up for the weekend' place."

Brian set up housekeeping in Los Angeles and went to work for Willy Bietak. Robin set up housekeeping on Lake Arrowhead and went to work for the Probsts. It never occurred to him to approach Carol and Walter for Broadway funding. Life seemed full of novel possibilities.

Robin among the Jays
Robin threw himself into his new life.

"Carol and Walter, bless him, were just wonderful, but I also think the three of us were incredibly naïve. We had our project, and I was ready to jump in with two feet, as I always am. It was a wonderful, wonderful, thing. It still is. Carol and Walter had such a vision about what they wanted to do. Walter was the mathematician of the project, making sure that Carol was happy. Nothing was impossible for him to do for that woman. I've never experienced devotion to someone's passion the way Walter was devoted to Carol's passion for skating. That was what drew me to Ice Castle in the first place. I think the most important thing is that it's there because of the love of the sport. There is not one nut or bolt in any part of that complex that isn't there through the love of skating and because of one man's desire to create something that would enhance what gave his wife pleasure through her whole life. Few places are built on those foundations."

One cold, rainy day, Carol and Walter drove Robin to a desolate spot in the middle of the pine woods in the town of Lake Arrowhead, not far from Blue Jay. The acreage in question was an abandoned children's summer camp that had just become available through foreclosure. Among its rustic structures were a residence hall, lodge, pool and Jacuzzi, amphitheatre, office buildings, and twenty-four knotty-pine cottages. A flat area at the top of the property could accommodate a second rink. Walter brimmed with ideas.

What did Robin think?

"It was overwhelming. The only thing I had to work from was my personal experience: what I would have loved to have had if I'd had that opportunity."

The buildings were salvageable but in need of repair and refurbishing. Carol planned the Country French décor. Little by little, twelve acres of wooded mountainside metamorphosed into a residential camp with a sixty-four-bed dormitory, a game room, bungalows for older students, a heated swimming pool, a 3,000 square-foot dance pavilion with a Bio-Spring floor for ballet, jazz, aerobics, and conditioning, a video-screening area, and a lodge containing a kitchen, dining room, and weight room. Talented skaters and coaches populated the complex. It was a far cry from Robin's unhappy days in the lonely bed-sitter.

Carol and Walter built the Lake Arrowhead rink, unlike the one in Blue Jay, specifically for competitive skaters. Because it was on private property, it couldn't be used for public purposes. That gave Robin the idea to banish hockey boards.

"Why do you need boards if you're not going to play hockey?" he asked.

Carol, ever the figure skater at heart, knew, "That was an assurance that we *wouldn't* have hockey."

On Robin's suggestion, large windows let in natural light. Mirrors lined the far wall. The Training Center rink was a dance studio with ice.

Robin invited Garnet to teach with him. By then, she had met her future husband and was ready to settle down. They established a team-teaching system. While Robin was away performing or competing, Garnet offered his students continuity. She took them to competitions when he couldn't, and both retained their flexibility. In the early days, when enrollment was low, they occasionally had the Blue Jay rink to themselves. Garnet felt lucky.

"The place was empty. We went in there sometimes at six or seven o'clock at night, surrounded by the trees, the mountains, and the open air. Robin put on music and went off into his own little world. It was beautiful. I watched him from just inside the private lobby. He could go on for three hours without stopping, putting on different pieces of music and interpreting them."

When Robin asked Garnet, "What did I do on that step?" she realized how valuable Brian had been to Robin.

"His skating is such a gift. He doesn't have to do a jump for me. I don't think people are going to realize this for another ten or fifteen years, but because of figures being gone, skating will change and become more acrobatic. I think Robin is the last of a dying breed, especially of the British-trained skaters. Those edges, and those great knees that he has! When you watch him skate across the ice and do a spiral, it's breathtaking. You can't say that about a lot of male skaters nowadays. Unless you see them do back-flips and triple Lutzes—yes, that will hold your interest—but I wouldn't watch them stroke."

Robin was nervous at first about teaching young students. Nick, his brother's greatest supporter, pointed out that he need not have worried.

"As a coach and choreographer, he can do it all. He can teach them the techniques; he can show them how to do it; he can choreograph their music; he can teach them (as far as it is possible to teach it) to move with the music; he can draw set designs; he can visualize, conceptualize— and all this is taking a wider sphere as his career develops."

Robin's career was about to develop in directions neither he nor Nick imagined.

Aurora and Florimund

In the spring of 1987, Rosalynn Sumners was a green-eyed, strawberry-blonde beauty with a warm, open nature and an appealing touch of vulnerability. In the years since her Olympic disappointment, skating with Disney on

Ice, she had become especially vulnerable—but her outlook was on the brink of change.

The Olympic silver medalist had a pristine memory of her first encounter with Robin.

"After I won Worlds in '83, I was still a naïve little innocent thing from Seattle, and there I was—world champion. I remember the party afterwards. Robin took me under his wing. I was sitting on his lap, and I couldn't even breathe. I'll never forget thinking, 'I can't believe I'm sitting in Robin Cousins's lap.' I couldn't sleep that night—because of winning, of course, and then because people like Robin were paying attention to me. I never knew that kind of stuff came with it. I remember thinking, 'This is almost as cool as actually winning.'"

Four years later, Rosalynn played Princess Aurora opposite Robin's Prince Florimund in the televised ice ballet "The Sleeping Beauty." Rosalynn fell in love with one of the pairs skaters, Jonathan Thomas, which didn't stop her from sharing jokes with Robin. Whenever the prince awakened the princess with a kiss, they laughed and ruined the scene.

The high-pedigree cast rehearsed in Peterborough, England. Filming took place in Norwich, in a vacant military airplane hangar, the only available facility large enough to accommodate the sets. A construction crew poured 300 tons of concrete to level the floor; laid ten miles of refrigeration pipes; and built up a four-inch ice surface, one layer at a time. Within the cavernous structure, there were trailers for makeup, costuming, gym equipment, medical services, and catering. In free moments, the skaters huddled near space heaters.

Robin delighted in the opportunity to work with dance choreographer Lar Lubovitch.

"We found ourselves, with Lar, making what we would consider to be basic connecting steps into major parts of the choreography. To him they were wonderful, because he couldn't do them. I found a lot of places where I thought we should be jumping or doing *something*. Lar said, 'But why? These steps are so wonderful.'"

Lubovitch loved lifts, but not simple dance lifts. He wanted to create new ones, which was fine, but Rosalynn was the one "hanging upside down in the air in some guy's arms" while Robin and Lar adjusted her position. The lifts involved Rosalynn's upper body and rib cage. After weeks of unaccustomed pressure, her ribs said, '"Enough!" She woke up in acute distress, with sore ribs and labored breathing. Robin took her to the hospital. She had two cracked ribs. The doctors who taped them were afraid to inject a painkiller. The cracks were too near her lungs.

"There I was, lying on a stretcher in a hospital in Norwich, England, but Robin took care of me. We got through the filming. We did it in sections. Unfortunately, on the last day, when we were filming the really nice *pas de deux* that came after he woke me up, I was in so much pain. If you know that, and you watch the video, you can see how he is lifting me *so gently*."

When Rosalynn was put on hold recently, she heard

the familiar Tchaikovsky score.

"I didn't even want the next person to answer the phone. I hear it quite often, and I turned it into a competition number a couple of years ago, but still, to this day, when I hear that music, I can instantly put myself right back into that big airplane hangar. I can almost smell the building."

The project's production coordinator was Debbie Turner. She and Robin discovered two common loves: gin and tonic and old ballads and show tunes—a devastating combination. Robin was at his most mellow.

"Generally we went back to the hotel and had a couple of gin and tonics. Then we serenaded the entire hotel, whether they liked it or not."

Star Spangled Ice

During the same spring as the filming of "The Sleeping Beauty," Robin and the Probsts established the Foundation for International Ice Skating Advancement to provide scholarships to deserving Ice Castle students. Robin inaugurated the *Star Spangled Ice* Fourth of July weekend show as a fundraising vehicle. He asked Rosalynn to skate in the premier edition and moved her into one of his many spare rooms.

Because the show was a benefit, Robin asked friends to donate their time. According to pairs skater Tony Kudrna, "It was interesting to watch those shows develop. Robin invited people he knew. They came in on a weekend, and he put the show together—the opening and the closing — just like *that*. So many people we work with want to make it hard (as if, in order to make it good, you have to make it difficult). Robin said, 'Do this, do that. Okay, now let's go have fun.' The audience liked it, we liked it, and there was none of the heartache that sometimes occurs with other producers, directors, and choreographers. I think that's a real gift of his. There was never any nervousness about pulling it off. It was, 'Just do it. It's going to work out.'"

Rosalynn stayed for several weeks as a guest instructor.

"Robin didn't just go in for a few patches and freestyles. I was there three weeks and saw him on the ice daily from five in the morning until seven at night. It wasn't as if he was running the show and then sitting back on the dock at the lake. He came home exhausted at night and still cooked barbecues and invited people over."

Robin regretted that he didn't have more time to spend with some of his students.

"Things had started to kick in for me. I was not around at some key points when I needed to have been."

Erik Larson spent the 1987-88 season on an Ice Castle scholarship.

"That was great talent—as with many of Janet Champion's students with whom I've crossed paths. Janet had a passion for skating, and Erik was the same. His style and quality were born of that. We had a brilliant year. He did win some things, but, for me, it was exciting for him to be the one people talked about."

Ice Castle hosted the Southwest Pacific Regionals, where Erik won the senior men's title. Future world bronze medalist Nicole Bobek was seventh in novice ladies.

Festival on Ice

Meanwhile, Willy Bietak had hired Robin to appear with Tai and Randy in Festival on Ice, opening in December at the Dorothy Chandler Pavilion in L.A. Robin habitually taught at Lake Arrowhead, drove two hours to all-night rehearsals, then returned to the mountain in the morning for another workday.

Nick's family flew to America for the holidays. Garnet volunteered to help them find their way up the mountain while Robin rehearsed. By the time they reached San Bernardino, it was 9:00 P.M.

"You can't go up there," she told them. "You'll never find that place on your own."

Nick, Helen, Thomas, and James spent the night with Garnet.

The next morning, they drove to Robin's house, only to find the roads closed behind them. They were snowed in. Robin had no trouble in his four-wheel-drive Subaru, but when Nick ventured out in a rental car, he slid off the highway. After a beautiful, snowy Christmas, Nick and his family drove down to Los Angeles, saw Festival On Ice, and spent several nights in a hotel, compliments of Uncle Robin. There was much to celebrate: 1987 had been full of challenges, hope, friendship, and new prospects.

Robin toured for several months with Tai and Randy. As spring burgeoned again on the mountain, his sky looked blue and crystal clear. Just over the horizon, however, thunderheads began to gather.

The Black Hole: Mortality Revisited

Robin had that sinking feeling. There was something wrong with his right knee. Cartilage trouble again? He didn't have much left. Although he hid the first hints of trouble, friends began to catch him grimacing when he stepped onto the ice. He couldn't do what he wanted to. That was frustrating and acutely painful.

On the day of the 1988 Fourth of July show, Robin limped off the ice. His eyes filled with tears as he entered his office with Garnet and turned to look at her helplessly.

"My performing days are over. I have to start doing other things, finding out what else I'm good at."

He had resolved to postpone his third knee operation until after the show. Meanwhile, his interior voices argued.

"I'm never going to skate again. This is it."

"So this is where I am. Fine. I have a great job."

"But—!"

"I remember being absolutely distraught on the afternoon of the second Star Spangled Ice. I was going into surgery the following day for what I knew was going to be the last time. There was no way I could go through that again. For some reason, I had it in my head, as I had never had before, that that was the last time and the last show that I would ever skate. Garnet happened to be on the receiving end of that one."

Rosalynn, back for another show, also glimpsed his pain and fear.

"One day he was trying to skate. He got off the ice, and he was crying. He thought he would never, ever skate again. He was worried about the surgery, and he was scared that it was going to be career-ending. We talked, although there's not much you can say. It wasn't as though I could assure him that his career *wasn't* going to be over."

Rosalynn stayed at Robin's house to look after his dogs. When he hobbled home from the hospital, she was there to help. She left thinking that the initial stress and fear had been the worst of it.

"He was kind of okay with being laid up. He was

taking a bit of a break."

Robin had put on a good act for his guest.

Garnet perceived "a big, emotional struggle."

"After he had the surgery, I remember him being really depressed for a while, thinking it was over for him. I think it was insecurity on his part. 'My gosh, what am I going to do? I know what I *want* to do, and I may not be able to do it anymore.' He was starting to think more along the lines of producing shows and coaching."

During the previous recuperations, Robin had been young and resilient. A thirty-one-year-old body was a different story. Although the first two surgeries had been invasive while the third was arthroscopic, the third just didn't go as well. It was Robin's second operation on the same knee: interior and anterior.

"It took me forever to get back on the ice, forever to even contemplate a three-turn. It was not good."

After three weeks, Robin could walk. After four weeks, he rode his mountain bike to the rink.

"That's when Dick Button came along. I thought, 'Great! That'll do it. I'll get back into skating again.' I was barely in shape. I barely got myself together."

In favoring his knee while skating, Robin absorbed the strain in his lower back, with excruciating results. He performed at Landover that December in a brace. Later he regretted competing—the only regret in a long career.

"It was the first time I just couldn't do what I wanted. I thought, 'When you get out there, you'll do it,' but my body wasn't in a position to cooperate, and I suffered for eight months."

Garnet alluded to his physical condition, though she might have been analyzing his psyche:

"I think it took about a year before he was totally back 100 per cent. Then he started to worry less about having another occupation. After two years, you would never have known. I thought he looked better than ever."

There was something that Robin alone could fully appreciate: in addition to the absence of cartilage in his right knee, he no longer had enough ligament support to keep the knee aligned. It was so loose that, under stress, it pronated nearly a quarter-rotation. As a result of the 1988 surgery, triple jumps were a risk he could not afford.

"I have so much mobility and flexibility in my knee joint, side to side, and the rotation of a triple jump has to be so fast and so exact on the landing, that there's no room to land anything other than textbook properly, which no one can guarantee doing. It's not that I don't have the desire, or that I can't do triples—I've done them now and again— but it's simply because I cannot risk landing from triple rotations."

Robin didn't correct those who assumed that his triples had vanished with age. In truth, though, age had little to do with it.

"He may not be doing triple jumps like the younger guys," Stephanie Andros remarked, "but he has so much other material, no one misses it."

Jo did miss the triples.

"Although I'm not into quad jumping and all that kind of thing, I did love the way he skated—the athleticism and the jumping and the artistry. I have to be honest. I do care about the lack of jumps. I like to see what he's always done, and I know he can't."

She worried that there wouldn't always be an audience.

"I think there will be," Fred assured her. "There are those who will go just to see his artistry, as they did with John."

Stephanie was satisfied to watch him stroke.

"One thing that's unique to Robin is the lovely modern movement that he has applied to skating (that I haven't seen any up-and-coming skater do). One of my favorites of the later champions is Kurt Browning. He's excellent, and so is Brian Boitano, but they don't have the suave ability that Robin has been able to apply to ice."

Surrogate Families

In late 1988, Robin had something to take his mind off his troubles: Garnet's wedding. His principal role was designer of the gown. How long did it take to come up with the general design?

"I'd say it was about three dinners," Garnet estimated. Robin measured the time in gin and tonic.

Bored on the mountain, Robin drove down to San Bernardino for dinner several nights a week. Afterwards, he and Garnet talked. Bridal shop wares struck her as "ordinary." She wanted something unique. Robin designed her dress from start to finish. He knew her style. She gave him a further idea of what she had in mind. Then he began by sketching dress parts: skirts, sleeves, bodices, necklines, and trains. Once they had finalized the design, he researched places to buy fabric.

When an Ice Capades dressmaker came to the house every month or so, Robin supervised.

"This is wrong."

"That is right."

"This makes her stomach look fat."

The forties-look gown in pearl-beaded satin had mutton-chop sleeves, a long, detachable train, and tiny folds in the front of the bodice pleated by a specialist. Robin had the connections from his work with skating costumes.

On his suggestion, Garnet ordered long, elegant sprays of birds of paradise, irises, and gladioli.

She had just one disappointment.

"Robin was one of the first people we told. We wanted to set a date when he could make it. He was supposed to be in our wedding, but about two months beforehand, another obligation came up."

Garnet married Bob Fiordalisi on May 28, 1989. Robin became a regular visitor in their home at the foot of the roller-coaster highway that swooped up the mountain. The year they bought the house, Robin was invited to do a show in Garmisch-Partenkirchen. He and Garnet knew a duet called "Mr. Monotony." When he accepted the show offer, he made her a part of the package. The producer balked at paying her airfare, and her own money was tied up in the house that she and Bob had gutted and were rebuilding.

"That's not a problem," Robin jumped in. "I'll pay her airfare."

Garnet was impressed.

"He knew it would be fun for me to do, and there was not even a hesitation on his part. He did get reimbursed for it later on, but it was never an issue with him. That's another window into how he thinks and who he is."

When Robin couldn't go to England for Christmas, Garnet and Bob invited him to share theirs. Late one Christmas Eve, the guests in the living room noticed a flicker of movement outside in the yard. It was Robin doing back-flips. He used the picture window as a proscenium arch to frame his cavorting and miming.

"We were laughing so hard, rolling on the floor, watching him perform for us on our front lawn," Garnet recalled. "Then he had my husband, Bob, a nonskater and a nondancer, out there learning how to do skating moves. It was one of the best Christmases we ever had."

When Garnet and Bob's babies came along, Robin felt avuncular. Three days after the birth of their daughter, he was at the door with a homemade gift: hand-painted baby shoes decorated with sparkles.

"We'll keep those forever," Garnet promised.

Robin sent birthday cards to the Fiordalisi children and anniversary cards to Garnet and Bob.

"How does he have time to remember?" she wondered. "Our wedding anniversary! My husband doesn't even remember it."

It was the same with Tony and Terry Kudrna.

Competitive skaters as teenagers, they had joined Ice Capades separately in 1979 and found themselves skating together two years later as Terry Pagano and Tony Paul. As adagio skaters, their challenge was to differentiate themselves from the pairs who joined the show after winning international medals. They met Robin in Detroit in 1984. In 1988, he was instrumental in bringing them to the Ice Castle to coach.

Robin had always been a "pairs freak."

"Irina Rodnina will testify that at every practice at a European or world championship, she would know exactly where I was sitting. I never missed one practice that they were on. Pairs short program was always the day before we did figures, and Carlo got sick of telling me to go home and go to sleep. He knew it made me feel good to watch the pairs."

Robin had a gift for choreographing pairs, though he didn't know all the technical intricacies. He liked the yin and yang, the permutations, the spectacular effects that pairs could achieve. He involved Tony and Terry in many of his projects and egged them on to ever more inventive tricks—over Terry's protests.

"On the floor when we were lifting, he was always right there, wanting me to try something more daring. When I saw him coming, I said, 'Go away.'"

Robin was thrilled when the Kudrna family expanded.

"When he found out Terry was pregnant, it was as if he were going to be an uncle. He was so excited. He keeps in touch with us, asks about the children, sends them presents. He's just like family."

It was the same way in 1985 when Celine and Vin's daughter was born. When Vin was out of town on business, Robin hiked around Manhattan, lulling Olivia to sleep in a baby pouch nestled against his chest.

He formed many of his longest-lasting friendships with couples, with and without children, because he missed his own home and family. In London, there was Trish and Mike; in Denver, the Wylies and Fassis; in New York, Vin and Celine; in Lake Arrowhead, the Kudrnas and Fiordalisis.

Robin was excited when his own family visited Lake Arrowhead. Fred invariably romped on the grass with his grandchildren. To watch him play, Garnet mused, was like watching Robin.

"I always thought that Robin looked a lot like him. There's Robin in thirty or forty years."

Fred and Jo couldn't visit America often. Angina and osteoporosis sapped Jo's stamina, but as Garnet said, "She kept sending her boys over. Nick came, then Martin came, then Nick came again. They traded off. I know Robin cherished that, because he is family-oriented, although he doesn't have a family of his own right now."

As Brian Klavano remarked, "Robin's great with kids. He shares with the whole world what others share with their families."

On the other hand, Robin is "great with kids" because he remains one himself—like another great English character, Peter Pan.

"Oh, absolutely," Brian agreed. "He'll never grow up. He can't—but he'll never grow tired either."

In 1988, Robin's nephews Tristan and Robin skated in the late-summer Ice Castle show. Robin was as proud as any skating father, readying them to perform.

Young Robin could skate, but Tristan had never tried. His skills were less than rudimentary as he teetered in a hockey helmet. According to dad Martin, "He was there, but he wasn't exactly skating."

Tristan took to the sport. In September 1995 at Swindon, history will note, he assumed one of Uncle Robin's titles: novice champion of Great Britain. In 1996, he won the primary title, then moved up to fourth in juniors.

When Carol Probst heard the news, she said, "Oh my gosh, I'm getting goose bumps."

Doug Mattis

The 1985 U.S. junior champion, Doug Mattis, finished seventh, tenth, and ninth (twice) as a senior before moving to Lake Arrowhead to work with Robin.

"Robin took what was meant to be energetic in my skating but ended up being frenetic, and he was able to calm it down, stretch it out, and somnambulize it. He was able to communicate to me that clarity was probably preferable to content, and he taught me a lot of things to do on ice skates that I had *no* idea were possible before."

Often when Robin worked on a competitive program, he began by asking the skater how he wanted the audience to feel at the end. Did he want them to applaud loudly? Did he want them to laugh? Did he want them to sit in stunned silence? If the skater didn't have an answer, it was unlikely that he would communicate coherently with his audience or judges. What statement could one make through the elements to create an impact? Robin had often answered that question in his own mind before he asked Doug, who saw through the subterfuge.

"Sometimes I felt that he created situations where I would inevitably choose what he wanted me to skate to. That was fine, because there was a benefit in having me on his side of the choice. That's one of the things about Robin: his overwhelming enthusiasm. You end up being swept up in it and seeing things the way he does."

Robin, at a slender six feet, carried off moves that were less attractive on Doug, a self-described "five-foot-five-and-a-half, kind of athletic, short, choppy guy." Their efforts were "hunt and peck." Doug relied on Robin's judgment and was willing to try almost anything his mentor suggested.

While Doug progressed up the U.S. skating ladder, others remained entrenched in the top spots. In 1990, a fall dropped him from fifth place to eighth. That July during *Star Spangled Ice*, Robin staged a revival of "Body Moves." Garnet, Terry, and Tony joined amateurs Jeri Campbell, Craig Heath, and Doug.

"I don't think we realized what a great number it was until performance night. We were dedicated to Robin (certainly I was) and to everything he wanted us to do choreographically. We could see that the number was neat and fun, but the crowd reaction was so overwhelming that we could feel it growing as we performed."

When the 1991 Nationals loomed, Robin thought that Doug's back-flip would make a fitting signature to his amateur career. The move was still illegal, but Doug agreed.

"I think it was suggested kind of wryly. Robin knew it would be up to me, but he did put conditions on it. He wanted to make sure that I had done the best long program

I could possibly do before I did the back-flip, so that it wouldn't be a statement of sour grapes. It would be a triumph."

In Minneapolis, Doug was tenth after the short program with virtually no chance of a medal. He skated his long program as well as he could, then grinned and tossed off a back-flip. The judges reacted as though he had made an obscene gesture at them. They missed the point.

Doug was someone who recognized Robin's worth.

"He's one of the few people in skating that I can honestly say the word 'genius' about and not be contested by too many people. He doesn't have a full idea of how gifted he is, and I think that's nice. Things come so easily to him that a lot of people in the industry have taken his offerings for granted to this point. In retrospect, when they look back at how Robin has changed our sport, they'll be more appreciative."

Bright Lights, Big City

When cool weather arrived, the Probsts moved to Palm Desert. Brian enjoyed the warmth of L.A. Robin spent his days, months, and changing seasons in the mountain solitude that was both the Ice Castle's principal charm and its major drawback.

During his recovery from surgery, summer turned to fall, which turned to winter. He began to go stir crazy surrounded by rusticity—not to mention snow, pea-soup fog, and frigid winds. As reserved as he was, he was never a loner. He craved the cultural and social life of the city.

One day he phoned Nick.

"I'm thinking of branching away, going into Los Angeles to find work."

Nick assessed the situation.

"Robin was the director of a rink. He had his gold medal. He had his skaters. There he was. He had a steady, traditional skating career all mapped out in front of him, but he was frustrated."

"Go for it," Nick urged. "You only get one chance."

Robin planned a concentrated teaching schedule in order to spend more time in Los Angeles. In early 1990, he bought a home in Beachwood Canyon and began to commute most weekends, choreographing programs to audio tapes as he zoomed up and down the mountain. That led to exasperation for Garnet. She thought when Robin left the rink that his choreography was set, but it continued to grow in his mind. When he returned to Lake Arrowhead, he accused her of getting the steps wrong. She summoned her patience and explained that the steps were exactly as he had left them at the door.

Robin's new hideaway was below the *HOLLYWOOD* sign, accessible via a labyrinth of narrow, twisting roads lined with fenced, hedged private compounds. From the street, the dwelling looked small and utterly bland. Its tall, vertical brown boards turned outward to the left of the tiny kitchen to allow for a nondescript gate, then continued down Hollyridge Drive to form an ugly, impenetrable fence. Beyond its deceptive plain brown wrapper, the dwelling was larger than it looked. It spilled down the hill in several levels. A wall of French doors afforded stunning views. Madonna's estate, visible across the canyon, was not one of them.

After a fire in the 1970s, the previous owners of Robin's house had rebuilt and redecorated it somewhat tastelessly. It occupied half a double lot. The other half was dominated by an award-winning swimming pool. Two years after buying the property, Robin began planning a massive renovation to add a third level and expand the existing two-bedroom home to four thousand square feet.

Though Robin threw several large catered parties, he usually lived a quiet life—quiet except for the barking of his dogs, Winston, Fergie, and Thumper: part Labrador retriever, part Doberman pinscher.

According to Brian, "The dogs' barking drove some of the neighbors crazy. Robin was never a good trainer of his critters. He was gone too often, so he spoiled them when he was home."

The simultaneous ownership of two houses was the outward manifestation of an internal tug of war. Robin's loyalty and need to please began to conflict with a greater force that pulled at him, unbidden, from the world beyond and from within. His restless creative urge demanded appeasement. He longed to cross new frontiers. As always, those frontiers soon loomed into view.

The Return of the Gymnast

In 1989, a new construct was born: a combination of figure skating and gymnastics, a "Symphony of Sports." Robin, with his gymnastic flair, was in on the ground floor.

Holly Turner, a San Francisco marketing executive, sold the idea to Lever Brothers and ABC's "Wide World of Sports." A production team helped her work out the details. Robin oversaw the skating, Paul Ziert the gymnastics. The show benefited the Women's Sports Foundation.

Top athletes assembled at the Dobson Arena in Vail, Colorado. The skaters were Robin, Katherine Healy, Rosalynn Sumners, Brian Boitano, Barbara Underhill, and Paul Martini. Bart Conner, Peter Vidmar, Cathy Rigby, Kristie Phillips, Charles Lakes, Lori Fung, Jim Hartung, Dianne Durham, Wendy Hilliard, Michelle Berube, Mike Rice, and Marcia Frederick were the gymnasts.

Ziert choreographed routines for a forty-square-foot mat. Patches of ice on each side were connected at the far end by a narrow ice passage. Gymnastics equipment lined the sides of the arena.

Robin chose and edited the music. His selections ran the gamut from Khachaturian's violin concerto to David Bowie's "Absolute Beginners" and local pianist Mickey Poage's "Mount of the Holy Cross."

The idea behind "Symphony of Sports" was to blend the two disciplines, highlighting their similarities and drawing strength from their differences. Ziert experimented with mirror imaging, counterpoint, and crossover.

Gymnastics tends to be a sport of explosive bursts, like a skater's jumps. Lyrical passages smoothed the new routines like a skater's glide. Music, theatrical lighting, and costuming were other elements new to the gymnasts. Only women's floor exercise was set to music.

"I like it a lot," Olympic gold medalist Conner told the *Vail Trail*. "You worry less about getting through the gymnastics skills than making sure you're right on the music. The whole production value is teaching the gymnasts a lot. I hope we can come away with a better feeling about how we can really make magic with a sport."

Perhaps because the body aesthetics are similar, there is a high positive correlation between fans of the two disciplines. "Symphony of Sports" was a hit. There were new shows in September 1990 and October 1991. With each year, there was more integration. Robin, wearing biking shorts, tried his hand at gymnastics choreography and ended up somewhat wiser, with severe rug burns.

A nucleus of athletes performed in all three productions: Robin, Bart, Rosalynn, Dianne, and Wendy. Nadia Comaneci joined them in 1990. (She and Bart have since married.) Brian Orser, Peggy Fleming, and Peter and Kitty Carruthers skated in the 1991 edition. Robin brought in Tony and Terry for the second and third shows. With Terry's gymnastics background and their acrobatic approach, they were naturals to blend the two media.

Robin, like Renaissance men before him, showed a knack for invention. He had the idea of building a portable gymnastics bar. He and Tony designed it. Then Tony had it built by a stagehand in Las Vegas, where he and Terry were performing. The metal device was six feet long with handles that turned on bearings. There was a rectangular, cage-like attachment for Terry that Robin dubbed "the human rotisserie." It looked like a barbecue spit with parallel skewers. Terry's pet name for it was more blunt: the ovary-buster.

Robin and Tony each held one end of the bar with Terry in the middle. The three skated together, then Robin and Tony lifted the bar and skated while Terry performed aerial acrobatics.

Robin had always loved to pairs skate, but *he* wanted to be thrown. Tony tossed him higher than the boards in a throw double Axel. The feat aired on "Symphony of Sports" as the credits rolled.

"Robin's so big. I got underneath and threw him as high as I could. He and I have pretty good lifts, too. I can get him in a press lift. There's another one called a Detroiter that he didn't think I could do."[17]

They nearly died laughing.

"It looked great," was Terry's opinion. "Robin's so *long.*"

Robin was attracted, as always, by the opportunity to fly through the air. Several years later, Russian acrobats on the Torvill and Dean tour gave him the idea of flying over the ice in a mechanical contraption. He had already talked to Peter Foy in Las Vegas about combining the skating motion with flying.

"The Ice Capades have their flying, but I'm thinking more in terms of hand grips, self-propulsion as opposed to mechanical propulsion."

It hasn't happened yet, but it's just a matter of time.

Song and Dance Man

In the summer of 1990, Paul Blake was the Executive Producer of the largest theatre in America, the Muny in Saint Louis, Missouri, an open-air, 12,000-seat amphitheatre. Four good-sized trees framed its stage like a proscenium arch. Paul decided to mount a production of *Cinderella*, a musical written by Rodgers and Hammerstein as a television vehicle for Julie Andrews. He thought that it might be magical if, when Cinderella went to the ball, it turned

---

[17]In a Detroiter, a skater spins his partner (who is rigid like a horizontal plank) in an overhead lift using one or both arms.

out to be a skating party instead.

"If we flooded our orchestra pit and had people ice skating in winter costumes in the middle of July, it would be kind of fabulous."

That decided, he needed an ice skating prince. His original idea was that the prince would be a mere consort for Cinderella, the star. Then he found Robin.

"I was so taken with his talent and his enthusiasm for the project that I thought, 'Why don't we make the prince a star and make Cinderella someone who doesn't skate necessarily. When she finally meets Prince Charming, she's so in love, she can do anything. Then she walks down the steps of the ballroom, takes his hand, and starts spinning.'"

That was the break for which Robin had been waiting since age six.

Vocal backup was ready in case the experiment failed, but when Robin sang at Paul's piano, the production team said, "This is better than expected."

Rachelle Ottley, singer and actress, had skated on artificial ice in Broadway's *Meet Me in St. Louis*. The producers had initially approached Robin when the plans called for real ice in a big production number, so he knew that Rachelle had at least minimal skating credentials.

They eyed each other on the first day of rehearsal.

Robin thought, "Can she really skate?"

Rachelle thought, "Can he really sing?"

Admittedly, Robin's résumé was short. Since *A Night of 100 Stars*, his only song-and-dance gig had been the Adelphi Theatre's anti-drug benefit, *The Just Say No Show*. However, as Rachelle reckoned, "You don't get to be an Olympic champion without a few talents in your bag." She found Robin a quick study, good at picking up harmonies.

Rachelle had skated competitively until age fourteen, when she tore her Achilles tendon. After majoring in theatre at UCLA, she performed with the national touring company of *Cats* and in regional productions. She was too busy to maintain her skating.

"What I have is what's left, not what I *could* do."

Her first thought was, "Oh, God! I have to skate with this Olympic champion?"

Robin set an irreverent tone by referring to the cast as the "ice people" and the "dry land people." When Rachelle's husband, Peter Kiklowicz, arrived on the scene, he found Robin and Rachelle making fake skating motions while Robin mimed the glass slipper scene with Rachelle's gym shoe. Suddenly Robin got the urge to run across the cement floor sniffing the shoe, to Peter's amusement. The next day Robin greeted him by saying, "Hello. I get to kiss your lovely wife."

Paul pondered what period to evoke for the light-hearted comedy with contemporary twists of dialogue. If the costumes were too Dickensian, it would look like *A Christmas Carol*. If there were too many hoop skirts, it would look like *Gone with the Wind*. He settled on a "fantasy Biedermeier period" with long, billowing skirts lined in plastic. Without the liners, ice spray would have soaked the costumes.

As skating choreographer, Robin brought Tony and Terry into the production, along with several other people whose skills he knew. The rest of the ensemble were what Rachelle called "the coffee club at the local rink."

"The nice thing about Robin is that he uses what you *can* do and doesn't get frustrated over what you *can't* do."

When Robin choreographed and skated, he felt secure. However, the prince had a major speaking role, and then there was the singing to contend with. In the company of seasoned Broadway pros Nancy Dussault, Adolph Green, Phyllis Newman, and Gretchen Wyler, he wanted to hold his own.

Adolph was a character. His wife, Phyllis, assured Robin, "Now and again he'll get his lines wrong, but don't worry about it. He'll get it right on the night."

There was a scene in which the prince complained about the ball.

"We were sitting around with the script one day, and Paul decided that the line should be, 'I suppose it's better to be chasing one girl than to be chased by a whole female ice hockey team.' Come to the first public performance and Adolph turns around to me and says, 'It's better to chase somebody than to have a football team after you.' Nobody laughed. I thought, 'Well, of course they're not going to laugh, because it doesn't make sense. He's supposed to be talking about women, and he's talking about men.' I wasn't ready for that. It was my first foray into making it up as I went along."

Barbara Sharma and Lois Foraker, the ugly step-sisters, agreed that one of them should skate at the ball. Lois laced on rental skates and teetered around with a learner plate on her back.

According to Paul, "We all made it our job to let Robin feel at home, because we knew he was a fish out of water when he was on dry land, as it were. We all adored him, and we all thought he was wildly gifted. The skating was extraordinary, but his whole love of musical theatre was obvious. He instantly was like a kid in a candy store. He couldn't get enough of it."

Paul fondly observed Tony and Terry's dedication.

"He was always lifting her and tossing her through the air. She was always landing in his arms. I had never seen anybody being lifted and tossed so many times in ten minutes. They constantly kept rehearsing. They never didn't rehearse—and this was on dry land. It was very funny. We found them all just terrific."

Rachelle's skating ability didn't come to light until her transformation by her Fairy Godmother. While she sang "My Own Little Corner," Terry doubled her in a dream sequence. In the garden at the ball, Rachelle and Robin sang "Do I Love You Because You're Beautiful?" while Tony and Terry skated as their doubles in the background.

Paul particularly enjoyed "No Other Love," a solo inserted for Robin.

"When Cinderella left him, and he was left alone with the slipper, he rushed down the stairs and went out on the ice. All the lights turned blue, and there was the gorgeous Richard Rodgers song, and the chorus would be singing this big vocal arrangement. He'd be skating; he'd be spinning; one set would be rolling off, and another set would be rolling on. It was dark, and the stars were out. I would sit in the audience every night, and the audience would just go, 'Ahhhh.' Their breath would be taken away."

As for Robin's acting, "It got better as we did it. He's a natural, and he's totally fearless. He's the consummate professional. We all felt that we'd found a kindred spirit. He's from ice skating, not from the theatre, and it's a very different world, but we found someone who is totally of our world. He's not Robin Cousins the star going in to do something because he's Robin Cousins the star. He tries to do a good job, the best job that can be done."

Taping for TV stops for commercial breaks, which allows time for costume changes—something without a parallel in live theatre. Robin rearranged the ballroom scene so that it made more logistical sense. In general, though, he kept a low profile in matters of dry land. He was a neophyte—but he was also a sponge.

The heat and humidity were intense for sweaty athletes in flannel, plastic-lined costumes. Another drawback: airplanes flew overhead. Rachelle wasn't bothered.

"I did a show two years ago down in San Diego, at Starlight. They stop the show for the planes, because it's right in the landing pattern. In the orchestra pit, there are red lights. You'll be in the middle of a line, and if you see the red light go on, you have to freeze. An airplane will go *vroooooom*. A little yellow light comes on, and then the green light, and you go on. It's really interesting when you're in the middle of a song. I didn't notice it at all at the Muny compared to that."

The beauty of the setting and the camaraderie that Robin relished outweighed the inconveniences.

"I have to say, when you get to a certain level, there is a sense of humor that everybody has. Sure, everything has had a serious and straightforward edge, but I have yet to do a show where it's been absolutely serious 'beyond the beyond,' as Toller would say. You find out that people like Phyllis, Adolph, and Nancy all conduct themselves, as I would, with the utmost respect for the project that they're working on, but absolutely 100 per cent as human beings. You take *it* seriously, but I don't think you can ever take *yourself* too seriously."

On the Cutting Edge

Not long after *Cinderella* closed, Lee Mimms phoned Robin about a movie project, *The Cutting Edge*, a contemporary boy-meets-girl story set in the intersecting yet incongruous worlds of hockey and figure skating. Director Paul Michael Glaser needed a skating choreographer and technical advisor.

"This movie is going to happen," Lee told Robin. "They want to have a meeting with you."

No fewer than seven scripts for films involving skating had passed through Robin's hands. *The Cutting Edge* was not the best, but it had the most commercial potential. Robin went to the meeting excited, yet without illusions.

"I was going to meet Paul Michael Glaser for the first time. I grew up on 'Starsky and Hutch,' so it was going to be a big thrill for me. I also knew that I certainly wasn't going to be the only person they interviewed."

"We are blind," the filmmakers told Robin. "We know nothing about figure skating. Can you deliver?"

"Yes," he said with alacrity.

He was the kid at Christmas again, opening an unexpected gift. Then the practical adult Robin slid into his black BMW convertible and asked himself, "Do you know what you have done?"

"As quickly as I said yes to them, I could also say yes to myself. Yes, I know what I've done. I won't have a problem saying, 'What exactly do you want? Is this okay?'"

Before deals were done and contracts signed, Robin talked to Tony, whom he planned to hire as his assistant. Tony took one look at the original script and cringed.

"This isn't going to get made."

Robin, as always, operated on cockeyed optimism.

Paul and writer Tony Gilroy handed over the script.

"Here. Rip it apart."

The story was short on reality. First, there was the premise: a hockey player, converted into a figure skater, teams up with a top-ranked pairs skater and wins the Olympics.

They asked Robin, "If you took Wayne Gretsky, could he do this in four or five years?"

"Gretsky? Possibly. Given every conceivable break, this all could happen."

When Robin went to New York in November to skate at the Christmas tree lighting, he auditioned four of the finalists for the female lead: Kate Moseley, a rich, spoiled pairs skater whose sharp tongue had alienated all her partners. She had nowhere left to turn.

Although she was not the best skater, it was a twenty-three-year-old ingenue with a "little pixie face like Winona Ryder's" who grabbed Robin's heart.

"This girl was falling on her can, rolling around, getting up, wiping herself off, waltzing around with the music in torn jeans, with a baseball cap on backwards. It was the energy I connected with."

The girl wasn't embarrassed when she fell. She was enthusiastic, full of questions, and never complained about the rental skates.

The actress was Moira Kelly. Her résumé included the television movie *Love, Lies and Murder* and the Dustin Hoffman film *Billy Bathgate*.

"What do you think?" Paul asked Robin.

"She's not anywhere near as good as the girls I auditioned in L.A., but if anybody is going to be able to exude what the girl in the movie has, I think she can do it."

"I'm glad you said that, because her screen test was great. She's going to be a huge star, and she's my personal choice."

Robin took Moira to Sky Rink and watched her stroke backwards, do crossovers, and execute three-turns. She was a typical Long Island public session skater.

Paul chose D.B. Sweeney, a rising young actor with Broadway, TV, and film experience, to play the role of Doug

Dorsey, a brash Olympic hockey player sidelined from a professional career by damage to his peripheral vision, then handpicked by Kate's coach to undergo a metamorphosis.

As Robin noted dryly, "The boy supposedly was a hockey player. That just means that he used to have his own pair of skates. It's more difficult, obviously, with men in general. The hockey was the important thing to D.B. in the movie, not the figure skating."

In that sense, D.B. was perfect for the part. His character, like his real-life persona, went kicking and screaming into the world of sequins and roses.

Sweeney wasn't Robin's number-one pick.

"He was Paul's first choice. Paul had pretty much made up his mind. I had seen another actor at the same time I saw Moira at Rockefeller Center. He had just come off a hit of a movie that I hadn't seen called *Ghost*, and he was in an off-Broadway play called *Some of Us* at the time. He was a classier-looking man—and skater—than D.B. To me, he had more of a Gretsky feel. The one thing that I didn't want was for the character to be a brute all the way through. I quite liked the idea of him becoming a little more sensitive to the girl's thoughts and ideas, and, in doing that, looking the part—but D.B. does clean up well, I have to say."

Evelyn Kramer gave Moira and D.B. a crash course. The late Bill Woehrle, a dancer and John Curry skater, did stretch and ballet work with them to teach them to move, stand, and hold their upper bodies as skaters do, and to walk with a recognizable gait.

Robin's next task was to hire real skaters.

Rachelle Ottley was a natural to play Lorie, the second-ranked pairs skater, which required more acting than skating. Lorie seduced Doug away from Kate. Robin chose pairs skater Kevin Peeks to play her partner, Brian.

"I had worked with Kevin in Festival on Ice and

various other shows. He had a wicked streak that made him great for Brian. We sent him a script and said, 'Would you mind playing this rather prissy character which is a bit of a cliché type?' We thought we'd have fun with it."

Robin hoped that Peter and Kitty Carruthers would double D.B and Moira. Peter's skating had the "rawness" that suggested the energy of a hockey player, and he and Kitty were masters of the material Robin planned to display. When the two couldn't be scheduled, Robin and Tony found themselves short a key ingredient just a month before shooting.

Then Robin had another idea.

Sharon Carz and Doug Williams had won the U.S. pairs bronze medal in 1990 but had dropped a place in 1991. Robin telephoned Sharon and invited her to work on *The Cutting Edge*—alone.

"In all due respect to Doug, he is too polished, far too finished, and a foot too tall, but if this is something you feel could work, I would love to use you. You look like Moira's twin."

What Robin didn't know was that Doug and Sharon had already dissolved their partnership.

"I'd love to," Sharon answered.

Paul had seen several men at Nationals who were the type he had in mind for D.B.'s double. They weren't available. Then Robin remembered John Denton, fifth behind Carz and Williams—another stroke of luck.

A prosthetics workup revealed that John's facial features were near-perfect matches for D.B.'s

The advantage of using John and Sharon was that they didn't have a history or a recognizable stylistic identity as a pair. Robin could start from scratch, which meant starting with what Paul wanted from the actors. John and Sharon, in wigs and facial prosthetics, became malleable extensions of D.B. and Moira.

People who walked onto the set while Sharon and

John were skating often remarked, "Wow, Moira and D.B. have gotten good."

Suspending Disbelief

Robin moved to Toronto in March and spent the first three weeks experimenting with Sharon, John, and some Canadian pairs teams. He indulged poetic license as he put them through throws, lifts, pair spins, death spirals, and side-by-side jumps. The work was videotaped and sent to Paul in Los Angeles for review and comment. In the end, the Canadian pairs added Robin's moves to their repertoires.

"It was an important playtime: 'You have recess. Go do whatever you want—and make sure you remember what you do.'"

Robin found "recess" infinitely more interesting than the games period at Henbury Comprehensive. He and Tony made notations for each piece of choreography. They devised a system using small pieces of paper: first page, move one, point A to point B; second page, move one, point B to point C. Then the filmmakers could break down elements from their own perspective. They could see where the action started, how it moved, and where to place cameras. There is no skating notation per se. Choreology, which few can read, is dance-oriented. For the most part, skaters rely on memory and videotape.

The chief challenge was to reconcile the filmmakers' need for fantasy with the skating public's demand for authenticity. Robin pointed out to the bosses, "A lot of people know figure skating through television. If you're going to break rules, which it seems to me you're telling me you want to do, let's broadcast that ahead of time, and let's *really* break them."

As he considered the possibilities, he mused to Tony, "We have to mix pairs and adagio to the point where it becomes acceptable to a knowledgeable skating audience who'd then go, 'Yeah! Why not?'"[18]

One day, Paul ran out of script. He called Robin to a meeting.

"We have a big problem. The skating is too good. They get to Nationals, and we believe it. They make the Olympic team. We don't need to see them win the Olympics. That's too trite. The story's over. We need something else, something that's never been done before."

Robin told Tony, "It's a gin-and-tonic moment. We need to go away on this one."

They sat in a small lounge at the Inter-Continental Hotel. After about a third of a bottle of gin, Robin had a revelation.

"It has to be dangerous. Kate has thrown down the gauntlet to Doug. Now he has to throw it back at her. It has always been her, her, her, and him giving up. Now let's see if we can make *her* give up. We haven't made her do anything yet that we didn't know she could do. I want to give it another twist. I want him suddenly to turn around and say, 'Okay!' But she's not ready for that—and the okay has to be out there. I mean, *out* out."

Tony objected. "We can't do that. It's illegal."

"Illegal, shlegal. We're past that point. Look at what we've been doing. We're using spotlights for competitions! We're in that realm. It's like the guy driving the motorcar. You know the car can't do 900 miles per hour, but you also know that he needs to drive it at that speed, or else he's not going to catch the bad guy."

"Well, okay. They should do a bounce spin."[19]

---

[18] Adagio skating differs from conventional pair skating in that it doesn't adhere to the strict rules for ISU competition. It is more acrobatic; includes spectacular lifts, more sustained than in pair skating, and without the requirement that the man revolve (no more than three times) throughout the lift; and permits carries on the partner's back, shoulders, or knees, as well as hand- or foot-held spins. The only constraints on adagio skating are fear and lack of imagination.

[19] More graphically described as a head-banger: the adagio trick, illegal in

"And he should let her go."

"Yeah, and she smashes head first."

"That's what would happen if you did it with Terry, but if you actually filmed the bounce so that, from the camera's point of view, she is vertical when you let her go, she could, theoretically, fly straight up."

"Then you'd catch her and put her down as if it was a double twist."

"Exactly. Let's go see the big cheese and find out what he thinks."

Robin told Paul, "I have an idea for you. We're way out there in terms of skating, but I think it might be what you want. We can make it look stunning. It doesn't exist, so we're going to have to create it."

Until then, Terry had been at home in California. Robin and Tony flew her to Toronto and showed Paul a bounce spin and adagio lifts.

"Fine. That's what we want."

"Right," said Robin and Tony. "Here's the deal. The bounce does this, she flies, and he catches her. In real life, if he were to release her on the way up, she would probably catch herself heading over the top of the barrier face first, teeth in the back."

Paul was sold. They called the move the Pamchenko, after Kate's coach.

Terry returned to California, got herself organized, then flew to Toronto to work on *The Cutting Edge*. Meanwhile, Robin and Tony set about breaking down the big move into filmable segments. According to the revised plot, Kate and Doug would be denied at Nationals—forced, in skating parlance, to wait their turn. Should they continue to play it safe, to play by the rules, or should they go for broke at the Olympics with the illegal ace in their pockets?

ISU-sanctioned competition, in which the man holds his partner by the ankles and swings her around him in circles with her head inches from the ice at the bottom of each revolution.

It was Hollywood. Of course they would go for broke.

The naïveté of some of the cast and crew astonished Robin.

"What was bizarre was that there were people who had watched the way we were filming, and when we were actually filming the stunt, they wondered at what point in the day Tony and Terry were going to do it. When we were filming it sequentially, it made perfect sense to the non-skating people. It wasn't a stunt, as far as they were concerned. As far as they were concerned, we were filming it that way because we could only do it a piece at a time from the camera's point of view, but at some point they would get an overview of the whole thing. I thought, 'They're sitting ten feet away from this *dummy* that is screwed into a platform, and they are *buying* it, hook, line and sinker.'"

Persuading an audience to suspend disbelief would not be a problem.

The filmmakers wanted a movie that was nothing like *Ice Castles* or televised competition. They wanted to make *Flashdance* on ice. That was fine with Robin, as long as he could guarantee the integrity of the context surrounding the elements of fantasy. He was fastidious about the minutiae: skate laces, blade sounds, entrances and exits, flowers, camera placements, "kiss and cry" décor, reading material for the audience during ice cuts. The moviemakers were in an alien land.

"It has been exhausting. I want to make sure that nothing on my end goes an inch out of place. I have to be on guard for any major *faux pas*. When you're working with people in this industry for the first time, you're often treading on glass. I was overly-meticulous at the beginning. I didn't want anyone to say, 'That's really not what we wanted.'"

The Cutting Edge involved fictional characterization during factual times: the four years between the 1988 and 1992 Winter Games. For the fantasy enactments of the U.S.

Nationals and Olympics, the art department designed fake programs. Robin obtained event footage so the creative department could hire extras who resembled judges, coaches, members of the media, and spectators.

For legal reasons, some things were done incorrectly. During the Olympic scenes, authentic mascots and advertising were banned. The Olympic rings had to be the wrong colors.

Paul loved the idea of the judges wearing headphones. Robin asked, "How can they hear the music?"

"No, they're hearing it through the headphones," Paul argued. "This is all new. This is something new and technological that was done specifically for this event."

The director was also stubborn about spotlights.

"I like to watch skating, but I couldn't tell you the difference between the pro skating events and the regular skating events. They're all on television around the same time. Some have spotlights. Some don't. Sometimes the world championships have spotlights."

"Well, those are the exhibitions," Robin explained.

"*I* don't know that."

At first, Robin was too precise in doctoring the script.

"I corrected every nuance from a skater's point of view. That's not what they wanted. They wanted a fantasy that could possibly happen at a *stretch*—and movies are made that way on purpose. I always thought that it was because they didn't know the subject well enough. They know the subject matter fine. What they do not want is reality, so it always has to be, 'Well, could it happen?' You have to say, 'If you really thought about it, could it possibly happen if someone were *stupid* enough? Yes. The answer's yes.'"

The pressure on Sharon and John was intense.

"It has been hellish." Robin remarked. "They've had to deal with getting to know each other, learning what

Paul wants during the acting, learning the movie business, and being nobodies—and having all that happen at the same time. When the novelty wears off, the real shit happens. You have to stand around for six hours to do a thirty-second double toe loop. I never realized how many people were involved in three seconds of moviemaking. My background is theatre and TV, and it doesn't come close. *Nothing* comes close."

The Magic of Moira

Rachelle had a particularly tedious scene.

"There was one shot that Moira and I did where she comes to the door, I answer the door, and she catches me with *him*. It took forever for them just to get her to bring her sunglasses down so that they would line up perfectly under her eyes. She must have stood there for forty-five minutes on a broken foot so that her eyes would be exactly right. That was the shot. No words, no dialogue, nothing but that."

Broken foot?

Although the bosses had told Moira that she was *not* to skate at lunchtime, she couldn't resist. She slipped and tried to save her Walkman.

Robin was not pleased, but he didn't say much.

"You can't smack a child when she knows exactly what she's done."

Originally, all the skating scenes were to have been shot at the same time. Moira's accident precipitated much rescheduling. Robin canceled his plans to skate on the Tom Collins tour.

The cast threw him for a while. He needed to design equipment that allowed Moira to appear to skate without actually wearing skates on her feet.

"There are a few scenes—I don't know that anyone will be able to pick them out—where she's not skating. If anybody can do it, Moira will, and she did."

According to Rachelle, "There's a scene in which Doug walks into a room carrying Kate over his shoulder, ostensibly because she's drunk. It's really to hide Moira's cast. It was a good idea to carry her in that way, but, if you'll notice, he sits her down on something, and she stays there. She's wearing a long coat. Then, later in the scene, she's crawling on her hands and knees looking for an earring. Well? They made do with the situation."

Robin rigged a chair on wheels to bring Moira to normal height.

"In the sequence when they're playing hockey together and Doug gets hit in the eye, she's not skating. It's me pushing her on that chair for all I'm worth. I'm on bent knees, crouched behind her, pushing and spinning. Of course, when you're looking at the body, that's Sharon."

Robin and Tony had designed a scene in which Kate glided past a mirror, checking upper body positions. At that point, Moira was strong enough to hold a decent arabesque without wobbling. It was going to be a long shot because, as seen through the mirror, the door at the back of the ice rink would open and in would walk the ex-coach. But there was a broken foot to deal with. As much as Robin pushed Moira on a dolly, Paul continued to protest, "It's not right. She doesn't look as if she's skating. She looks as if she's sliding across on something."

It suddenly occurred to them that, rather than change Moira or the dolly, they could change the mirrors, which were in panels. If you switched one slightly off angle to the others, that created a rippling effect as she skated past. It completely changed the feel, but it did instantly make it look as if she were skating. In the movie, as she rippled past the mirrors, you could tell that she wasn't skating *if* you looked at her—but you were not watching *her* at that point. You were watching her reflection.

Moira was not the only one who came through like a trouper. The Canadian pairs impressed Robin.

"The kids from Kerry Leitch's school are probably the most respectful and incredibly disciplined group of skaters I have ever worked with. One team stood around for three days without shooting anything, in costume and full makeup. Not a peep out of any of them. Not a word. 'Fine, we'll see you tomorrow.' When it has been time to deliver, they've said, 'How high do you want us to jump? How many times?' It has been a treat to work with them. Kerry has instilled something in them which I haven't seen since I worked with Gladys Hogg in England. That was the way we were brought up—to do as we were told. These amateurs have been working on the movie set like seasoned professionals, whereas—"

Whereas D.B. Sweeney was not the easiest person to get along with. One popular amusement was the crew-sponsored weekly contest to determine what the initials D.B. really stood for. *Delightful Boy* was not the answer that sprang to everyone's lips. Some of Robin's theories were inventive.

Moira, *au contraire*, was a joy.

"Typical of an actor, she was more interested in what goes on in a skater's head than what goes on in the body, because it's what goes on in the head that then dictates how the body reacts. If you know what somebody's thinking, then you know how he would stand or look. D.B.'s body language gave him away. Moira's never gave her away as not knowing what skating was about or what being a champion was about. Getting her off the ice was the problem.

"Whatever Moira does, she does intently. There's a lot of personal incentive for her, because she's fresh and new. It's not a game to her. It's a business. I connect with her for that very reason. She's unbelievable onscreen. She looks every inch a national or international figure skater before she sets foot on the ice, just by the way she stands and holds herself—and she is unbelievable *on* the ice, in presence and carriage. She sells it. She looks like she's been skating all her life. If she had been a figure skater instead of an actress when she was fourteen, she would have been at Nationals."

Double, Double, Toil and Trouble

The filmmakers created illusions: Moira and D.B. skating; Moira and D.B. falling painfully and repeatedly; Moira and D.B. performing a trick that no human could survive. Robin used multiple layers of doubles: John and Sharon, trick doubles, fall doubles, a dummy, and Tony and Terry.

"A girl who, for her living, throws herself off burning buildings was launched at thirty miles an hour by Tony Kudrna on a bounce spin and thrown across the ice. We've used Moira, we've used Sharon, we've mixed and matched to the point that there's so much going on that you cannot tell who's who. They have those children's cartoons: find Waldo. It's find the real Moira, find the real D.B."

How Moira stopped and how Sharon stopped were two different things. After Moira was filmed stopping, Robin had Sharon's skate sound dubbed in.

Paul loved it when skaters dragged their toe picks and scratched to a stop. Robin informed him, "You just gave it away. You're panning like this on her face. She's gliding. She's lovely. She's stopping correctly, but the sound is not right. It's like having an opera singer open his mouth and sound like Mickey Mouse."

Paul strove to achieve what he termed "that subjective, impressionistic view of the realm of figure skating" by using a number of unconventional filming techniques. The idea was to convey the energy of skating. It didn't hurt that, with the same techniques, he could camouflage the doubles. Other choreographers might have seen those techniques as limitations. To Robin, they were challenges.

"I don't do what people expect. You're only going to

see a snippet of this, a snippet of that, but I don't want it to look like the same snippet that you would see on ABC's 'Wide World of Sports.' I don't want to shoot skating like it's ever been shot before. We've been trying to get inside skating—to show energy on the screen that skating has never been able to show before, unless you see it live.

"The way I've done it, which has been the best way for Paul and me but the worst way for the skaters, is to choreograph the routine and set it with the music. Then, once Paul has seen it through the lens, as he shouts, we re-arrange. That's where it gets tough. I don't know anybody who'd ever bothered filming a pairs sit spin only between the shoulders and the knees of the two skaters. You get the incredible energy, and you can see everything you need to see. It's all right there."

Much choreography was determined based on the view through the lens, which in turn was determined by lens size and type; speed of motion; whether or not the frames were doubled up. Some of the footage looked like bad home movies. The ability to convey the raw energy of pairs skating rather than conventional fluid movement fascinated Robin.

"You print the same frame three or four times, then repeat it, and it becomes jagged. It gives an instant throw-back of energy without showing a whole spin or jump. I don't want to see the eight crossovers it takes to get to the lift. I want to see what his face is telling me while they're doing the lift."

Tony operated a Pogo Cam, skating inches from the action.

Robin helped to design a contraption that he affec-tionately called Fat Albert: a large rotating platform out-fitted with cameras and lights. It allowed the equipment and actors to revolve together. The focus and lighting remained constant as the actors simulated skating.

Robin told Paul, "If you mix and match properly,

with the right edits, no one is going to know—as long as you don't stay on them long enough for the body language to give away the fact that they're rocking back and forth."

Robin, Tony, and Evelyn Kramer spent hours watching each other skate. In the end, they found a different model.

"Rather than try to get Kate and Doug to look like the average skater, we used Toller for an example. He has such upper body motion when he skates. We were getting into many different ways of utilizing just the upper body."

Robin and Tony draped themselves over chairs, analyzing how Moira could simulate a death spiral while Paul spent six minutes shooting a head move or a hand clasp. The filmmakers were lamentably ignorant of the skaters' limitations. They asked the impossible. Sometimes they got it.

Paul wanted a map.

"How about one team doing a lift, coming this way with the camera. Then, when they get to *this* point, I want two other teams behind them doing throw double Axels."

It was a logistical nightmare. Paul wanted to signal instantly that something big was happening. How do you convey the excitement without telegraphing the moves? By eliminating all the "in between." Robin had to provide five elements within forty-five seconds.

"How do we get there the quickest?" Paul wanted to know. "We can cut to someone in the stands, but when we come back, I want to see another thing happening."

Actors hit their marks. Skaters more often aim in a general direction. Timing and rhythm are key. Space is secondary. A diver can't guarantee that he'll hit the same molecules of water two dives in a row. Nonetheless, Robin had to say, "Yes, we will guarantee it, and if we're here until two o'clock in the morning, we'll get it." He choreographed pairs moves like compulsory figures, so they could be repeated in the same place with identical timing.

Robin wrote dialogue for Kate's Russian coach, Anton Pamchenko, played by English actor Roy Dotrice. He and Roy scripted informal scenes like practice sessions on the spur of the moment. Paul might tell them, "We need lines for Anton at this point. What would he say?" After the two brainstormed, Robin translated their ideas into broken English.

"I find myself pushing certain people I know into characters. There's a lot of Carlo Fassi in Anton: in the way he speaks, in getting the words backwards, in the genuine affection he has for the girl. There are a lot of little things there that people never saw between Carlo and me."

Robin's job included providing six to eight musical selections for each of more than thirty-two cues, matching the music to the characters.

"Some of it's recognizable. Some of it's not. Some of it's original. Some of it's not. I've been able to mix and match, which has put me in pig heaven. You know what I'm like with music."

Robin was also in "pig heaven" on Olympic-size ice. Tony thought it was a pity that the filmmakers didn't use more of Robin's own skating.

"He isn't cut out to be behind the scenes yet. He would have liked to be in the movie more. We skated during lunch, and he loved to get out there so everybody could see that he could do it. I think he had a job right after the film ended, so he did need to skate, but as soon as the producers and directors were standing around watching, he'd start doing back-flips."

The extras returned from lunch early and yelled from the stands, "Back-flip, man! Do the back-flip."

It takes a quick eye to discern Robin's appearances on film. He performed many of the pratfalls in the toe pick sequence.

"They couldn't afford for John to get injured, which is why it's me. *I* could get injured, because I didn't have to double the split twists. Trippity-trip-splat was me—then D.B. came along and just slid onto the ice."

In the same scene, Robin's hand reached for Moira's and missed. Later his hands and feet appeared when Anton placed diagrams of the Pamchenko on the ice.

Robin played a cameo off-ice role as well. He and ice dancer Judy Blumberg ad-libbed simulated television commentary. Someone had the idea of dubbing over their voices. The result in Robin's case was far too similar to his own example of an opera singer sounding like Mickey Mouse. The producers feared that his English accent would confuse movie audiences. Instead, the commentary was inane, both in voice and in substance.

"It was silly," Tony agreed, yet it was easy to see how it happened.

"Somebody decides, then nobody thinks about it again. There are so many decisions to make every single day. That's the amazing thing that both Robin and I found difficult to believe: how much time people are willing to spend on something frivolous and tiny. We never realized all the time and effort that goes into it. People put their lives on hold and go to a movie set sixteen hours a day for six or seven months. He and I agreed that it was fun to do it once, but we certainly wouldn't want to make a life out of it. It's one-dimensional."

Albertville Redux

The staging of the Albertville Olympics approached the scale of the *Ben Hur* chariot race. Two thousand extras moved around the Copps Coliseum in Hamilton, Ontario, like an army on maneuvers. Robin found their treatment embarrassing.

"They hired extras, but they didn't dress them. They said, 'Show up. These are the requirements.' What I wasn't prepared for was how rude they were going to be to those people. There would be fifty or sixty people dressed in winter clothes, woolly hats, and furs. The casting director would come to me and say, 'We're going to pick out the five that we need.'

"I would try to be quiet and say, 'That lady is not really dressed right.' He'd say loudly, 'She has too much makeup. No. You go. We don't need you. Go change your clothes.' He spoke as if they had no pride. It was like putting them in front of a firing squad. 'No. Do you have anything nicer that you could wear? If you could come back tomorrow with a better-looking dress—!' That's the industry, and it's like that all the way through. They don't care what they say, because they write checks, and they're in charge. If sensitivities get trampled along the way, it's no big deal."

An ad had appeared in the local paper: "Wanted: Men, women and children to act as the cheering crowd during the film's Olympic figure skating finale. Applicants must be dressed in winter clothing (green is preferred) and over the age of 12." Someone hadn't told the creative team that skaters viewed green as bad luck.

Two thousand extras didn't come close to filling the Copps Coliseum, a new facility seating 17,000. The solution was a trick used in other movies: *The Natural*, for example.

Photos of people in audience poses were blown up to life-size, printed on cardboard, and cut out. The same few shots, including images of Robin, Paul, and producer Dean O'Brien, were reproduced by the hundreds and scattered strategically throughout the arena.

To disguise the subterfuge, the staged events were filmed in spotlights rather than in the bright television lighting associated with real competitions. On film, with the haze of dry ice, the cutouts looked eerily real. In person (so to speak), they were both amusing and alarming. The cast and crew called them "the freeze-dried people."

One day in June at the Copps Coliseum was memorable for sheer whimsy. A group of extras at one end of the ice looked like fugitives from Saint-Moritz in their Day-Glo parkas and furs. A group of *faux spectateurs* relaxed in the adjacent stands—the groundlings, judging by the preponderance of gym shoes and baseball caps. A teenager played a noisy hand-held electronic game, unthinkable in a real skating audience.

Tony stood on a rotating platform, twirling the dummy. Time after time he flung it aloft while Terry, Moira, and Sharon (all dressed and coiffed to match the dummy) remained on standby. Tony struggled to find the correct angle of release. The idea was to film the dummy at the instant it flew vertically from his hands.

At the beginning of the Pamchenko learning sequence, Kate suffered a messy accident. Enter the stunt double, in boots with rubber blades. She wasn't planning to skate. All she had to do was land with a thud. The rubber protected Tony and D.B. from gashes.

It took ten minutes to persuade Tony to release the stunt girl. He was so protective of his wife that it went against every instinct. She assured him, "No, no. That's fine. I'm used to this. I jump off buildings."

Tony and Terry worked on the bounce spin for three days. There were multiple takes for multiple camera angles. When Paul asked, "Can you do one more?" Terry said, "Of course." She did as many as he needed. It was her chance to be in a movie, and she wanted everything right. After shooting, she flew to California with a disfigured face. The centrifugal force had burst her blood vessels.

Tony developed tendinitis. He had scars where Terry's boot grazed his arm during the twist lift.

The big trick sequence was a collage. Tony and Terry performed the bounce spin. He and the dummy filmed the hand release. He and Terry executed the twist lift. Then he and Moira did the set-down, while the camera focused on Moira's face. With her hair flying, she looked as though she had done the whole sequence herself.

As Robin observed, "Between the real people and the dummy—which just looked so hideously ridiculous—it's great on camera. You'd never know, but it was a scary few days."

The film includes footage of Sharon skating with D.B. and of Moira skating with John. Moira became proficient enough that the camera could look over John's shoulder as she glided and spoke her lines.

Much of the best skating fell to the cutting room floor: several hours' worth, by Robin's estimate. Among the cuts were throw triple Salchows and triple twists. The director didn't want to dilute the impact of the Pamchenko.

The actors hadn't seen the daily rushes. Rachelle waited for a sneak preview in a darkened theatre, hunched down in her seat muttering, "Oh, God." She was relieved when the audience howled with laughter. At some points, she thought, "If I had known, I would have done that a little differently." Overall, though, she was pleased.

"You don't know until you see the whole thing. They just call you in when you're shooting your part. It was funny and entertaining, and that was the main thing."

Robin first saw the film at a preview screening at the L.A. studios, surrounded by teenagers with rating cards. It tested in the eighties and nineties.

As a feature designed to appeal to a wide audience, *The Cutting Edge* pushed some gratuitous buttons. Whereas flamboyantly gay Brian, wanton Lorie, and the Weiderman twin in lederhosen sent movie audiences into paroxysms, skating fans weren't equally amused. Still, the film nudged the sport into the mainstream.

It had a good premier week with the sixth-highest box office in the United States, behind *White Men Can't Jump*, *Basic Instinct*, *Wayne's World*, *My Cousin Vinny*, and *Ladybugs*. Reviews were generally positive. Robin was told that it pulled MGM out of the red. It was a huge date movie, and it generated large-volume video rentals.

The Cutting Edge stirred some interest among the crew. Virtually everyone on the set put on skates at some point and got hooked. According to Tony, it also raised the consciousness of the filmmakers.

"Paul Glaser really got into the skating and seeing what it was all about. The producer, Dean O'Brien, came up to Blue Jay and saw a couple of Fourth of July shows. He still has an interest."

As for Sweeney, don't look for him in Ice Capades.

The Faces of AIDS

Long before *The Cutting Edge*, Paul Glaser suffered a tragedy. In the course of a blood transfusion when their first child was born, Paul's wife, Elizabeth, was exposed to the HIV virus. Before she knew her status, she passed it to her children, Ariel through breast-feeding and Jake *in utero*. Elizabeth was diagnosed with AIDS in 1986. In 1988, seven-year-old Ariel died an AIDS-related death.

Elizabeth began a fight to save Jake. There were no pediatric drug protocols. HIV-positive children were often banned from school and shunned by neighbors. When Elizabeth and two friends established the Pediatric AIDS Foundation, Hollywood's initial reaction was hands off. Paul threw himself behind his wife and son. He went into directing, saying, "Going behind the camera was the only way I could keep myself sane."

Until he met the Glasers, Robin had never confronted the specter of AIDS.

"Then, suddenly, I was working and living with a family under a death sentence: a husband who had to look on, never knowing when the virus would move into its active stage; a wife and mother who might die before her remaining child, a lively and beloved son, ever grew up."

In June 1990, Elizabeth established the annual "A Time for Heroes" picnic and carnival for HIV-positive children. Hollywood rallied to help. Times had changed.

In 1991, Robin and Paul missed the event due to filming delays. Elizabeth was upset. The next year, they were there with bells on. The event took place at the Brentwood estate of Robert Taylor. Ronald and Nancy Reagan rubbed elbows with Mel Gibson and Dustin Hoffman. What fascinated Robin was that the celebrities were there to work, not to shmooze. Their booths dotted the mansion grounds. Robin Williams distributed ice cream bars. Tai Babilonia and Meryl Streep ran a fishing game. Robin worked with Mary Lou Retton on a balance beam. The highlight of his day was being photographed with Barbra Streisand, who was helping children throw Ping-Pong balls into fishbowls.

"Even the celebrities were celebrity-spotting. If somebody had wanted to universally and quickly wipe out Hollywood, that was the event to do it. You see these lists all the time, and you say, 'Oh yeah, right. These people are never going to show up.' All of a sudden, there everybody is, in jeans and T-shirts, just having a good time."

Elizabeth died in 1994 at age forty-seven after entering pediatric AIDS into the national lexicon.

By then, Robin had lost several friends to AIDS. The deaths of Robert McCall in 1991 at age thirty-three, Brian Pockar in 1992 at age thirty-two, and John Curry in 1994 at age forty-four (to cite three of many) left the close-knit skating community shaken to its foundations.

Robin sought to organize a fundraiser in Southern California. He contacted each figure skating club from San Diego to Santa Barbara, asking them to allow their skaters to participate. The only positive response was from Pasadena.

"It was a little disconcerting," Robin told the L.A. Times. Nobody wanted to be linked with the cause. When he decided to plan *Skate For Life* in England, he swore that no more doors would slam in his face.

The BBC televised the gala benefit for CRUSAID, the Terrence Higgens Trust, and local AIDS charities on May 15, 1993, at the year-old National Indoor Arena in Birmingham. As producer, choreographer, talent scout, and star, Robin planned the choreography in his London flat, then went to the Solihull rink and ran through all twenty roles. The affair was a critical and humanitarian success.

At a party to wrap up the festivities, Robin made a speech that impressed Toller Cranston.

"I can't remember what he said, but I knew that I was seeing a great person speaking from the heart. I was, if one dares say this, kind of proud of him. I was so happy to be there. I might add that I was sort of vaguely brilliant that night as well. You're never absolutely sure whether you belong in the group, but Alan Weeks, the announcer, had fortified me with the energy and the ego that you need. He said, 'Ladies and gentlemen, this is the person who has changed the face of figure skating, who has revolutionized the sport and is a major star.' Of course, I threw myself into the splits and was never better."

Robin regretted that *Skate For Life* fell short at the bank.

"It was a financial disaster. I just figured that we would, in this country, be as quick to respond corporately as they were in America. Fortunately for AIDS organizations, but maybe unfortunately publicly, AIDS was trendy to be associated with at that time. Corporate America was almost fighting within itself to be involved. That was not the case here. I know CRUSAID and Terrence Higgens Trust were able to get some things donated, but certainly not to the extent that we wanted to. Promises kept coming, so we kept organizing. You get to that point where you can't pull the plug. We knew before the gala happened that it wasn't going to be a success as a fundraiser. It was a success in terms of visibility and a huge artistic success, but not what I had seen [financially] from Rob McCall's show and 'Heroes.' I think I was rather naïve in that respect, but I don't regret it."

Easing on down the Road

Over a period of several years, Robin grew away from Lake Arrowhead, towards Los Angeles. Then he grew away from Los Angeles, towards the world at large. He was in good shape. He had offers to perform. New creative avenues opened up. During his last years at the Ice Castle, he was there more in name than in body. Carol Probst empathized.

"He had that operation on his knee, and he thought that was the end of his career. Then, when he started feeling so good, and his knee was good, and he was back doing his back-flip, he still had another year, year and a half, to go on his contract. We could tell he was champing at the bit, wanting to go do other things, so we just tore up the contract. We said, 'You can't hold somebody with that talent to a piece of paper.' He saw that he still had a lot left to do. We sniffed and said, 'Okay. Cut the apron strings. Go for it.' He had pupils, and he made sure they were taken care of. He did everything in the right way. We just love him. It was like a mom and dad letting their kid go off to college."

By the spring of 1991, Robin had one foot out the door.

"I've arranged the summer program so I can teach the kids when I *can* teach the kids. I have nothing pre-booked. I don't want people coming because *I'm* there. I want them coming because of the facility."

After all, he reasoned, students didn't go to the American Ballet Theater to learn from Baryshnikov. They went to learn from someone Baryshnikov endorsed. He had spent five years helping Walter and Carol build the complex, publicize it, and achieve excellence with its programs. If people were going there just for him, that wasn't what it was about.

"I absolutely thought I was in a position to stay put. Then I found out that maybe I wasn't, because there were other things that people wanted me for that they didn't want anybody else for. Then I skated again, and did Landover again, and thought, 'Wow!'"

Robin bought a smaller home nestled in a hill on Burnt Mill Road near the Training Center rink. Where the Ice Castle was concerned, he became less a resident oracle and more a roving ambassador. Carol doesn't remember the day she and Walter removed his name from their letter-head. It was too sad to contemplate. They were grateful to him for putting their rink on the map. By his example and through his influence, the teaching level had increased each year. Big-name coaches had relocated to the moun-tain, and international skaters had followed. Frank Carroll was one of those big-name coaches.

Not everyone was as grateful to Robin as the Probsts. He is convinced of a widespread perception within the skating community that Carroll's arrival, not his own, legitimized the facility. He sometimes found himself in a political climate that he hadn't anticipated and didn't understand. In his ingenuousness, he had failed to inquire about the provenance of skaters who appeared at his door.

"I guess you can't stop people coming up to the rink. What I didn't know was that the coaches that they nor-mally worked with didn't realize that they were coming. I personally took a lot of flak for that. Fortunately I was also stupid enough not to know about the flak. The politics of club-level skating are far greater than any politicking that ever could be done at the national or international levels. In my naïveté and stupidity, and I have to say Carol and Walter the same, we had no idea how insular and cliquey the L.A. figure skating community was. I came from a place where if someone said, 'Will you teach my child?' I automatically assumed it was kosher with their rink and club. Having grown up in England, I believed that communicating with coaches was the parents' job.

"Had I been teaching in America long enough to understand how things worked, I would obviously have spoken to coaches first. There were ten great, long-established coaches in L.A., and there *we* were, little upstarts. I was certainly not there to say that what I had to teach was better than what anybody else had to teach. I was just working in a facility that enabled me to do something that I had never had a chance to do at home, and that enabled kids to learn from a group of teachers that I happen to think were terrific, and still are. Some students had left coaches and started afresh. Some we mixed and matched with, but it did start to get blurry and grey. At competitions, I felt like an outsider. I always feel like an outsider, anyway."

Being a coach had ramifications Robin wasn't ready for. He was too close to his own ideals to understand why a talented young national competitor wouldn't aspire to more. If he saw empty ice, he suggested an extra practice. Students answered, "I've had my lesson. Why do I have to put in another hour?"

"Well, why not?" he asked himself.

He sometimes found that his desire was greater than his students'. Parents, too, were often more ambitious than their children. One day Robin was in the coaches' room, a small lounge at the front of the Training Center rink, trying to escape the clutches of a hell-bent mother. The only exit was through the lobby and out the front door. Like a treed animal, he grew cunning. The windows of the coaches' room opened onto the parking lot. He backed out, rear end first, while the other coaches egged him on and applauded. When he turned to head for his car, there stood the mother, witnessing his escape.

Robin acknowledged the incident with a cheerful "Oh, well."

"There are those skating parents who don't want to hear the truth about what their kids are capable of doing (good, bad, or indifferent). It was the end of the day, and I just said, 'I cannot deal with this mother again.' It was the fourth encounter of the day. I thought, 'My life does not revolve around this child.' Out through the window I went."

He grew frustrated when privileged children didn't appreciate their good luck. Without misusing or abusing the facilities, they failed to use them properly. There were many talented students who couldn't be bothered to work and many hardworking students without talent.

"Natural talent is sometimes not the best thing to have, because you abuse it. The desire to do something is far more important."

Lake Arrowhead was another stage in Robin's education.

"It took being around a place like that and having one or two students—and only one or two—who thought the way I did, who wanted to work the way I worked, and a lot of kids who were just there having fun, to make me think. I loved working there. It was a great time. But, at the same time, it was the wrong time."

His friends saw the writing on the wall. Garnet, in particular, had always believed that coaching was the wrong career path. She thought when he began, "Robin, not now. Do that later." At last she got her wish.

Old Circles, New Tangents

During the 1991-92 season, Robin's skating life came full circle. The World Cup Champions on Ice tour reunited four of the Saint-Gervais five: Robin, Randy, Linda, and Charlie.

The show toured small North American markets from November through April in theatre and arena versions. Robin's contributions were his Rachmaninoff piece; either "Blue Serenade" or "Busy Being Blue"; and "Walk of Life" in the first-half finale.

He came to view the subtle, understated *Adagio sostenuto* from Rachmaninoff's Concerto No. 2 in C minor as a choreographic turning point.

"When it came together properly, it was one of those great moments. There were a couple of pieces—my Rachmaninoff was one, and the *Romeo and Juliet* that Klimova and Ponomarenko did—where it didn't matter if you were in an arena or in a theatre or in a barn (as we played in some places), as long as the atmosphere worked. There was a big gap between the end of the number and the applause, which is how you know it is one of those numbers. I knew when I had a good go with that one. It has been one of my favorites ever since."

Robin found the Champions on Ice tour less than euphoric.

"I have to say that it was quite a cheap show. A first-class hotel tour it was not. The buses were not great. It wasn't what we had expected. Liz Manley, on more than one occasion, was on the phone saying, 'We're not doing this!'

"We got to one of the cities in Florida and showed up at a hotel/motel that was pretty rank. When Liz and I walked into our rooms, we could see each other through the wall. There was a hole the size of a fist. Liz decided, 'Enough. We're moving.'"

They skated either on postage-stamp stages or in full-size arenas. The smallest venue they played was Wilmington, Delaware, where the theatre was deeper than it was wide. Everyone performed his program sideways. As had happened with *Festival on Ice*, Robin frequently had to dash into the wings in order to get a runup for his back-flip. (In one *Festival* venue, he ran out the stage door and back in through the loading dock in order to work up sufficient speed.)

"It was pitiful, but we did have a good time. Still, it's not something I would race to emulate anytime soon."

By the end of the run, Robin was on the brink of renovating his Hollywood house. Then Torvill and Dean invited him to tour with them. He flew to England during the summer—a temporary detour, he thought. Instead, it was another of those defining moments, undetected as it passed, that set him on an entirely new course.

Bedford Square

The symmetrical façade of Number One Bedford Square had an upscale, well-cared-for look. The forest green door in its white Palladian doorcase was topped with a fanlight and flanked at shoulder level by crossed spears. A riot of violet, red, and pink flowers spilled over the cornice.

The door opened onto a vaulted atrium painted in soothing shades of off-white, buttery cream, and colonial green. Vases of mauve roses and pink alstroemeria perfumed the air from their sunny perch on a round wrought iron table by the window. On the perpendicular wall, a ceramic medallion, inscribed in white letters on a sea-blue background, proclaimed:

> *C. Mackintosh*
> *Producer*
> *flourishes here*
> *1988 - ∞*

It was the sanctum sanctorum of Cameron Mackintosh, the best-known musical theatre producer in the world. His Midas touch had gilded the likes of *Les Misérables*, *Cats*, *The Phantom of the Opera*, and *Miss Saigon*.

Somewhere in the rabbit warren above the vaulted ceiling was an office that belonged to Nicholas Allott, Executive Producer for Cameron Mackintosh Limited of London. The godfather of Allott's second child was Robin's friend and fellow skater Haig Oundjian.

In the early 1990s, Robin had hatched a radical idea. He wanted to continue to bridge the gap between skating and the theatre. The vehicle he had in mind was a show from the 1980s called *Abbacadabra*, built around the hits of the group Abba. Alain Boublil (who wrote *Les Misérables* and *Miss Saigon*) had adapted the music for Mackintosh's stage production. Robin hoped to turn the musical into a theatrical ice show.

"The *Abbacadabra* thing shows you how my brain works. There's a compilation album called *Hey, Mr. Producer,* which is basically songs from all the shows that Cameron has produced. In his program notes, he says that although *Abbacadabra* was a great success, something was missing, and if he ever had the chance to find a way of producing it again, he would. It occurred to me that maybe what was missing was ice."

It was Haig Oundjian who made the phone call to Nick to pitch the idea and help Robin obtain the book. Nick and Robin, who had been introduced at a party years earlier, began exploratory talks. Meanwhile, Robin met with Boublil. The project reached a dead end, but the wheels in Robin's head continued to turn.

"If you don't ask, you don't get. All they can do is say no. Nick actually did think it was not a bad idea. Alain had some reservations. Of course, after I read the script, I realized why. What did come of that was a lengthy conversation with Nick Allott that connected the skating with the theatre and then left me with the theatre and took the skating away."

In midsummer 1992, Robin met Nick for a drink. Arriving for the first time at Number One Bedford Square, he tried to seem blasé. Cameron Mackintosh's offices! It was Oz, the North Pole, and the Oval Office rolled into one. It was the Golden Milestone, *point zéro*, the epicenter of musical theatre.

During their comings and goings, Robin and Nick passed Darinka Nenadovic on the stairs. Darinka (universally known as Dinks) was the production administrator for *Cats* and *Five Guys Named Moe*. She and Nick had a project under discussion: a national tour of *Cats*, scheduled to begin the following summer. They wanted to launch it with a star name. The chance meeting on the stairs was a favorable convergence of the planets. While Robin, oblivious of it all, crossed the pastel atrium and exited through the big, green door, Dinks and Nick said, "Well, maybe we could think about *that*."

Dinks had always thought of John Curry as the ballet dancer of the skating world and Robin as the athlete. She had never watched Robin perform live, so she went to see him several times in Chris and Jayne's show at Wembley.

"I was amazed. To do the stuff that he was doing on ice, I found that absolutely extraordinary. I found it fearless as well as artistic."

One night, Robin invited Nick to see the show. They met afterwards for a late supper, and Robin proposed an even more grandiose scheme than *Abbacadabra*. He had seen the 1948 Gene Kelly movie, *The Pirate*, and thought that it would be fun to adapt it as a musical. He saw himself as the swashbuckling romantic lead. Rather than skate, he would dance.

As a child, Robin had idolized Gene Kelly. He was thrilled when the *New York Times* dubbed him the Gene Kelly of ice. There were parallels. Kelly was an athletic dancer. A Depression-era bricklayer and ditch digger, he brought a blue-collar vigor to an effete, overrefined world. He explained, "I belonged to the sweatshirt generation and wanted to make the dance, in costume and movement, akin to the world we were living in."

On the day Robin was to meet Kelly, the actor was ill and sent an apology. His photo traditionally decorates Robin's dressing rooms.

In a way, Gene Kelly was to Fred Astaire what Robin was to John Curry: less fancy, more attainable. By some miracle, could Robin become Gene Kelly off the ice? If hard work could make it happen, he was ready.

After watching *The Pirate*, Nick didn't think much of Robin's idea.

"Listen, if you are going to make the bridge from skater to theatre performer, you should first of all cut your teeth gently."

People established in one medium, Nick explained, aren't necessarily able to make a natural transition into another medium that requires similar, but not identical, disciplines. Moreover, their high profiles leave them exposed if the effort is less than overwhelmingly successful. Critics wait to dance on their graves. Better to minimize the risks.

Robin agreed and asked what vehicle might be appropriate.

"I think *Cats* would be good for you."

Cats was a dancing show that required enormous athleticism: one point in Robin's favor. Although he'd had some voice training, he wasn't naturally a singer, but the score was able to accommodate some deficiencies. Finally, *Cats* was a company show. Robin could be one of a group with featured moments. He was eager to audition.

Dinks went to see Christine Cartwright, the artistic coordinator of *Cats* in London, a pleasant woman with a bright laugh and a halo of red hair. It was her job to restage the show for the new tour.

Dinks told Chrissie about Robin.

"This idea has come up. What do you think?"

"Well, I don't know. I'm game, but we're going to have to meet him and see whether he can do it."

Privately, Chrissie was enthusiastic.

"I got excited, because I remembered seeing him skate. I saw a classical dancer, really, with a fantastic flow to the movement. I'd never noticed it until I'd watched John Curry skate. Then, when I saw Robin, I thought, 'Wow, that's *it* again.' No one else seemed to have that. They had brought something new to skating, from what I could see. Suddenly I could relate all that I knew about dancing to what they did. I could see the similarities, and I almost wished that I could do it. We're restricted on a solid floor, whereas, on skates, they just skim across the ice with their hair blowing back, their costumes following them, with, apparently, such ease. It looks as though it provides so much more freedom, somehow, than we have as dancers."

Some years earlier, Chrissie Cartwright and Gillian Lynne, the choreographer of *Cats*, had auditioned John Curry and had worked with him on the role of Munkustrap. Nothing came of it, but Chrissie thought that if Robin could sing and dance well enough, he might be considered for the same role. Dinks agreed.

"Robin is lean, tall, and statuesque, and Munkustrap is the leader of the cats. All the little ones come to him to make sure everything is all right and to ask advice. Robin physically fit the bill. That role has to be a presence on-stage."

Some members of the *Cats* creative team were skeptical. "This is Nick Allott foisting something on us," they suspected.

"Just give him a chance," Nick told them. "He has huge enthusiasm for an artist of his status, albeit in another medium, to want to come and work with us. We should respect that and give it the attention it deserves."

Robin was willing to risk rejection. Beyond the chasm of defeat dangled the shining Gene Kelly dream.

"I did those auditions quite happily. I had nothing to lose. It was something I had wanted to do as a child. I didn't start out as a skater. I started out as a dancer, a gymnast, singing in school choirs and things. Only through seeing skating live did I realize that *that* was a version of dancing that, to me, was more individual and completely different. I was fulfilling my childhood fantasy and original goal: to be in musical theatre."

If nothing else, Robin would walk away with an honest, constructive opinion. In November, he hid his nervousness and joined Dinks, Chrissie, a dance captain, and Martin Koch, the Cameron Mackintosh musical super- visor, on the *Cats* set at the New London Theatre.

As Chrissie watched Robin approach, her first thoughts were, "He walks so beautifully, with such good posture. He has a nobility about the way he moves."

For more than an hour, the experts put him through his paces. First they gathered around the piano and had him sing numbers from the show. Martin wondered why Robin knew them by heart when he hadn't seen the show since 1981. What Martin didn't know was that when Robin learned songs, he remembered them for years. *Cats* had made a particularly great impression on him.

Next Robin learned a dance routine and demon- strated it for the panel. From his point of view, the singing had gone relatively well. Surprisingly, it was his feet that didn't cooperate.

"Thank you," Robin was told. "We'll be in touch."

The initial, cautious consensus was, "Okay, it's not the strongest voice in the world. He's a natural dancer, but there are inherent problems in his style. He'll need to do some work."

According to Dinks, "He was so eager to learn and to do. I think we all felt afterwards, 'There's something there.

We should take this further.' We couldn't make a decision at that stage. We knew what he needed to go and do and then come back again to see whether he could pull this off. He obviously had the determination and the will and the love of the theatre."

The drawback everyone noticed right away was that Robin had little flexibility in his ankles. Normally what they looked at first were a dancer's feet. Robin's were stiff. He had enormous fluidity of motion; he was a dancer from the shoulders to the shins; but from there down, he was absolutely solid. He was used to being laced into skating boots.

Robin was asked to spend two months improving his flexibility and his singing voice. Though Nick knew and liked him, he could easily imagine him saying, "I can make a fortune skating and doing other things. This is an awful lot of hard work to put into a company show." Nick wouldn't have blamed him.

"We weren't sure whether he'd actually commit himself, but of course, being Robin, he did."

Bow to Tolly
In December, Toller Cranston crossed paths with Robin in Santa Rosa.

"We were perfect foils for each other. From all reports, Charles Schulz's Christmas extravaganza never hit such heights as when we were there. I watched Robin every night, and I suspect he watched me every night. We watched to be inspired. Robin had something that I actually could have strangled him for. (Maybe I have it, too. No one's ever said that I do.) He had an ability to conjure up fascination and mystery when he did nothing. I hated him for that."

Toller had pooh-poohed Robin's allusions to stage work.

"During that Santa Rosa show, he did something so

fantastic that I had to reassess everything."

At the cast Christmas party, Robin incorporated the skaters in impromptu lyrics. To the tune of "Deck the Halls with Boughs of Holly," he sang, "Deck the halls and bow to Tolly."

"My God," Toller thought, "he really can sing."

A New Tune

Robin's name didn't ring a bell. In voice teacher Florence Riggs' busy life, Olympic Games came and went without notice. But when he appeared in the detached music room off her back garden, he made a good impression.

"I thought he was terribly polite, and I noticed what an incredibly handsome man he was, but there was also a genteelness to him, an elegance."

Florence had no qualms about teaching him.

"I know, by the discipline that it takes, that anyone who's a dancer (and since he skates, he dances also) is going to be a good student—and Robin was. One of the best. He's incredibly professional. I always knew he would be prepared for his lesson. He's good at focusing on what he wants to do, and then, if he doesn't have the material or the skills for it, he knows where to look to find them."

Florence detected a good ear and a lyrical voice.

"He has a somewhat fuzzy quality to his voice that makes it earthy-sounding. It hits you in your heart. It's not the kind of voice you would expect of someone who was singing opera. He has a musical-theatre type of voice that can grow more and more along those lines. Certainly he understands a lyric very well, because he dances a lyric very well."

She warned that her exercises might seem silly or produce socially unacceptable sounds. Robin became adept at the lip trill, the sound that children make when they imitate motorcycles.

"To do it in a scale, and to do that over and over

again, that's what helps to develop the voice. Robin has such wonderful discipline, and his voice really grew. The fuzziness was something that he was controlling a lot more, and he was singing with a lot more clarity of tone."

Florence pronounced him a baritone with a good top end and had him vocalizing up to high C. There were areas that needed "cleaning up": the *passàggi* between his head voice and his chest voice, where there were shifts in resonance. His vibrato needed development.

Some people have natural vibratos. One day Florence told Goldie Hawn, "You're using a vibrato on every note. Let's do a little styling. Hold off on the vibrato."

"What do you mean?"

"Just sing a straight tone with a flat line on it."

"I don't know how to do that."

Florence had to teach Goldie to hold her vibrato still.

"If you know how to bend a lyric, bend a note with feeling and emotion, then you don't need a lot of vibrato in your voice."

Florence drew analogies between how Robin handled his body when he skated and how he handled his voice. The complicating factor was that different types of breathing were involved. Skating and ballet breathing were "pulled up," whereas breathing for singing was diaphragmatic, dependent on the heavy-lifting muscles.

"With singing, the chest is up, but you're not holding it up, and you're not holding in your stomach. You're allowing the breath to move downward, so when you take that breath, it's as though you're sitting at the bottom end of a column. That's where you get your support. That's one of the things that Robin did have to learn: breath support and how to sustain the voice. He has good breath control."

At first, Robin found the breathing difficult.

"One of the things with skating is that we always try to pull stomachs in and pull everything up into the chest. Florence said, 'I want to see your stomach move in and out.'

It was so alien to me to pull everything down. The one thing I did find, when I think about it and when I do it properly, is that my voice lowers. I found it frustrating to begin with, because it was theory. I didn't want to have to think, but with Florence, it was theory that made sense and worked. She had little diagrams. 'This is what's happening here.' We could make bad noises on purpose and then clean them up instantly."

Singing and dancing simultaneously presented a different challenge. The key, according to Florence, was to build stamina. She suggested vocalizing while jogging up and down stairs.

She made tapes of Robin's lessons so he could use them for daily practice. The work in the studio was her "guidance system." It was the work away from the studio that paid dividends. Robin did his exercises in the car.

"You're driving along in southern California with the roof down, and people think that you're having a fit. As self-conscious as I am, I did find myself instantly shutting up and looking the other way so I didn't have to see people's reactions."

Florence made Robin feel, for the first time, that he had something legitimate to work with. She helped him to spit out Munkustrap's narration of "The Aweful Battle of the Pekes and Pollicles." When it was time to audition again, he was ready.

According to Nick Allott, "He'd done it. He was terrific. They really wanted him."

Before offering Robin the role, Chrissie consulted director Trevor Nunn.[20]

"How would you feel about Robin?"

"I admire him so much. I'd be thrilled to be able to work with him."

---

[20] Of *Nicholas Nickleby, Peter Pan, Les Misérables, Starlight Express, Sunset Boulevard, Aspects of Love,* and *Chess.*

At home in California, Robin received the message via his agent: "Get your jazz shoes on. We're delighted to have you on the *Cats* team."

Only then did anyone mention that the tour began in Bristol.

Robin phoned his brother Nick.

"I have a part in *Cats*!"

"But that involves singing."

"Yes?"

"Yes, Rob. Singing, you know?"

He knew that he had his work cut out for him. He didn't want the company to think that he had been hired for his name.

In Nick Allott's book, "He wouldn't have gotten the role if he wasn't any good. We would have taken him, probably, straight away if he had been ready the first time we saw him, but we said, 'Go away and do some work,' and that's what he did. He earned his place in the company. Clearly he had an advantage, inasmuch as he was a name, and we had friends in common. Had someone rung up and said, 'I'm a skater, and I want to be in *Cats*,' we would probably have said, 'Yes, very nice. Send in your c.v. and we'll send you into an open audition.' Because he was who he was, he jumped the queue. We did give him special attention when it came to his audition, but it proved to be entirely justified. Had it not been, then we would have said, 'Thank you very much. This is not your art form.'

"We've had major rock 'n' roll stars wanting to play roles in our shows. In the end, you just have to say, 'Thanks very much, but why don't you stick to filling Wembley stadium?' It's an odd feeling. In Robin's case, he was someone who could draw a crowd, and there obviously was interest in what he was doing, but had we not been absolutely convinced that he could do the role and walk away with a great set of reviews, then he would never have gotten the part."

N i n a

Florence helped Robin with "Nina (from Argentina)" for the London benefit *Mad About the Boy*, a salute to Nöel Coward at the Lyric Shaftesbury Theatre. May 16, 1993, was his moment of truth as a *chanteur*.

"A couple of other people had apparently expressed interest in 'Nina,' but I got first dibs on it. It was a flamboyant piece, a samba, rhumba, cha-cha kind of piece—something that could be fun and not taken too seriously. I thought, 'You can't try to be serious next to this cast.' The other times I had done those events, I was a novelty factor, as were television celebs or journalists. You muck in for a good cause, as it were. It's nice if you can go in as a novelty factor and come out as somebody who's serious about his craft."

"Come watch the tech rehearsal," Robin told Brian Klavano. He hopped onto the stage for his run-through with the live orchestra, playing nervously with his shirt cuffs as he sang. During the instrumental interlude, he told the director, "I sort of thought I'd do some footwork. What am I going to do? Just stand here for eight bars?"

"Oh, yes. Footwork. Could you move? Anything!"

By Brian's assessment, Robin's voice was "adequate but not spectacular." He went back to Robin's flat thinking, "Hmm. He just sort of stood there and sang—but he'll be okay."

Robin admitted to being "a little understated."

"I hadn't heard the backup vocals until that afternoon. That was a bit intimidating, because some of those backup singers had voices of death. I thought, 'I can't sing lead in front of this.'"

That evening, Fred, Jo, and Brian settled in at the theatre and held their breath. Because it was a dark night in the West End, the cast featured many of its top voices.

According to Brian, "All of them came up and sat in a *chair* and sang, stood over *here* and sang. Very little movement. Finally Robin's turn came up. He came out and flung himself against the proscenium. There was a smattering of applause. Well, he proceeded to tango and sashay and *Olé!* to the entire song. He gave it a whole physical presence—which nobody else had done. He brought the house down. They'd been giving good applause, but that stopped the show. The crowd brought him back out. They were blown away by the caliber of his performance."

Jo and Brian stood to applaud. Then Jo turned to Brian and said simply, "Well! He doesn't often surprise me."

How a Dog Man Became a Cat

Rosemarie Ford owed her career as a television presenter to the first British *Cats* tour. She was promoted from Bombalurina to Grizabella and got to sing the show-stopper, "Memory," on the very night that Andrew Lloyd Webber sat in the audience. He invited her to sing in his Royal Variety Performance tribute. There Bruce Forsyth saw her and asked her to join him on "The Generation Game."

When her second *Cats* tour came along, the tall, dark-haired beauty didn't worry about starring with an ice skater. She knew he would be professional. Besides, she had always loved skating.

"For the outsider, the interest very much began with John Curry. Comparing the two, I preferred Robin. He was more jazzy. I think he, and John as well, brought real dance onto the ice. That made it more pleasurable to watch. John was safe. Robin was exciting. Suddenly he was doing back-flips on ice. He had you sitting at the edge of your seat."

When Rosie, a Yorkshire girl, went to London as a young dancer, the first show she attended was Holiday on Ice. Later, she saw Electric Ice.

"It was lovely to see a theatre show with ice skating. I was amazed that they could actually contain it in quite a small space and do all the things they were doing. It reminded me of *Song and Dance*."

Rosie realized from that experience that Robin could function in an ensemble. One can imagine what reservations the rest of the company had. Robin could have been a prima donna.

Dinks bluntly assessed how things might have been.

"It could have swung both ways, but it was more likely to swing the way of 'I'm obviously fabulous on ice, so therefore that means that I'm fabulous on the stage.' If it *had* gone that way, without a doubt he wouldn't have achieved the success that he achieved. He has an amazing discipline, and he just wants to learn. He is more than happy to be taught and told and told off. He'll take notes. He's not starry whatsoever (quite wisely). I don't think he could have been, under those circumstances. Nobody would have been bothered to give him the time of day."

Robin and Rosie met at a press conference in Bristol. Each of them said a little piece. Later they watched the news in the theatre press office. First Cameron talked. Then the camera cut to Rosie walking to the podium. Just as she opened her mouth, Robin appeared onscreen. She never quite forgave him for the tape editor's indiscretions.

On the morning after "Nina," Robin strode down Rosebery Avenue to Sadler's Wells. The Cranko Studio on the uppermost floor stood at the summit of a mountain of stairs. A long, narrow balcony offered fresh air and a view. The studio itself was bare: a wooden floor, a piano, a few chairs, and four walls lined with barres and mirrors.

There Robin first met Trevor Nunn. The titular director of all *Cats* productions liked to spend the first day with each new company initiating the dancers into their strange new feline world. Nunn explained the origin and evolution of the show. Then he talked through the characters while the dancers made notes. He told each prospective cat three key words: meek, aggressive, humorous, inquisitive, each was highly individual. The object for the dancers was to internalize their traits.

Inhibitions flew out the window when Nunn consigned the cast to all fours: touching, feeling, rubbing, rolling, communicating through body language. The dancers worked to develop their characters and postulate theories to explain them. Each stood up individually and portrayed a caricature of his character through a story line. The cats learned about one another by asking, "Where do you come from? How do you feel? What do you like and dislike?"

Certain cats instinctively avoided each other. Others became territorial or sought protection. Robin found it odd but fun. Chrissie had thought that it might be difficult for him.

"For dancing, there's not enough of that improvised work done in training. We're forever being told, 'You must have your arms here. This has been handed on for three generations. This is the position. Exactly this.' We don't have the freedom to say, 'A little bit off to the right will be fine.' I presume that it was the same for skating, because of the question of balance. I found that Robin was free and receptive and brave in the experimental and improvisational work. It's usually quite daunting for most dancers. Presumably it's the same for skaters."

Trevor Nunn, in his wisdom, by breaking down their barriers, had turned a group of dancers into a company.

That was the first day of a grueling five-week rehearsal period. Chrissie soon discovered in Robin a trait that many dancers lacked: single-minded commitment. He worked, and he worked overtime.

"We have unions in the theatre, and they say you have to have certain breaks. That's fine and right, but Robin said things like, 'Don't do this now. I'll do it on the break.' Wow! Nobody ever says that to me."

She overheard a young cast member tell Robin, "Chrissie says we have to work on this together."

"Fine, but we won't go over it now. I'll do it on my break."

"Well, okay," the dancer agreed, thinking at first that Robin didn't want to bother with her.

Robin explained to Chrissie, "When I was skating and doing it without money, I had to use every hour that I could find. There was no question of 'I don't get paid for that' or 'I don't work my breaks' or 'I have to finish at a certain time.'"

When he walked to his flat from Sadler's Wells, he listened to *Cats* on headphones and sang along. One day, some fellow dancers passed him in a car and tried to attract his attention. At the next rehearsal, they mocked his oblivion.

"You were really gone."

"You're all used to it. This is new to me. I have a lot to catch up on."

They found it amusing that Robin was still going like the Energizer rabbit, even after a twelve-hour day.

"I was absolutely terrified that I was going to be left behind. I didn't pick up the Jellicle ball as quickly as I wanted to, and I was afraid that I wasn't going to be able to dance it as well as anybody else. You can only allow yourself to get so far behind before you lose it, and I was not prepared to lose it."

Robin commandeered empty studios. One Saturday, he had a revelation: he was *skating* all the choreography, moving it out as though he had an entire arena to fill. He told himself, "If the rest of the cast were here, you'd have played ten-pin ball with them all."

In skating, Robin had the luxury of space and independence of movement. In dancing, he was confined: both by four walls and by someone else's choreography.

"I suddenly realized that, unlike ice, you can choreograph twenty minutes in a three-foot-square piece of stage. From that point, I had my feet underneath me more, and I was a lot more coherent with what I needed to have happen. It took me a good two months after the show opened to be as comfortable doing the choreography as I was singing and doing the staging and the acting—which became comfortable quickly."

Katherine Healy had turned her figure-skating background into an advantage.

"That was something that stayed with me in my dancing: the sense of movement. It's how you use a stage in a theatrical sense; how well you cover it, how well you command. Skating rinks are about three times the size of most normal stages, so I was pretty used to enormous performing surfaces. Sometimes when you have dance choreographers working in the medium of figure skating, they get a bit stationary. Things get vertical instead of using the possibility to move."

Robin found that he had to adapt to the relative verticality of dance choreography while capitalizing on his freedom of movement and ability to command.

He was frankly surprised to find the dancing difficult. Chrissie called him "clod-footed." She introduced him to flexible ankles. He began to use them in new ways, with resultant tendon problems and sore feet and calves. The cat persona exacerbated the problems.

As Chrissie explained, "Every movement of the foot is like a paw peeling off the floor. We had to emphasize working through the feet. He actually did that quite naturally, which surprised me. I'm sure he had to work at it and concentrate on it. Because of Robin's way of working, everything was done with a great deal of detail. He did it outside the rehearsal room, I suspect. I don't remember having to say, 'No, go though your feet. Flex your ankles.'"

In skating, Robin's knees, thighs, and gluteus maximus muscles bore 90 per cent of the force, with his body low and his weight slightly forward. For dancing, he had to become more upright and adjust his center of gravity.

Learning cat mannerisms was one of the interesting challenges. Hands and fingers became a major focus. Palms were never raised.

"It's always knuckles and claws. You find yourself scratching your nose with your wrist."

Because Munkustrap was the protector, ready to pounce, Robin learned a high, open stance with rounded shoulders and a hunched back. At one point in the show, he spent a full nine minutes with his back hunched, shoulders tense, and arms in a broken *port de bras*. Only his eyes moved. He developed muscles on top of muscles from holding the pose.

According to Chrissie, "His role was a princely character. It was able to use well his good posture. There was a cat involved as well, which wasn't upright. What we had to do was get the balance between the upright bearing of the prince and the closer-to-the-ground movements of the cat. Like everything, it grew with Robin. There was a stage where I thought, 'It's going to take a while.' Then suddenly it was there. He never came back the following day having taken a step back. It was always a step forward."

Robin admired Chrissie's passion.

"I learned so much from watching her, because she knows the show so well. She has every nuance in her brain, every lyric, every step and movement that those cats take on the stage. Every time she was watching, I could see her eyes going. She kept saying, 'There's no leeway. It has to be this way. That's how it was set.' That's not an easy task, to keep it looking so fresh, but you don't teach that. That's what comes from the heart."

The only air conditioning in the Cranko Studio was the occasional breeze that wafted in off the balcony, bringing with it humidity and street smells. At the end of one stifling June afternoon, Rosie and Robin appeared in the doorway with a large tub of ice cream and enough cones for the whole exhausted company.

Robin adored that hot, sweaty studio.

"Baryshnikov was rehearsing below with the White Oak Project. I thought, 'Fonteyn and Nureyev worked in this room, and Baryshnikov is below me!' We got to meet, and I saw the company perform. They were fabulous."

The majority of the *Cats* dancers were youngsters straight from school. Robin, Rosie, and the late Tony Monopoly were the acknowledged heads of the company. They set the tone and led by example.

"Tony was absolutely God to everybody. He was Dad. He was the most affectionate person. Old Deuteronomy spent most of the rehearsal sitting on the tire. We never got to his part. Whenever there was a break, everybody gravitated to him. They leaned on him and put their heads in his lap. Gravitating to the nest—and the nest was the tire and Tony. Lovely, lovely man. It was great fun."

Rosie found in Robin the same sort of empathy.

"Grizabella is a cat who has fallen on hard times, so many of the male cats talk about her. Every time she comes onstage, they snicker at her. We improvised within our characters. Most of the time, I'd sit by the piano, then try to move out into the midst of it. They'd be hissing and spitting at me, trying to get me away. Then I'd scuttle—well, as fast as Grizabella *could* scuttle—back to the piano, or wherever I was sitting."

Robin hissed and clawed like the others, but softened it up with a wink. He told Rosie, "I feel so bad that we're all baiting you like this."

As characters emerged, Robin developed a theory.

"Munkus had to be personable to Grizabella from a distance, whilst keeping his authority and not letting the rest of the tribe know that he understood what she was going through. Chrissie had said, as had Gillian and Trevor, 'There are things you will find about your characters that other people haven't found. We're only giving you guidelines.' I said to Rosie, 'You know what? I think Grizabella was probably Munkustrap's first.' She might have been the one who introduced him to the feline frenzy, as we like to call it. Deep down, although he had to (on behalf of Deuteronomy) keep her distanced from the young ones, he needed to let her know that he did understand and like her. He had a little flame for her, because he'd had a big flame with her earlier. That kind of worked for her, too."

Despite the fun of character development, the weeks of rehearsal were punishing. Rosie found *Cats* the most demanding musical to dance.

"I don't think there's much that you can get that will top that. You have to get through the burn—the 'Jane Fonda burn.' You have to get second wind every night, eight times a week. It's very hard mentally. You say, 'How am I going to do it? I don't have the energy.'"

All the young dancers went through the same torments: living on sandwiches; in tears because all they could think of was resting their weary bones; wringing wet with sweat from morning 'til night.

"Chrissie Cartwright is very good," Rosie said. "She won't let up. She knows that, in rehearsals, she has to keep pushing it, pushing it, so that people reach the level of fitness to get through the two-and-a-half-hour show. I don't think I ever saw Robin lose his temper. He was always calm and placid, which is amazing."

That was on the outside. Inside he knew that *Cats* was the hardest work he had ever done.

One day he went to a physiotherapist. Since he was there as a dancer from *Cats*, the man didn't make the connection with Robin Cousins, the skater. He ticked off a list: "You have *this*, you have *this*, you have *that*. How come you're dancing?"

"I'm not really a dancer. I'm an athlete."

"Well, that would make sense."

They went through Robin's history. The physiotherapist stared in amazement.

"You're very lucky, you know. From what you're telling me, you're still able to perform at at least 70 per cent of what you would be doing if you had no injuries at all."

That was a perspective that Robin had never considered.

"It's something I've lived with for the whole time. There are people who probably still, to this day, have forgotten because of what I've done, but by rights I should not be doing anything but barely walking at the moment."

He enjoyed one advantage, according to Dinks.

"He's very healthy, very fit. It *is* the most arduous show to do, without a doubt, and everyone who's ever in it says the same thing. Everybody stays with us for no longer than two years. We have that rule. It's for both them and for us."

Three factors contributed to the difficulty: the need to simultaneously use multiple talents; the fact that cast members rarely left the stage; and the unusually detailed choreography.

"Few musicals require all those ingredients *and* the standard of choreography—and then, on top of that, to have to create areas of it for yourself; and on top of *that*, you have to learn how to be a cat. Robin had to be able to sing; he had to be able to act; he had to be able to dance—all at the same time—and various styles of dance, not just one. He had it in him, because it came out, but he still needed to start from scratch."

Robin's spring and rotation were useful. At the end of the ball, he threw in a triple tour adapted from skating. The dancers were intrigued, especially by the rotational speed. He showed some of the classical dancers what for them were "cheat" jump techniques.

Stage presence was something else that Robin brought to *Cats,* according to Nick.

"It's something you're born with. There's nothing

striking about Robin physically when you meet him, besides the fact that he's an enormously nice man, very warm and affectionate, but when he's onstage, he just lights up. I didn't know whether he'd fit into a company, but he did. He stamped his presence on the show as a member of the company. Quite clearly he was the leader, without necessarily dominating. It's a fine balance to achieve, but I think he did it.

"Deuteronomy is the older leader, the grandfather of the company, but Munkustrap is the head of the herd. He's a stag, if you like. Robin has that kind of showy, masculine presence without it necessarily being in your face. He has the delicacy, the grace of movement, that a dancer has, but he's also overtly male onstage. He has a confidence about him which the character needed to exude, which meant that he could draw in the younger members of the company."

It took Robin two hours to learn to apply Munkustrap's makeup. He took notes as Karen Dawson explained the application stages.

"When in doubt, more powder," she said. Sweat bled through quickly. Some cats got the job down to fifteen minutes, but not all patterns were equally elaborate. Even with practice, Robin's transformation took an hour—but it was riveting.

"The first day Karen was in working with everybody, people disappeared every now and again and came back two hours later in normal rehearsal gear and just the face. It was strange. The only way you could recognize who they were was by what they were wearing. You totally lose the structure of the normal face, the cheekbones and eyes.

It's odd to look at various photographs that I've seen of companies of *Cats*. You keep thinking you're seeing somebody you know, and you're not. The costume and the makeup and the size of the body are pretty uniform worldwide. If the character needs to be five-foot-five, it needs to be five-foot-five. There are traits that go all the way through. When I saw the guy who took over for me when I left the first company, it was like looking in a mirror. He was about my build, my height, and had identical makeup on. There are only subtle changes from one person to the next. The minute the makeup goes on—and the makeup is so intense, and the wig, and the costume—you do *become* something. I've never looked in the mirror and seen Robin Cousins."

Robin wore the wig and makeup between shows, which amused his backstage guests.

"From my point of view, it was just *me* talking to them. Of course, you forget what they're looking at. They were talking to makeup and hair."

Each cat had two identical Lycra costumes that were rotated for repair and cleaning after each performance. Munkustrap's was black and white with furry shins and shoulders and a silver-studded black leather collar. By the time Robin put it on, he wasn't playing a cat—he had become one.

Back to Bristol

The Hippodrome was turned inside out. The orchestra pit and eight rows of seats were removed to make way for a ramp that allowed the cats to run into the audience. A lift was installed below the stage to shoot them up through a trap. Thirteen truckloads of scenery outfitted the auditorium as a giant garbage dump replete with 2,000 pieces of cat-scale refuse: cereal boxes, tin cans, broken dishes, an auto body, all three times life-size. State-of-the-art sound and lighting systems were installed. Fiber optic technology turned the ceiling into a canopy of twinkling stars, while giant fans created smoke effects.

The scene was surreal the first time the cast walked onto the set. The dancers behaved like cats, prowling, pur-ring, growling, immersed in their characters. They sought out areas where they felt at ease and shunned uncomfortable places. It was hard to believe, but they were acting territorial.

On July 5, 1993, the pressure was intense. The premier of a new *Cats* tour was a big event. Much of the first-night crowd had come from London—including Cameron Mackintosh, to see his new show for the first time.

Robin was not the only débutant.

"We had maybe six or seven cast members who were fresh out of school. Fabulous dancers. It was all very exciting. They were making their débuts at eighteen. I was not, but I have to say that I did *feel* eighteen."

Trish Bernays was enthusiastic after early misgivings.

"I remember thinking, 'What is it going to be like?' I'd heard him sing, but I'd never heard him sing publicly before, and I was waiting to be thoroughly embarrassed. He was excellent. Within two minutes, I'd forgotten it was Robin. It was a funny feeling, though. I was quite uptight about the whole thing."

At the final curtain, the audience stood, to a man, and cheered. Dinks particularly noticed Fred and Jo's reactions.

"They were desperately proud of that opening night. I don't think any of us will ever forget it. Those curtain calls! I remember seeing Jo afterwards. She said she was just so moved to see her son up there and everyone cheering, waving, and carrying on. He'd done it. This is what it was all about."

Cameron Mackintosh hosted a party at the Swallow Royal Hotel. Spotlights shone on the façade bedecked in gold balloons and *Cats* banners. Five hundred guests sipped champagne, feasted on oysters and prawns, and carried on, in many cases, until four or five in the morning.

Grizabella's Ascent

Rosie was afraid of heights. She loathed the moment when Grizabella ascended to the "Heaviside Layer" on a tire.

"Once in a new venue, the tire got a bit temperamental. Sometimes the damn thing jiggled. Every time that

happened, Robin reached out and grabbed my hand to re-
assure me. I was so frightened that I sat down. I kept
thinking, 'This thing is going to drop.' He stood practically
under the tire, holding my hand as if to say, 'It's all right.'"

He caught hell for that. If the tire had crashed,
Rosie would have been safe enough—but not Robin.

Lessons Taught, Points Taken

During the Bristol run, Brian Orser arrived to work with
Robin on his Landover numbers, "Calling You" and "Deeply
Dippy." The two compared the preparation of young dancers to that of young skaters. Skaters, they agreed, were
essentially trained to compete—but not well enough trained
to meet the challenges of competing on a national and
global stage. When they turned professional, tour life was
a shock. Many were ill-equipped for the physical grind
and the need for self-reliance.

Dancers, at least in Europe, were prepared for professional life by special schools that trained them in their
teens. They adapted more easily than skaters. Skaters,
Robin decided, could benefit from formal warmup, standardized instruction, and increased self-discipline. He was
impressed that some of the younger cast members, the
"heavy-duty dancers," took forty-five-minute or hour-
long classes on their own before the general-conditioning
warmup, even on two-show days.

"The leg is required to go 180°, and you work very
hard. 'The Jellicle Ball' is devastating for some of them."

Munkustrap didn't dance the entire ball. His numbers, "Pekes and Pollicles" and "Old Deuteronomy," led,
back-to-back, into the first-act finale. Even stepping in
and out of the ball, Robin recognized how hard it was to
dance it properly.

Chrissie Cartwright hazarded a guess as to what else
Robin learned from the dance world.

"He had problems to put up with, niggling things

that weren't always taken care of. Not everyone has his commitment to working and to detail. It's hard to put up with other people not having it. He learned to do the same thing night after night and keep it looking as if it was the first time he'd done it. He learned, probably, a sort of humility, too. It's humbling to have to do things that you're not used to doing: for example, the improvisation. He was prepared to look foolish—and didn't look foolish, in my opinion.

"From beginning to end, the moment he was on-stage, he *was* that cat and that character. There was never a glimpse of anything else. We try to achieve a balance between a cat and a human being, sort of the character of a human being within a cat's body. What we're trying to say is, 'You see, cats are very much human beings at the end of the day. They go through the same emotional states and relationships as humans.' His performance was always true. He's very sincere."

Some of the luxuries of the dance world took Robin by surprise. He didn't expect a dresser to pick up after him. On the road, a skater took care of himself. The theatre industry seemed indulgent by comparison.

Robin and Simon Rice, Mr. Mistoffolees, discussed what the skating world could teach dancers. Simon was Royal Ballet School through and through. When a dancer went to the studio, he took a class. He didn't just dance. He did the prescribed steps, in the prescribed manner, over and over. A skater often went to the rink just to skate, training on his own for hours. A skater with a gift for choreography created programs for himself in his personal style.

"The individuality, which is what I think has made skating so special, is what they are envious of, and the fact that we can turn fifty thousand times without blinking an eyelid. They came to watch when I was working with Brian, and they looked at the speed, travel, and the fact that we can spin forever without getting dizzy."

What some of the dancers learned from Robin, in the view of Chrissie and Dinks, was professionalism, commitment, and care. He taught them to work hard and play hard. He modeled warmth and generosity, onstage and off, and helped to create a harmonious atmosphere, which inevitably told in the production.

Robin was embarrassed to hear their assessment.

"It almost sounds as if I gave classes in it, but I didn't even know that I was doing it. It's strange to hear what people say about you. I guess, in anything, if the leader is right, everyone else follows—but I never considered myself the leader. That was just the way I do things and the way I am."

Cats, with four months in Bristol, became the longest-running show in the Hippodrome's history. Robin signed on for a ten-week Liverpool extension that was to span Christmas and conclude at the end of January. He planned to interrupt the run to fly to Boston for "Skates of Gold," a televised exhibition by Olympic gold medalists. A second brief hiatus would allow him to compete at Landover and the Challenge of Champions.

He had been off the ice entirely for months. With serious skating in the offing, he began driving from Liverpool to Deeside, North Wales, to pick up what ice time he could—four hours a week.

In the past, he had stopped skating without having trouble returning to the ice. During *Cats*, it was a different story. Skating was a general struggle, especially jumps. The takeoffs were fine, the rotations were fine, but the landings were nosedives. His body positions were "out of whack." He was puzzling over the situation when Simon, who had been sidelined with an injury, arrived at the theatre brimming with enthusiasm.

"I'm so happy that I got to go back and take classes with the Royal Ballet and recenter myself. The rake of the stage had pushed my weight way out of proportion."

A light bulb flashed over Robin's head. The stage on which he had been dancing was a foot and a half higher in the back than in the front. Spending every day pitched forward, he had compensated by changing his center of gravity.[21]

"I didn't even consider that it would be a problem. It didn't enter my mind. It has been horrendous dealing with that. Now that I know that's what it is, I don't feel quite so bad. I was scratching toe picks and tripping, and I just couldn't figure it out. Then Simon mentioned the rake, and that was it."

Robin took off just a day and a half for "Skates of Gold." He missed the Saturday evening performance to fly to Boston. On Sunday, he performed in the ice show, then changed from his costume to street clothes in a cab on the way to Logan airport. His night flight had him in Bristol by Monday morning. Monday night, he was onstage again in *Cats*.

Several weeks after the Liverpool run ended, Robin did BBC Olympic commentary. While he and the two chief skating presenters worked in the London studios, he stayed with Rosie, who had left *Cats* after Bristol. One day Rosie was upset. She phoned her mother and sobbed into the receiver.

"Next thing I knew, Robin had brought some tissues and put them on my lap. He's a very caring person, and I do love him dearly."

Dinks shared that view.

"Robin loved *Cats*, and we loved having him. He fit in brilliantly and stayed with the show far longer than I

---

[21] A study published in the *American Journal of Health* by Dr. Randolph Evans of the University of Texas suggested that dancers who performed on raked stages had three times the average risk of injury. The American industry standard, one inch per foot of stage space, was likened by neurologist Evans to "standing on a ski slope."

hoped he would. What's exciting is to watch his skills develop. The natural talent has come out in a big way. Not that anything he did onstage in *Cats* is as demanding physically, probably, as some of the stuff he does on ice, but the courage he had in taking that step is extraordinary. The wonderful thing was that none of it was born out of arrogance. It was, 'I want to give this a go. Will you help me?'"

Nick added, "I suppose he's a courageous man to switch disciplines at a quite advanced age in terms of the physicality that's required. There's very little cynicism in him. I'm sure he worked his heart out to get where he got in the skating world, and then to turn around and say, 'Okay, I'm going to do it again in another medium,' you have to have an enormous sense of optimism. He could easily have fallen on his face. The fact that he hasn't, and that he's reestablished himself in something else and still remains as nice a man as he is, says a lot about his approach to the work."

They all kept in touch.

"We shall stay friends," Dinks vowed. "In this business, it isn't always like that. People are flighty and pop in and out of your life. I don't feel that with Robin."

His ties with England were soon bound tighter than anyone could foresee. He went home to America restlessly pondering a blueprint for a new future.

8. A Renaissance Man Returns to his Roots

*I*n mid-March, Robin flew to England to spearhead the annual show for Cancer and Leukaemia in Childhood International (CLIC).

Over the years, he had participated in CLIC's fund-raising efforts. In 1993, he became a trustee and began overseeing the annual gala. Months of work came to fruition on March 20, 1994, in the charity's eighteenth-birthday celebration. Robin led off the parade of stars in a variety show at the Hippodrome.

He returned to California, where his ties were complex. By then, however, his reflections had crystallized. Plans had been set in motion. A personal relationship gone sour was just one of several catalysts.

Robin had been asked to kick off the second-year *Cats* tour.

"Without hesitating, I said yes—not really thinking that I didn't want to get stuck in a role. Maybe I should have said, 'No, I want to find something else,' but I said yes. I think I knew in my heart that that would give me the reason that I wanted to come back to England."

Lee Mimms was finding Robin work in America, but it wasn't the kind that would launch him in the right direction.

"It would possibly have helped me to go sideways, but it wasn't going to make me go forward. I felt that I was on a roll. The momentum was moving, not at a great speed, but in the direction that was getting the juices flowing, getting the brain back in gear. There I was, having done *Cats*, on a speaking basis with Cameron Mackintosh and Nick Allott, having put my foot in the door. I needed to say, 'Where do you think I should go from here?' It was a question of finding the right agent."

"I'm going to change London agents," Robin announced to Brian as they stood on the balcony of the Hollywood house.

He told Brian first, because Brian knew and liked Janet Mills, the outgoing agent.

"She was a big fan and a great family friend and had been instrumental in getting *Cats* organized, but I felt that Janet was not going to be the person to say, 'That wasn't good.' I almost thought that, in her eyes, I could do no wrong. That's great, but it wasn't going to serve its purpose. I also felt that, in the long run, it was probably going to destroy our friendship, which was far more important than whether or not she could get me into a West End show or onto television."

The new agent, Jan Kennedy, was better connected and more in tune with the English theatrical world. She would push Robin more aggressively, he thought.

"That was a difficult transition. It still hasn't been resolved 100 per cent, but it was the right decision. Jan handled Rosie, so we had met. We had three or four conversations on the phone. Then I had lunch with her. I thought, 'I really like this lady.' She knew I was doing the second tour of *Cats*. It was during that time that we got ourselves organized. I knew, when I went back to England the second time, that that would be it."

Between the end of March and early July, Robin put his Lake Arrowhead house on the market and found some tenants for the Hollywood residence. Winston and Thumper went to a new home. (Fergie had already moved in with Fred and Jo.) He relegated the rest of his life to storage. The day after *Star Spangled Ice*, he boarded a plane bound for England, shortly to join a partially recast *Cats* production for a fall run in Newcastle and Southampton.

Fred wasn't surprised.

"I always said he would come back."

Jo was another story.

"Robin loves America, and I am amazed that he's back here. I think it's that when he came back to do *Cats*, which was the first long period he had here, met up with all his friends, then went back in the middle to do something in America, he decided he had missed contact with his family—not us, necessarily, Fred and I, but the boys—to be able to ring them up, go out to lunch with them, meet up with his nephews. I think that although he was enjoying life in America and leading a full life, he suddenly missed the contact with home."

Tony and Terry thought the move made sense.

"He missed his family. A lot of changes have taken place in the last couple of years, but I think he's where he wants to be now."

Brian was a pragmatist.

"He was going to auditions in America and looking to

get into theatre, but it finally made sense, when the *Cats* offer came along, to go back to the country where he is known on every street corner."

As Celine said, "He realized that time was flying by. His oldest nephew, Robin, was suddenly fourteen, and his parents were getting older."

Trish knew that Robin would come home in the end.

"I think his roots are deep here. They always have been. Then, Robin has been a great one for moving on when some things no longer work, for whatever reason. I don't think he says, 'Oh, what a shame.' He says, 'Oh, never mind. Let's start again.'"

Robin found Trish close to the mark.

"I happen to think your own destiny will guide you in the direction that you need to be guided in. Sometimes that is the wrong direction, in order to be taught a lesson. If it works, it works. If it doesn't, fine. Next! That time on the balcony with Brian was probably the first time I'd actually orated the thought. We all have great ideas and aspirations, but the finality is saying it."

Robin's visits to England over the years hadn't convinced him that he was missing anything. Time, maturity, and experience changed his perspective.

"Living in Britain, being home, is completely different than it was when I was seventeen. The timing was right. You can go to shop after shop, looking specifically for something, and never see it. A week later, you're looking for something else, and within three minutes you see what you spent hours looking for."

Something frightening happened almost immediately to reinforce the wisdom of Robin's decision. In August, on the day after his sixth grandchild, Oliver, was born, Fred had a heart attack.

Robin was in Newcastle, near the Scottish border. He heard the news at the end of the *Cats* matinée. There was no air service to Bristol, and the last direct train had left.

As upset as he was, friends didn't want him to drive.

Nick, who had gone ahead to Bristol, was in a bad state. He feared they were going to lose Fred, and he couldn't erase from his mind the thought that his brother wasn't there.

"Where is Rob?" he repeated distractedly. He was worried for himself and Jo, but most worried for Robin.

"I still regard him, as I suppose all elder brothers do, as vulnerable. He's easily touched by emotion. He handles grief very badly, as I do."

Robin drove the three hours to London and slept briefly at his flat. By the time he arrived at the hospital, Fred had begun to pull through.

"He was the last person we would have expected that to happen to. My mother, yes, because of her frantic life-style, but my father? I guess, in the end (as they said), the one thing he never does is complain. He internalizes everything, as I tend to do, and it all became rather too much for him. As one of the doctors said, with the know-ledge that we have of the heart, sometimes actually to have an attack is the best thing. Then you're able to compensate and look after it, whereas before you wouldn't have known anything was wrong. Cardio people are so clever now, but it was extremely scary nonetheless. Once we knew Dad was in good hands, we turned our attention to our mother. The rock of Gibraltar was suddenly turning a bit into pebble dash."

After the crisis, Fred and Jo simplified their lives. They sold Baridon House and moved to a flat in London. In time, they found their dream bungalow in Borough Green, a short train ride from London and not far from a town on the Sussex coast where Robin had begun negotiations to buy a house of his own. He was, at heart, a homebody, a creature of his family.

"We're very much our own persons, but collectively we all have a bit of our family in us. We're happy on our own, but we're also extremely happy to get together. The nice thing about our family—and it has had to be that way— is that it's one of those families that functions okay when it's apart, and when it's together, it functions as if it had never been apart."

His friendships were the same. He liked to pick them up where he left off. The people in his life were ones who could do that, too—or put up with it.

When Robin decided to move home, he had a talk with his niece, Claire.

"America is on the other side of the world," he explained to the childish face tilted up towards his.

A little voice said, "Does this mean that I'm not only going to see you on the television anymore?"

It occurred to Robin that he had seen his brothers' children little, if at all, in the course of a year. He enjoyed being around them, having them visit, and talking to them on the phone.

In England, Robin was able to involve himself in Tristan's skating. He choreographed his nephew's novice program but kept a low profile.

"What I don't want to do is start to be a focus. Let him do his own thing. Let people see him for what he is, not as my nephew. Now that he's at the point where people are taking him seriously and the judges really like what he's doing, I'm trying to get a bit more hands-off."

Tristan was well-grounded in the fundamentals at the Stevenage Training Center. Robin saw some parallels to himself. One was a touch of precompetition nervousness, worse if Uncle Robin was around. Another: "He has *big* jumps. He does like to launch himself."

Martin had returned to the familiar fray.

"It's worse. Tristan is small, and he's younger than when I really got interested in what Robin was doing. He's more vulnerable, and he's definitely *mine*. I shared Robin with two parents and another brother. It's incredibly

nerve-wracking, and I guess we're just starting to understand what my parents went through.

"It's odd in a way. We still try to keep it under
control. Obviously we know what Robin did. We know what
it took to get there. After Tristan won his first national
title, someone asked, 'Is he going to be like his uncle?' I
said, 'Hang on a minute. Tristan's just got on the bottom
rung of a ladder that Robin got to the very top of, and it's
one hell of a big ladder. There's an awful lot to do between
where he is now and where you're talking in terms of
emulating Robin.' But it's great to have someone else following in brother's footsteps."

Tristan would rather be himself than Robin Cousins's nephew, in his father's opinion.

"People always, whenever they talk to him, will
want to talk about Uncle Robin and what Uncle Robin did.
There's no avoiding that, but he's not setting out to be like
Robin—or do what Robin did, even. He's setting out to do the
best he can, the best way he can, having Robin's help
whenever he can get it."

The financial pressures of training in England had
changed little since Robin's amateur days. Tristan, as the
novice and primary champion and a member of the British
training squad, received no help from the N S A. As Martin
said with an ironic laugh, "Nothing changes in this country."

Young Robin, born during the 1980 Olympics, lost
interest in serious skating. He preferred to draw. As for
Claire, "She likes anything done with dancing and jumping, and she has the most beautiful natural voice."

The youngest, Oliver, may yet be Fred's footballer.
He learned early to line up the ball like a pro and drill it in
a straight line—"but it has to be left foot."

At the end of 1994, Robin made several transatlantic
trips: to the Canadian *Elvis Tour*, then to the North American Open in Cleveland. He skated to Kenny G's "Alone" and

Sam Harris's version of "Satan's L'il Lamb."

A freak injury during the fight scene with Macavity put a damper on the end of Robin's *Cats* run. The culprit was the battery pack that he wore in the small of his back to power his microphone.

"The pack jarred something in my lower back, which completely seized it. Whilst there wasn't a lot of pain, there was zero mobility. Normally in the London production of the show, Munkustrap has time to take the pack off before the fight. Due to changes in the production that I was in, and to the fact that I was actually in a lot more of the show than other Munkustraps, there was not an opportunity for me to leave the stage to tape or remove the pack.

"We had choreographed the lifts and the throws and the rolling around on the back perfectly comfortably. I always tried to make it as authentic as possible, because I can't think of anything worse than a choreographed fight that looks like two people dancing together. As it was supposed to be quite vicious, the last thing I wanted to do was prance around the stage. We did tend to like to get a little bit carried away. Towards the end of the run, when your body's so in tune with it, that's when the problems happen. I certainly wasn't in a position to bounce around between the stage and the ice."

With a viral infection on top of the injury, Robin flew to Canada again, catching a few hours' sleep before competing in the inaugural Toyota Canadian Professional Figure Skating Championships at Hamilton. With both ears plugged and his equilibrium impaired, he gave a subpar technical performance—Toller pronounced it the worst of his career. The next night, after a better artistic showing, Robin was sent to bed without an exhibition.

Three days later, his "Impossible Dream" earned a standing ovation at the Northwestern Mutual World Team Championship. Then he gladly headed home to an English Christmas.

The View from the Broadcast Booth

In March 1995, Robin sat in a glass cubicle suspended above the skating audience at the NEC Arena, on display like the crown jewels to anyone with good eyesight. The World Figure Skating Championships had arrived in Birmingham, England. Robin, as elder statesman, shed light by refracting it through his prism.

In the booth with him was Sue Barker. Below, in the tiered blue rows of the press box, Alan Weeks and Barry Davies provided play-by-play analysis and color commentary.

Davies had begun announcing for the BBC in 1984.

"Torvill and Dean were not the world's greatest talkers. I was invited to see if I could get them to say a few things."

At the Ottawa Worlds, the Civic Centre had tingled with anticipation on the day Chris and Jane were to skate *Bolero*. When the main generator failed, plunging the arena into darkness, most of the audience left to find dinner. In England, watching the couple win Worlds meant staying up until three o'clock in the morning. The only local affiliates that refused to broadcast the event at that hour were those in the Nottingham area, T & D's home turf. The BBC found that "just a touch amusing."

Davies worked with Robin during his early broadcasting career.

"His great forte is his enthusiasm for the sport. Apart from his knowledge, he brings it in an interesting style. He doesn't flap, which is a major plus in television. He's easy to get on with. If you throw him an idea, he'll come back, and he's certainly not reluctant in coming forward to give an opinion."

The British are more reserved than North Americans in their enthusiasm for skating as a spectator sport. Davies thought it a good sign when he noticed a well-known soccer hero in the crowd. The sport's popularity in

England is cyclical. Television ratings go through the roof during the Olympics. As with any other country, if Britain has a contender, there's a larger audience.

Over the years, Robin had learned to edit his complex thoughts and to formulate and present key points efficiently. His BBC training was to let the skating speak for itself. He made just one memorable gaffe in Birmingham. When the control room wanted him to end his comments, Davies gave the signal, a circular hand motion. When Robin had worked for NBC, the same signal had meant "Keep it going. Drag it out."

He knew that the sign had gone wrong when he saw the expression on Sue Barker's face and realized that he was supposed to *stop* talking.

Birmingham was not without its irony. There was Robin, the confident Olympic champion, the capable commentator, the pillar of adult society. All the while, an invisible part of him was the little boy who had trembled in the presence of the austere British judges. "Not today, Dearie" still rang faintly in his ears.

"There are maybe a couple of judges that I can speak to on a first-name basis, but that's it. It has changed a little bit, but at Worlds, I was not there from the association's point of view. I was there for the producer. I can't say it was comfortable the whole time."

The adult Robin laughed heartily at his quaking inner child.

A month later, he assumed the mantle of skating official at the Miko Masters in Paris. Although he enjoyed presiding with Carlo Fassi, he wasn't wholeheartedly flattered by the invitation.

"I was *most upset*, thinking they'd phoned to ask me to compete, but they were asking me to be a referee. That tells you, 'You're getting on a bit, Robin.'"

Robin was named Alan Weeks' replacement upon the death of the *éminence grise* just three months after his

1996 retirement. With Weeks' passing, Robin lost one of life's reassuring fixtures.

"When I was a child, I had to take naps on Saturday afternoon in order to stay up until eleven or midnight to watch skating competitions. It was always Alan whose voice told me all about the skaters, my heroes, on the screen. It was a good five or six years later that I met him for the first time when he was commentating on my skating as a junior. He was there when John won. He was there when I won. He was there when Jayne and Chris won. Then I got to be beside him. He had a long and illustrious career. He will be missed."

You're Going to Do *What*?

The telephone rang one winter day early in 1995. It was Jan Kennedy.

"I've put you up for something. Either you'll think I have a great idea, or you'll think I'm nuts."

"What is it?"

"*Rocky Horror.*"

Silence.

"Oh. Which part? Brad?"

"No. It has to be Frank."

Frank? Frank N Furter? The alien transvestite from Transylvania? Mother was not going to like that at all.

"I don't know. Do you think I can do it?"

"That's not for me to say. If you think you can do it, go for it. I certainly think you have the ability."

"Actually, I haven't seen the show."

"Well, they want to see you."

"So you've already put me up for it?"

"Oh, yes. They're sending the script and music."

"Fine," said Robin, none too confidently.

Richard O'Brien wrote *The Rocky Horror Show* in 1973 as a high-camp rock 'n' roll musical. The show and its movie adaptation, *The Rocky Horror Picture Show*, became cult classics with a core of diehard fans who persist two decades later in dressing as their favorite characters, shouting rude setup lines, and dancing in the aisles to "The Time Warp."

The plot sends babes in the woods Brad and Janet into the castle of Frank N Furter just as the extraterrestrial, cross-dressing mad scientist is about to unveil his creation, Rocky, a perfect specimen of young manhood. As the slider goes up, Frank belts out lyrics asserting his identity as a sweet transvestite from Transexual, Transylvania. Later, he seduces Janet and Brad. Yes, both of them.

Robin found the script witty, the role heavy-duty.

"It's quite a big part, and it's so revered," he told Jan. "Am I going to be able to get away with it? Do you think it will work?"

"I don't *think* it's going to work. I *know* it's going to work. I have every confidence."

"You don't even know me very well."

"I don't have to. I've sat in my office and talked to you. I know what you're about, and I think it's a great idea."

"Well, then, I'm off to audition."

Some of Robin's friends were apprehensive. He thought, "That's probably exactly why I should do it." What better way to break out of the Prince Charming mold?

Although director and coproducer Christopher Malcolm had begun his career with the Royal Shakespeare Company, among his credits was Brad in the original *Rocky Horror Show*. Christopher cast a wide net for Frank. When someone suggested Robin, he wondered, "Would a skater have the necessary elements?"

Both men were headed for Los Angeles. Robin, Christopher, and Jeff Rizzo, a musical-theatre conductor hired as accompanist, met in a rehearsal room at Screenland Studios in Burbank. If Robin was nervous, it didn't show. He chatted about *Cats* and *Cinderella on Ice*, then sang "Sweet Transvestite" and "I'm Going Home."

Jeff found Robin's voice full, his pitch solid.

"It was obvious that he was familiar with the material but not overly rehearsed. In fact, that was probably the first time that he had sung the songs with piano accompaniment. He did exhibit a strong understanding of how he wanted to perform the material and seemed to have a good time doing so."

Christopher was surprised by Robin's voice and impressed by his confidence. "I think we should go with it," he told his associates.

"I couldn't get over how willing he was, how enthusiastic he was, how malleable he was as a performer. It's very unusual for an actor. I've been brought up in the purely theatrical world, so I know actors inside out. It was refreshing to find someone who was so totally committed, completely focused, and enthusiastic to try anything, even if it didn't work. He slowly and carefully built his performance."

Robin developed theories about his character.

"I think that Frank is a very together person. He's quite calculating, even though he is really *not* responsible for Rocky and everything else. That's Riff Raff's role, but Frank has the gall to take credit for it and be in charge. I actually find him quite a good character to play. Because he's not human (which people tend to forget), he doesn't have to act with human characteristics, so things can be sort of strangely, abnormally normal. Some people have a hard time playing horrible people, and I wasn't sure how I should play him. Christopher said, 'Don't worry. You'll find your version.'"

Christopher conceded that, if there was one facet missing from Robin's portrayal, it was "an innate selfishness, that kind of innate hostility" that the character typically exudes. Robin couldn't find it in his heart to be rude to the audience.

"The audience can be cheap. They can do what they want, but Frank will not be cheap."

Robin created a meticulous Frank.

"He is *so* meticulous in the creative aspects of his life that I don't think he would be that clever with everybody else and not be that way about himself. When you look like Frank looks onstage, the last thing you need to do is give it any help."

Robin rationalized away his squeamishness.

"He can look like that and still be a truck driver. He's quite happy being a man who likes to dress up in women's clothes. He's certainly in control and commanding. The nice thing about the show is that you get to play a bit of everything. You get to be funny. You get to sing. You have a death scene. Shakespeare it's not, but it does appeal to my wicked sense of humor. Sometimes you see the world taking itself far too seriously."

Makeup, a neatly coiffed auburn wig, silver high-heeled shoes (size twelve), a basque, a garter belt, and fishnet stockings: that, for Frank, was conservative. The costumer had simplified the outfits.

"I want to see more body," he announced to Robin. "Oh?!"

Robin had to put the gear on, have a look at himself, and decide, "Do I want to stand like this in public?"

"I've had to wear some pretty hideous things in my time. Even with *Cats*, it was a strange costume. I still am self-conscious until the lights go on in terms of what I look like backstage, but it's part of the role, so you get on with it. It's certainly not anything that I'm going to add to my wardrobe, although I quite like the leather jacket."

Robin ran and jumped in the six-inch heels, breaking a few in the process. Wearing them on a raked stage hurt his feet and threw off his balance.

The heavy makeup presented an irony. When *Cats* ended, Robin had told Helen, "No more of this stuff on my face now. It's going to be so exciting to find another job when I have a human face." Then what did he go on to? *Rocky Horror*. Rather than creating a grotesque effect, he chose dark colors, subtle reds, a "neoromantic" look. What he didn't want to do was resemble a drag queen.

"Men can't be threatened or turned off by Frank. For women, he has to be inviting. I find the whole thing quite strange, actually."

Christopher cautioned Robin, "Don't overact. You have to remember what you look like." Robin was taller than anyone onstage, with a presence born of years of skating and a role that screamed for attention.

The first time Robin, Brad, and Janet ran through their love scenes, it was ten o'clock in the morning. They had just met. Robin quipped, "They're the only people I've made love to before I've taken them out to dinner."

Rocky was an audience-participation event. The

regulars knew the script by heart and had repertoires of cutting remarks. Because Frank and the Narrator were allowed to talk back, the directors yelled out comments during rehearsals.

"No," Robin gulped. "They're not going to say *that*."

"You bet," remarked Narrator Nicholas Parsons. "You'd be surprised what they say."

Robin thrived on the give and take, raised as he was on the interactive element in skating. Still, rehearsals didn't fully prepare him for live, screaming, dressed-for-Halloween audiences.

"It is euphoric to go out and have 'Sweet Tranny' happen the way it does. The challenge every night is to get through those sliders (deep breath right before they go up) and plow through it."

Trish Bernays saw *Rocky* in previews.

"I don't know if you've ever been to anywhere as suburban as Woking. Robin was sweet. He got tickets for our neighbors as well. We didn't tell them fully what the show was about, and we walked in to be surrounded by various young men dressed up in high-heeled shoes and fishnet stockings. It was an interesting experience, but our neighbors loved it. It's so different from what Robin's done before. I always think Torvill and Dean are rather pompous, rather like the Queen Mother. It would be nice if one of them did something outrageous for a change."

Robin liked that dimension of *Rocky*.

"It was interesting, the week in Woking. I love going on the stage and looking at people pointing and saying, 'That's not *him*, is it?' As the show goes along, you basically show them why you are there. It's not just novelty. I do have the ability to do the material. If you've got the balls, really, to have a go at it, then, by all means, go. I feel comfortable onstage. I'm confident. With Frank, you have to be. Frank can *not* be vulnerable. Big trouble."

Rocky transferred to the Duke of York's in the heart

of London's West End. Throughout the summer of 1995, the theatre's white Palladian façade sported a life-sized head-to-thigh poster of Robin in dominatrix gear. Flanking the main doorway, the image dared all customers to leave their stereotypes outside. In the alley leading to the stage door, early arrivals loitered at the gates of pop culture, dressed in black leather and fishnet.

Robin's basement dressing room was large but hardly glamorous. Amidst couches, chairs, a small refrigerator, memorabilia, and *nature morte*, he peered into the mirror and became Frank. On the first night of West End previews, Dinks Nenadovic was amazed at the metamorphosis. She had been warned what Robin would look like, but that wasn't the same as being prepared. For twenty minutes, she sat with her mouth agape.

"It was extraordinary for him to have actually wanted to tackle something so different, musically and in every other way. Who else but Robin would do that?"

When he finished singing "I'm Going Home," he saw fans in the audience waving skating marks.

After the show, he asked Dinks, "Do you think I made the right decision?"

"Yes, I do. You're doing a wonderful job with it, but it's not just that. The point is that you're showing to everybody, whether they like it or not, that you are capable of lots more. Have your mom and dad been in?"

"No, they won't come."

"It's a shame."

Not necessarily, from Robin's viewpoint.

"The roles come along, and you audition. If it's something that you think is going to be good, will make you work, and will be a challenge, then you do it. I'm certainly not going to sit back and say, 'I'm only going to take roles that I think my mother is going to go and see, or that I think my fans will be pleased at.' God, no. That would be boring."

Fred and Jo attended the premier gala. Before show time, Fred became ill, so they went home. A month later, Jo was still debating whether or not to return. Her maternal inclination was to go, but she feared embarrassment—misgivings that Robin could appreciate.

"This would be the first time that she'd ever have to see me out of context, as it were. They wouldn't go to see it normally, so why come to see it just because I'm in it?"

Jo eventually got up the nerve to watch her son descend a flight of stairs in a garter belt. As he swung his long, fishnet-clad leg over the banister rail, it was hardly the future she had envisioned when "Fred" and "Ginger" played on Dingle Close. She understood why Robin had accepted the role. As an act of iconoclasm, it was absolute.

Christopher recognized from the outset that Robin could perform an emotion better than most Franks, but speech was an unfamiliar medium. Because Robin applied rigid discipline to his skating, it took him longer than some performers to realize that acting was organic. He fixed the role and stood still in the part. Then one evening Christopher noticed "extra bits, little extra nuances." Robin had learned to be an actor.

Frank N Furter traditionally gets bad notices. Robin's critical reviews, as expected, were mixed. Said the London *Times*, "He sings rock with some gusto, strutting in his suspenders . . . Unfortunately he has not got the luridly enticing looks of Tim Curry, immortalized in the movie. Cousins can dance, and does a witty send-up of a dying swan when Frank is finally zapped by Riff Raff, his extraterrestrial butler. But he is not wholly liberated in his platform heels. He also desperately needs to get his skates on when it comes to spoken lines."

Today suggested, "DO get your skates on to see Robin Cousins as Frank. He sings well and moves terrifically as one might expect of an ice dancer. What one does not expect of an ice dancer is such spindly legs. And when it comes to acting, he makes a good ice dancer."

Robin wished that he could have been reviewed further into the run. During two months in the West End and three months on fall tour, his skills improved. His acting reviews, by the time he reached Cardiff, were glowing.

Christopher appreciated Robin's trueness to himself.

"He's created a role which he's comfortable with, which the audience finds interesting and appealing. He's a sympathetic Frank. I have nothing but the highest respect for the man. The company are a very good company, and they're good because they're led from his example. I've done this show all over the world. We've had hellish companies. They always reflect who's playing the leading role. When you get somebody like Robin in the company, he provides a base; he provides a happiness, a real cohesive force. If I could tell you the problems I've had with actors! The guy is a dream come true. He's always there. I would never imagine for a day, unless he fell under a bus, that he wouldn't be onstage. He has that discipline and that absolutely sharp focus on his performance. I respect him probably more than any performer I've met—because of what he's done, what he's attempting to do now, the way in which he's put himself out there. There's no hiding, is there? He goes out and just does it."

Robin found commanding a theatre with 700 seats easier than commanding an arena. He liked being able to connect with the audience, all the way to the back of the dress circle. Above all, he was relieved to be in control, with his dignity intact.

"I don't ever want to be a novelty," he said with a shudder. The *Rocky* experiment was about proving that he was leading-man material. If he wanted a career in musical theatre, he had to be ready for anything. Then casting directors couldn't say, "Forget Robin. He doesn't do that."

Rosalynn Sumners and her fiancé saw *Rocky* during

a visit to Wimbledon. Robin pulled out a bottle of champagne, then took his guests to the Sports Café. Rosalynn laughed at the contrast.

"He went from fishnets, six-inch heels, and makeup to jeans and a T-shirt in a sports bar. We had a fun night. It was such a kick to see him. When he danced and had the whole stage to himself, it was totally like watching one of his skating routines, except in six-inch heels. I was on my feet, just howling. I knew what to expect, but not really— and then to watch him come out in *that*. It was too funny."

She drew the line at following in Robin's footsteps.

"Along with choreography and infiltrating some of his style into my skating, he taught me what it is to be a true professional. Then I saw him in *Rocky Horror*, and I thought, 'This is one thing you're *not* going to teach me, Robin.'"

Denise Biellmann and Michael Chack learned choreography from Robin during the *Rocky* run. Michael got the full backstage treatment.

"I hung out in Robin's dressing room and met the cast. He showed me how the stage worked, took me under his wing. He's a very nice guy."

Robin may have been, as a critic suggested, a little *too* nice to play Frank, but it was part of the learning process, the boundary-pushing. When he left *Rocky* at the end of the fall tour, he took Frank with him. Occasionally there came unbidden the flash of brash humor, the Joan Crawford voice, the haughty demeanor, the impudent thrust of the hip.

"Oh, my god," he gasped. "I'm Frank N Furter."

Michael Chack

Michael Chack, an American Olympic-eligible competitor, brought Robin his long-program music from the Patrick Doyle soundtrack *Mary Shelley's Frankenstein*.

"Robin put the music on, skated around, and tried

wild footwork. He threw himself into the air. Wherever he landed, he landed."

Some things hadn't changed in a quarter of a century.

"The nice thing about him as a choreographer is that he doesn't give you *his* style. He wants to bring out your best qualities, your best line, and develop them."

They worked briefly at Queens but found it crowded with public sessions (something else that hadn't changed). Then they went to Alexandria Palace, where Robin assessed Michael's strengths and weaknesses.

"Show me how you do a spiral. Show me how you spin. Let me see you jump."

They inventoried the necessary elements. As Robin played with the music, he came up with moves that Michael imitated.

"It may look great on him but look horrible on me," Michael said ruefully, "because he has legs for days."

Michael reminded Robin of Doug Mattis: short, strong, and good with steps. As they worked, they listened for hidden beats and unexpected nuances. The opening jump went on a big boom.

"This would be great for an opening triple Axel," Michael suggested.

"Well, no," Robin disagreed. "I hear triple Lutz-triple toe."

"Oh, yeah. You're right."

Robin didn't like the end of the piece, so he found another Doyle soundtrack, *Much Ado About Nothing*, and edited it onto *Frankenstein*. In the final pose, Michael's hand rested on his hip in a masculine gesture. Robin struck the same pose, then reversed his hand and dropped his hip into a slouch.

"*This* is how you should end."

"Excuse me?" Michael laughed.

He was looking at Frank.

Before Michael left, Robin warned him, "If you skate great, I did the program. If you skate horribly, I don't know who did it."

Denise, Denise

Denise Biellmann, 1981 world champion from Switzerland, was often willowy and lyrical as an amateur. As a pro, she followed her own lights, adopting a modern, angular, fast-charging idiom. In 1995, she was ready to try something new.

Robin offered her a handful of musical choices. She selected "When I Look in Your Eyes" by Linda Eder.

"I never do things like this," she told him.

"You should, because it's beautiful."

The number they produced was similar to what Robin might have choreographed for Rosalynn once upon a time.

"It's quite lovely. No drums, no boogie, no off-the-beat disco dancing. Without even trying, Denise has some of the most beautiful lines and nice stretch. It wasn't as if I was trying to make her do things she didn't understand. People need to see Denise slow down, take her time, and enjoy the skating that she does, because it is incredible. She is so disciplined and well trained."

By the 1997-98 season, Denise had an entire repertoire of Cousins choreography—and some high competition placements to show for it.

Not in Kansas Anymore

Lakeland on an August day was sweltering even by Florida standards. On the blacktop outside the Lakeland Center's truck entrance, the temperature was marginally tolerable as crew members on break soaked up some rays.

By contrast, the arena was bracingly cool. Skaters in warmup gear, dancewear, and grunge assembled in front of rows of orange-cushioned fold-down seats. Robin, in khaki slacks, a long-sleeved burgundy T-shirt, and a tan baseball cap, and Cindy Stuart, in a black tie-on skirt and leotard, issued instructions for the day's rehearsal of *The Wizard of Oz on Ice*.

Robin spoke with a note of self-mocking humor.

"We're going to run precision with all heads—and all feet. Then, from 11:30 until 12:45, we're going to do the set changes with the crew (no music), just to organize who comes on first; to prioritize the changes. Everybody has to get out, but the person who has to get out first is the person who has to go the farthest. Stage awareness is what we need."

"Oooooo."

The skaters feigned awe.

"And set awareness. It's just like a giant jigsaw puzzle. After lunch and all afternoon, we're going to do bugs and trees. If you're not a bug, a tree, a solid tree, or a spare, you have the afternoon off."

The marquee at the corner of Lemon Street proclaimed, "Toto, I don't think we're in Kansas anymore." That was obvious.

At lunchtime, Robin and Cindy took chairs onto the blacktop. Robin nibbled at a pasta salad concocted in the condo that producer Kenneth Feld had provided for his month and a half in Lakeland as special choreographer and creative consultant for *Oz*.[22] He was working with Feld for the first time.

"I equate him with Cameron Mackintosh. Give those men what they ask for, and they're the greatest people in the world to work with. They both have been there. Cameron was a stagehand. He swept the stage. He knew what he wanted. The same with Kenneth. He grew up around the circus and all that. He knows what he wants, and he knows

---

[22]Feld produced Walt Disney's World On Ice and owned and produced the Ringling Brothers and Barnum & Bailey Circus.

how to get it. I expect to be yelled at and reprimanded if I don't deliver the goods I have promised to deliver."

Coincidentally, Cindy had begun her skating career with Feld's first ice production, Ice Follies and Holiday on Ice. Later, as an understudy in Holiday on Ice, she met her husband, Jeremy, an English drummer with the tour. In the middle of the 1981-82 season, she and another understudy took over the slot vacated by a pregnant Katie Baxter. Cindy didn't want to be "just a replacement."

"The funny thing is, I didn't have red hair then, and I refused to dye it red. I am not Katie Walker! But it kind of helped when I did dye my hair red."

On January 8, 1995, she found a message on her answering machine.

"Call me. I have a show to work on, and I'd like you to assist me."

Robin knew that he and Cindy were on the same wavelength. He didn't find many like her—regardless of the fact that she had almost killed him once, yanking him off the ice by the collar at the end of the "Mr. Monotony" routine in Santa Rosa.

"Few people have the passion to make things work. You also have to be fortunate enough to have opportunities come along, and I've been very fortunate."

Cindy had been, too, especially for a no-name.

"Longevity in a business like this, getting to step to the other side along with somebody like Robin, is a gift."

Robin had begun work on *Oz* during winter meetings in Vienna, Virginia. The challenge in adapting a beloved movie was to create something unique that "didn't mess with what people revered." One obvious problem had no solution: six-foot Munchkins.

The *Oz* team sought inspiration in the book by L. Frank Baum, *The Wonderful Wizard of Oz*; in the 1939 film script and score; and even in outtakes. Robin's "Jitterbug" number was based on a film crew member's amateur video. The segment had ultimately been cut.

Robin had his early material videotaped. By the time he joined Cindy in her native Los Angeles, she had it memorized. Together with skating director Bob Paul, they spent ten days creating and making notations for the bulk of the show—three people conceptualizing and walking through a performance for a cast of forty-six.

Robin announced, "That's okay. It'll work." He could visualize it working. Bob was nervous all the same.

"What are the counts on that?"

"Don't worry. It's there. It will all fall into place."

Cindy took charge of the chart book, blending the music count charts and Robin's choreographic count charts.

"She found the common denominator, the bit between the head and the feet, and made it work so that whoever reads it, it reads the same. With the book that we have, if you wanted to put your own company together and put on *The Wizard of Oz*, you should be able to put the entire show together without once phoning us."

Robin counted and choreographed in phrases. "Listen to the music, and you'll hear the ritard[ando] and the boom. That's where the step goes" was more logical to him than saying, "It's on the five-six-seven-eight."

"If the music says one-two-three-four-ritard-boom, we write it down, and it becomes the ritard-bum-tiddy-bum step. It's simplified, but that's how I work."

He knew when enough was enough.

"It's the execution that makes something stand out. It may be intricate, but you shouldn't need a Ph.D. to figure it out. It's great to have all these steps and wild moves, but let's not forget that skating is about curves and edges."

One of Robin's first ideas was for the witch's guards, the Winkies. They weren't pretty-looking things. What if they wore their costumes backwards? What if the skaters skated west while the heads and feet pointed east? He raised the idea in a production meeting and Feld "just laughed his head off."

Robin was confident, but he needed to pin down the counts and speed. Another Feld cast was asked, "Can you make it work?" They successfully executed half the Winkies' pinwheel. The rest fell together in Lakeland.

When performance director David Browne tried out the Winkie costume, a boyish voice asked, "What are you doing?"

"*The Wizard of Oz on Ice.*"

"Oh, is that a Winkie guard?"

"How did you know it's called a Winkie guard?"

The term was never used in the movie.

"It's in the book."

By the oddest of coincidences, the well-informed boy was the great grandson of Jack Haley, the first Tin Woodman.

When Robin left for London to star in *Rocky* through mid-July, Nancy Barber, the girls' line captain (and Wicked Witch of the West) joined the Los Angeles group to learn the show. When the full cast assembled for

Florida rehearsals, the anticipatory buzz was a swarm of hornets. What was Robin like?

"I had no idea," said Nancy, "until I met Cindy. From working with her, I had the idea that they were a lot alike. Then I knew he'd be fun."

By the first day's end, he knew most of the forty-six names: American, British, Canadian, Russian, and Ukrainian. Nancy found him upbeat.

"He's serious when he needs to be, but even when he gets mad, he phrases things humorously. You get the point, but you don't feel that he's been condescending."

Robin had arrived in Lakeland with three-fourths of the choreography set. He made the rest up as he went along, with the full cast on the ice. He had been needlessly nervous about the Winkie number, the first segment they tried.

"Because it has nothing to do with normal skating, it's easier to learn. Instead of going heel-toe, heel-toe, it's toe-heel, toe-heel. My concern was that they would put on the backwards heads and it wouldn't be funny. It wouldn't work. They wouldn't be able to see where they were going, and they would bang into each other. You cannot look where you're going, because that means that the fake head isn't looking where *it's* going."

The Winkies moved in formation to low-pitched chants of *Oh-ee-ah, eeyoh-ah*. With their crocodilian faces, furry black feet, green claws, and odd gaits, they looked like something that Maurice Sendak had illustrated—and that was without the rest of their costumes.

Robin and Cindy worked together like a well-oiled machine.

He remarked, "We haven't started finishing off each other's sentences, but we're not far off."

One day he told Cindy, "You have to watch what we've just done. I think it's great." Cindy replied, "*You* have to watch what *we've* just done." Both groups were doing the same thing.

If Cindy, a lyrical skater, went overboard on softness, Robin spiced things up with tricky steps. Together they horrified the cast by announcing "class." Dread appeared on young faces contemplating the barre.

"We *are* doing class," Robin explained, "but if you want to be in jeans and T-shirts, that's fine. You don't have to be in tutus. We're not going to be screaming, 'Point your finger.'"

That sometimes happens in the skating world.

"You tell people, 'You need to go to dance class,' and they take it all too literally. They need to go and funk out and have a good time. They need to experience something other than skating. Just because someone says, 'I'm going to class' doesn't mean that they're turning into Baryshnikov. (Not that I could ever turn into Baryshnikov. Wouldn't *that* be just too wonderful.) I just think that people need to loosen up."

Cindy insisted on the daily company class to bring up the general skating level. She began each morning with group warmup routines: footwork repetitions with deep edges and classical body lines, outgrowths of the John Curry philosophy.

Nancy remarked, "In our training, we were taught how to jump and do spins, but nobody ever taught us how to really *skate*: how to use our edges and increase our control of body movements. I always dabbled in that type of skating. When I found out I was coming to this show, I knew I was going to do more of it."

Robin encouraged peripheral awareness.

"I'm peripheral, which is why I think the show has gone together so quickly. One of my biggest complaints with kids here is that if you asked them who had been on their immediate left and right for the last ten days, few of them would be able to reel off the names. They're focused internally, and they're focused on where they need to be at any given point, but I'm always thinking, 'If I know where *they* are, then I know *I'm* in the right place.'"

In teaching choreography, he associated feelings with steps—the actor in him. He wanted the poppies to feel like floating petals. The Emerald City characters adopted a "hoity-toity" attitude. In Munchkinland, the watchwords were "crazy" and "bouncy," with steps designed for swinging arms and maximum freedom. Feelings facilitated steps, and vice versa.

When two Poppies disappeared on a break, Nancy filled in but failed to correctly catch on to the formation. Robin announced: "I'm making a change. Your line captain screwed up. I *like* it. Everybody do *that*."

He had little patience for airheads and slackers, but he empathized with first-time professionals who still bore their amateur stress. A British pairs champion had been hospitalized with stomach pains. When Robin saw her training at lunchtime, he lectured "You have to leave all that baggage behind. I went through it, and it's not pretty. You're not *training*. You're rehearsing. This is your time to have fun with what you spent all those years training for."

Officially, Robin had nothing to do with the sets. However, the changes were done by the cast as they entered and exited the ice. The sequence required logistical masterminding. Robin solved another dilemma at the same time: Feld wanted the Kansas house in the finale, but the crew responsible for packing it up and hauling it to the next city insisted on loading it onto the truck early in the show.

Suddenly Robin ran across the ice.

"I've got it!"

The stage crew could pack up the heavy motorized equipment as soon as it had propelled the house through the tornado. Then the cast could skate out the light, empty shell for the finale.

Nor did Robin have an official connection to the

costumes, but that didn't stop him from making sugges-
tions. Flipping through the costume book, he called Frank
Krenz a genius. You could tell he wished he had drawn the
designs himself. The Munchkin outfits were a riot of
bright colors and odd shapes, while the Tin Woodman's was
structurally ingenious: laminated layers of wire mesh
covered with Latex and metallic paint.

Though a great dog-lover, Robin was forbidden to
touch the cairn terriers who played Toto. Jeri Campbell, as
Dorothy, trained several of them to run to her. Mark
Farrington, the Cowardly Lion, handled the dog trained to
run away from Dorothy.

While the corps of skaters hung out during breaks
on the snack-bar side of the arena, the production staff
worked from a long table opposite them. Once, Jeri left a
bag of dog treats among the papers, Evian bottles, coffee
cups, and assorted personal effects that lay in a clutter on
the table. Robin absent-mindedly reached in, pulled out a
chunk, and began to pop it into his mouth.

"Uh, Robin."

"Yeah?"

"Those are dog treats."

"Ugh."

Everyone had a laugh at his expense.

Epilogue

*I*n October 1986, Robin informed the London *Times*, "I'm retiring from professional competition on December 20, and that's something even my mother doesn't know I'm doing yet."

In April 1992, he told *Tracings* magazine that the Diet Coke Skaters' Championships had been his last competition.

"I think I've done everything I can do as far as competing is concerned. . . . I've been there and I've done it and I've won it and I'm over it."

In December 1995, he announced his competitive retirement at the Challenge of Champions in London. Veteran Cousins-watchers said, "We'll see." They weren't surprised when he finished second at the Legends event in September 1997.

Although he couldn't have imagined it in 1980, his professional competitive career had handily exceeded the fourteen-and-a-half-year span between his first step onto the ice in Bournemouth and his final amateur step onto the podium in Dortmund. Throughout, he had skated first for the audience; secondarily, for himself. The judges had ranked a poor third in his hierarchy.

While preparing for his final Challenge of Champions, Robin was immersed in other projects. When the *Rocky* tour ended in December, he joined the cast of *Cinderella*, a Christmas pantomime (with artificial ice) that played Birmingham throughout the early winter. Next he oversaw the successful 1996-97 Feld production *Toy Story*.

The following season, he repeated the pantomime in Woking, then created Feld's *Starlight Express*, a critical success in search of demographics. He pronounced the choreography some of his best.

In the meantime, after months of formalities, he concluded the long-awaited purchase of a Georgian row house in a small town on the Sussex coast. He sank deep roots behind a narrow, white façade that overlooked the Channel.

The quintessentially English house rose skyward in multiple levels: vertical living spaces rather than horizontal.

At the front of the ground floor, to the left of the entry hall, Robin indulged his talents as a chef in an enormous country kitchen. That was flanked on the right, beyond the hall, by a long, narrow "museum," where he lightheartedly displayed his skating mementos.

A vast bow window dominated the airy upstairs living room, affording a view of the enclosed central garden and a sideways glance at the sea. An interior courtyard made a lofty perch for a table, chairs, and a small garden, while an office and a music-storage area occupied the space above the "museum."

In the spacious third-level bedroom, several pairs of skates rested casually on the floor at the edge of an Oriental carpet, ready to soar again at the first opportunity.

The uppermost level housed a guest suite, soon to teem with visiting Cousinses.

On a sun-drenched cushion, a gargantuan black and grey tiger cat named Muffin-Pickle (an adopted London stray) completed the picture of domestic beatitude. Robin sang and whistled as he bounded about the premises, up and down the many half-flights of stairs.

He could skirt the garden, cross the street, and descend onto a quiet stretch of pebbled beach dotted with small fishing boats. Farther along, the wave-lapped shore curved past groups of summer sunbathers. Winter would bring shrill winds and high seas: dramatic weather that Robin relished.

Somewhere up the stony coast, there was an ice rink of sorts, barely large enough to merit the name. One evening Robin held a group of local youngsters spellbound. After he taught them some of the finer points of basic skating, the assembly moved *en masse* to a private meeting room a number of blocks away.

"What's your favorite color?" Robin asked a young skater.

"Red."

"What color is your competition dress?"

"Blue."

"Well, why are you wearing a blue dress if red makes you feel good?"

The children listened in sober fascination while their parents nodded agreement and took notes.

Later that evening, back in the tall, white house, Robin unearthed some videotapes that he hadn't watched in many years. There it all was: Miss Nash's music and movement class; the Olympic long program; *This Is Your Life*. Among the treasures was amateur footage of Electric Ice and Ice Majesty. Perhaps it wasn't too late after all to re-form his company and restage "Body Moves"—or to strike out in a completely new direction.

Robin confessed that the old urges were stirring.

"I closed the chapter on all that when I moved to Lake Arrowhead to teach. Then the knee surgery came, and everything else. It's only recently, as a result of the theatre, getting back a little bit into skating myself, that those thoughts have returned to haunt me. It is not something that I have to do, but it is something that I feel I want to, and I still *could* do.

"I thought all those demons were put to bed, but I guess they're not."

Perhaps Tony Kudrna understood it best.

"Some people would say, 'Yeah, I'm Olympic champion. I'm done. I can ride that to the grave,' but Robin is always opening another door and stepping through."

Amateur Competitive Results

Placements are for figures, short program, long program, and free skating (short + long combined).

1	1969	British novice championship (*)
1	1972	British junior championship (4, 1, 1, 1)
3	1972	European championship (18, 14, 13, 14)
7	1973	St. Gervais Grand Prix (14, 4, 5, *)
10	1973	Skate Canada (11, 9, 5, 5)
11	1974	Skate Canada (10, 4, 3, 3)
2	1974	British championship (2, 2, 2, 2)
11	1975	European championship (11, 8, 10, 8)
12	1975	World championship (15, 11, 11, 11)
2	1975	Skate Safari (2, 1, 1, 1)
2	1975	British championship (2, 1, 1, 1)
6	1976	European championship (13, 7, 5, 5)
10	1976	Olympics (14, 11, 8, 8)
9	1976	World championship (14, 8, 8, 8)
2	1976	Skate Canada (4, 2, 2, 2)
1	1976	British championship (1, 1, 1, 1)
3	1977	European championship (7, 2, 2, 2)
w/d	1977	World championship (10, 5, w/d, w/d)
1	1977	Skate Canada (2, 1, 1, 1)
1	1977	British championship (2, 1, 1, 1)
3	1978	European championship (5, 1, 1, 1)
3	1978	World championship (4, 2, 1, 1)
1	1978	British championship (1, 1, 1, 1)
3	1979	European championship (6, 1, 1, 1)
2	1979	World championship (5, 3, 1, 1)
1	1979	Rotary Watches International (1, 1, 1, 1)
1	1979	NHK Trophy Free Skating (n/a, 1, 1, 1)
1	1979	Ennia Challenge Cup (n/a, 1, 1, 1)
1	1979	British championship (1, 1, 1, 1)
1	1980	European championship (3, 3, 1, 1)
1	1980	Olympics (4, 1, 1, 1)
2	1980	World championship (5, 1, 1, 1)

w/d=withdrew; n/a=not applicable; *=information not available

Professional Competitive Results

1	1980	World Professional championship*	Landover
2	1981	World Professional championship*	Landover
2	1982	Pro Skate	Montreal
3	1982	Pro Skate	Vancouver
1	1982	Pro Skate	New York
1	1983	Pro Skate	Calgary
1	1983	Pro Skate	Vancouver
1	1983	Pro Skate	Edmonton
1	1983	Pro Skate	Toronto
1	1983	Pro Skate	New York
1	1984	Pro Skate	Tokyo
1	1984	Pro Skate	Sapporo
1	1984	Pro Skate	New York
1	1985	Pro Skate	Tokyo
1	1985	Pro Skate	Sapporo
1	1985	World Professional championship	Landover
1	1985	Challenge of Champions	Paris
2	1986	World Professional championship	Landover
2	1986	Challenge of Champions	Paris
1	1987	World Professional championship	Landover
4	1988	World Professional championship	Landover
1	1989	World Cup of Figure Skating	Ottawa
2	1990	World Professional championship	Landover
3	1990	Challenge of Champions	Barcelona
3	1991	World Professional championship	Landover
4	1991	Challenge of Champions	Oslo
4	1992	Skaters Championships	Cincinnati
2	1993	World Professional championship	Landover
2	1993	Challenge of Champions	Toronto
3	1994	North American Open	Cleveland
4	1994	Canadian Pro championship	Hamilton
3	1994	World Team Championship*	Amherst
3	1995	Challenge of Champions	London
2	1997	Legends Professional championship	Little Rock

*=team scoring
Information compiled by Lois Yuen

Name Index